Currency and Contest in East Asia

A VOLUME IN THE SERIES

Cornell Studies in Money

edited by Eric Helleiner and Jonathan Kirshner

A list of titles in this series is available at www.cornellpress.cornell.edu.

Currency and Contest in East Asia

The Great Power Politics of Financial Regionalism

William W. Grimes

Cornell University Press
Ithaca and London

First published 2009 by Cornell University Press
Printed in the United States of America

Library of Congress Cataloging-in-Publication Data

Grimes, William W.
    Currency and contest in East Asia : the great power politics of financial regionalism / William W. Grimes.
        p. cm. — (Cornell studies in money)
    Includes bibliographical references and index.
    ISBN 978-0-8014-4689-4 (cloth : alk. paper)
    1. Finance—East Asia. 2. Regionalism—East Asia. 3. East Asia—Foreign economic relations. I. Title. II. Series.

    HG187.E18G75 2009
                                                      332'.042095—dc22

Cloth printing   10 9 8 7 6 5 4 3 2 1

To Melinda

Contents

Figures and Table

Acknowledgments

This book is the culmination of over eight years of research, thought, writing, and rewriting that began in 1999. Initially, I meant only to revisit a theme that had been dropped from my first book. That theme was "internationalization of the yen," a constantly mutating debate that had resurfaced in Japanese financial politics every decade since the end of the Bretton Woods era. As I began my research in Tokyo that summer, the phrase had recently reentered political discourse, and I planned to better understand the domestic political economy of financial liberalization by tracking its use over time. Instead, I found a full-fledged debate about how to insulate Japan and East Asia from large-scale capital movements and fluctuations in the value of the dollar.

Although the phrase "internationalization of the yen" eventually fell out of favor in the political and policy world, even by 1999 its original meaning had already been supplanted by much more ambitious thinking about regional financial insulation that drew on the ideas developed by advocates of yen internationalization. This was an exciting topic to address—not only were some of Japan's most capable and intelligent financial policymakers and analysts involved, but a new era of East Asian regional cooperation was just beginning. It has been my great fortune to have been able to observe the whole path to date of ASEAN+3 financial cooperation, all the while having the opportunity to meet on a regular basis with leading participants and observers of those efforts. I am deeply grateful for their willingness to offer me guidance, instruction, and at times correction.

I carried out much of my research in multiple visits to Tokyo, visits that would not have been possible without financial and logistical support from a variety of sources. A fellowship from the Marion and Jasper Whiting Foundation supported a month of research on this and other topics in the summer of 2001; a Fulbright-Hays Faculty Research Grant allowed me to spend four months in 2005 focused on yen internationalization and financial regionalism. I also spent a month each in the summers of 1999 and 2000 using personal funds. In addition, over the years, I was able to make use of shorter visits sponsored by the U.S. Department of State, the University of Tokyo, the Institute for International Policy Studies, the Harvard Law School Program on International Financial Services (PIFS), the *Yomiuri Shimbun,* and the Policy Studies Group to conduct interviews and obtain materials. The PIFS annual symposia on U.S.-Japan and U.S.-China financial issues helped me to build contacts and knowledge, although actual discussions were off the record. A sabbatical leave from Boston University in 2005 allowed me to complete the bulk of my research and begin writing in earnest, and a book-writing grant from the Japan Foundation Center for Global Partnership in fall 2006 was instrumental in giving me the space to complete the initial draft by buying out my teaching responsibilities for the semester, in addition to sponsoring author's seminars in Cambridge and Tokyo that provided invaluable criticism and guidance. I am also deeply grateful to the Policy Research Institute (and its predecessor, the Institute of Fiscal and Monetary Policy) of the Japanese Ministry of Finance, which provided me with office space and support in the summers of 1999, 2000, and 2005, as well as to the Bank of Japan's Institute for Monetary and Economic Studies, which did the same in the summer of 2001.

I have been the fortunate recipient of guidance and instruction from a large number of academics and policymakers from various countries and organizations including Japan, the United States, China, the International Monetary Fund, and the Asian Development Bank. Several have asked to remain unnamed, but I am happy to express my gratitude here to Akira Ariyoshi, Masatsugu Asakawa, David Cowen, Toyoo Gyohten, Nobuhiro Hiwatari, Kenta Ichikawa, Kiyoto Ido, Naoko Ishii, Takatoshi Ito, Tadashi Iwashita, Mikio Kajikawa, Masahiro Kawai, Shigeki Kimura, Shūhei Kishimoto, Hidehiro Konno, Tarō Kōno, Isao Kubota, Yōichi Nemoto, Hideki Nonoguchi, Toshizō Ōhara, Takeshi Ohta, Naoyuki Shinohara, Sadahiro Sugita, Atsushi Takeuchi, Rintarō Tamaki, Takuji Tanaka, John Taylor, Noriyoshi Torigoe, Hiroshi Watanabe, Tatsuo Yamazaki, and Naoyuki Yoshino. I also benefited from comments from audience members at numerous talks in academic and policy venues in Japan, the United States, South Korea, and Iceland. In addition, I received research assistance at various points from Tamon Asonuma, Jennifer Donham, and Saori Nishida.

I am especially grateful to those who have read all or part of various versions of the manuscript and provided their frank criticisms and suggestions. The major venues for these discussions were the author's conferences sponsored by the Center for Global Partnership in 2006, which were attended by Thomas Berger, David Cowen, Toyoo Gyohten, Nobuhiro Hiwatari, Jonathan Kirshner, Yoshiko Kojo, Yōichi Nemoto, and Michael Smitka. Michelle Frasher-Rae also commented on several chapters, and Stephan Haggard, Saori Katada, and Yves Tiberghien provided significant input for an article in the *Journal of East Asian Studies,* parts of which appear by permission in this book. Two anonymous readers for Cornell University Press provided extremely detailed, incisive, and useful comments on the penultimate and final drafts of this book. It is a privilege to be working again with Cornell and with its remarkable social sciences editor, Roger Haydon. It is also an honor to be published in the Cornell Studies in Money series, edited by Eric Helleiner and Jonathan Kirshner.

In addition to giving me the time to complete my first draft and funding the two author's conferences, my grant from the Center for Global Partnership also provided the unique benefit of a three-member advisory group, whose members participated in the author's conferences and offered significant additional guidance. My advisory group was, I am fortunate to say, extraordinary. It was composed of Toyoo Gyohten, Nobuhiro Hiwatari, and Jonathan Kirshner. All three are long-time mentors and friends with the unusual ability to combine rigorous criticism with reassurance about the importance of the project. Toyoo Gyohten, who has been a crucial participant in all of Japan's international financial initiatives of the past thirty-five years, has been unstinting with his time and help ever since I first had the privilege to be his research assistant in the early 1990s. Nobuhiro Hiwatari is not only one of Japan's finest scholars of international political economy but was also the organizer of several conferences in Tokyo in 2001 and 2005, where I was able to develop several of the ideas presented in chapter 3. He read and commented thoroughly on two manuscript drafts, as the only person other than me who was able to attend both author's conferences. Jonathan Kirshner inadvertently introduced me to the power politics of international money when I sat in on his dissertation defense nearly a decade and a half ago, and I have been an avid reader of his work since. He has been exceedingly generous with his time and advice on this project ever since we first discussed the earliest results of my research back in the spring of 2000. I also salute the memory of Takeshi Ohta, whom I would certainly have asked to be part of the advisory group had he lived to see this project come to fruition. He was a wonderful mentor and human being, who brought extraordinary knowledge and experience to his self-assigned task of teaching me about Japanese finance and Japan's role in the world economy.

This book is far better for the guidance and comments of all these people. Of course, any errors that remain are mine alone. None of these individuals or institutions should be held accountable for them, nor should they be assumed to agree with my interpretations.

Finally, I express my deep gratitude to my family and friends for their support during this project. When I embarked on a four-month research trip to Tokyo in May 2005, I left behind my wife with our two-year-old daughter and ten-week-old son; after six weeks, they joined me, spending a hot and humid summer in four separate sublets and furnished apartments. I do not know how we would have managed without the support of many friends, especially Dave and Maki Fujii and Fred and Kendra Morgenstern, who offered not only moral support but also lots of baby equipment, toys, and even occasional transportation. My parents-in-law, Denise and Jim Stanford, supplied us with extensive care packages while we were in Japan as well as babysitting back home at crucial times when I had to spend time away for research and writing. They have also been consistently enthusiastic about the project. My parents, Joseph and Margaret Grimes, provided invaluable help at all turns, helping me to stick with the project even when I had my doubts about it. My father read the entire manuscript and individual chapters in various stages of completion. My mother, herself the survivor of a doctoral dissertation, gave me the diagnosis that I did not drink enough coffee to complete a book and would have to supplement with chocolate. I am fatter but happier for her advice. My children, Isabel and Will, have been enthusiastic in wishing me luck in completing this project, even though they do not fully understand the point of a book with no pictures.

This book is dedicated to my wife, Melinda Stanford. She did not write a word of it, but she deserves at least half the credit for its completion. Her willingness to spend a long, hot summer in Tokyo with very small children allowed me to carry out the most crucial part of my research. She threw herself into the challenge, pushing our double stroller around the local park and making friends through pantomime and sheer force of personality. Melinda and the kids have also endured many days when I have been traveling and many nights when I have had to work late in order to write this book. Through it all, she was instrumental in keeping me motivated to finish and to make the final product worthy of her sacrifices.

Abbreviations

ABF	Asian Bond Fund
ABMI	Asian Bond Markets Initiative
ACD	Asian Cooperation Dialogue
ACU	Asian currency unit
ADB	Asian Development Bank
AFC	Asian Financial Crisis
AFTA	ASEAN free trade area
AMF	Asian monetary fund
AMU	Asian monetary unit
APEC	Asia-Pacific Economic Cooperation forum
ARF	ASEAN Regional Forum
ASA	ASEAN Swap Arrangement
ASEAN	Association of Southeast Asian Nations (Brunei Darussalam, Cambodia, Indonesia, Laos, Malaysia, Myanmar, Philippines, Singapore, Thailand, and Vietnam)
ASEAN4	Indonesia, Malaysia, Philippines, and Thailand
ASEAN5	Indonesia, Malaysia, Philippines, Singapore, and Thailand (original ASEAN members)
ASEAN+3	ASEAN plus China, Japan, and South Korea
ASEM	Asia-Europe Meeting
BIS	Bank for International Settlements
BOJ	Bank of Japan
BSAs	bilateral swap agreements
CMI	Chiang Mai Initiative
CSIS	Center for Strategic and International Studies
DM	deutsche mark

ECU	European Currency Unit
EMEAP	Executives' Meeting of East Asia–Pacific Central Banks
EPA	economic partnership agreement
ERPD	Economic Review and Policy Dialogue
EVSL	Early Voluntary Sectoral Liberalization
FDI	foreign direct investment
FT	*Financial Times*
FTA	free trade agreement
G7	Group of Seven, an international forum for the governments of Canada, France, Germany, Italy, Japan, the United Kingdom, and the United States
GAB	General Arrangements to Borrow
GATT	General Agreement on Tariffs and Trade
GSP	Generalized System of Preferences
IMF	International Monetary Fund
JBIC	Japan Bank for International Cooperation
METI	Ministry of Economy, Trade and Industry (Japan)
MOF	Ministry of Finance (Japan)
MOFA	Ministry of Foreign Affairs (Japan)
NAB	New Arrangements to Borrow
NBER	National Bureau of Economic Research
OECD	Organization for Economic Cooperation and Development
OREI	Office of Regional Economic Integration (ADB)
PAFTAD	Pacific Trade and Development Forum
PAIF	Pan-Asia Bond Index Fund
PBEC	Pacific Basin Economic Council
PBOC	People's Bank of China ·
PECC	Pacific Economic Cooperation Council
PTA	preferential trade agreement
RIETI	Research Institute of Economy, Trade and Industry
RMB	renminbi
ROOs	rules of origin
SDR	Special Drawing Right (IMF)
SMEs	small and medium-sized enterprises
TAC	Treaty of Amity and Cooperation in Southeast Asia
WTO	World Trade Organization

Introduction

The Emergence of East Asian Financial Regionalism

The rise of regional institutions and initiatives in East Asia in recent years is a striking and new phenomenon. On this much, nearly everyone can agree. But what does that mean? Is East Asia the cusp of a regional revolution as governments emerge from decades, if not centuries, of political and economic fragmentation to build a cooperative order based on effective institutions? Or is the promise of a politically coherent East Asia characterized by peace and co-prosperity a dream that cannot withstand the bright light of reality? It is, of course, impossible in 2008 to predict the long-term effects of efforts involving varying and interlocking sets of issue areas and countries. Nonetheless, it is essential to begin to address the big questions about East Asian regionalism, given its potential to remake the political and economic map of the twenty-first century.

All attempts at regionalism arise from both economic and political motivations. At some level, the politics and the economics must push the same way for such efforts to be made at all. But what makes East Asia interesting as a region is that participating states' political motivations are mixed. In particular, differing preferences regarding the political and economic role of the United States add a frisson to the always difficult issues of designing regional institutions and investing them with power and capabilities. The premise of this book is that power matters and that patterns of regional cooperation will reflect not only opportunities for mutual gain but also competition for leadership among the great powers of Japan, China, and the United States.

To get a handle on the big picture, we need to work from the basis of concrete activities by governments and private sector actors. In this book

I examine financial regionalism—that is, attempts to reduce currency volatility, to create frameworks to contain financial crises, and to develop local financial markets—in East Asia. I argue that financial regionalism can best be understood in the context of great power rivalry among Japan, China, and the United States, and that it has profound importance for other aspects of that rivalry. The rapid rise of China as an economic and political power combines with growing regional economic integration to create space for both cooperation and competition.

This book contains the most detailed description and analysis of East Asian financial regionalism available in English. Financial regionalism is important but understudied: in this book I provide an accurate and readable account of the actual substance of regional efforts.

At first glance, financial regionalism may appear to have little to do with long-term security or relative power. After all, its goals are explicitly to improve and expand the functioning of domestic and transnational financial markets and to reduce the danger of currency crises and contagion. Such efforts in support of markets and mutual prosperity seem to call out for a standard political economy analysis that addresses such questions as: How can currency crises most effectively be prevented? What are the obstacles to the provision of regional public goods? Which economic actors gain or lose from regional financial cooperation, and how do they express their preferences to their home governments?

These are important questions, but they are essentially instrumental in nature. If we step back from the particulars of financial regionalism per se and, instead, think more broadly about this issue area as one aspect of a broader game of competition and cooperation among Japan, China, and the United States, then different questions arise. For example: How does the U.S.-Japan alliance affect Japan's willingness to promote regional approaches to currency crises that rival the International Monetary Fund? Can China be locked into a commitment to create an open financial system based on global standards before it is powerful enough to dictate its own terms? And what are the implications for U.S. economic leadership of a serious challenge to the global hegemony of the dollar? These are the issues raised, albeit in some cases incipiently, by East Asian financial regionalism.

Money and finance will necessarily be among the principal concerns of East Asian regional cooperation if it is to progress beyond a rudimentary stage. Today's attempts to design and shape institutions of regional financial cooperation will be decisive in setting the terms of future regionalism—we are now in a very real sense present at the creation of a new East Asian order. But there is also another compelling reason to focus on financial regionalism. In attempting to address currency-crisis management, financial market policies, and currency regimes, financial regionalism brings up fundamental issues of economic sovereignty and stability. From an analytical perspective, each aspect of financial regionalism raises a different set of choices for the states involved, making it particularly attractive as a lens through which to view the forces that shape regionalism in general. Thus, analysis of financial regionalism can lay bare deeper political forces in a way that trade negotiations and environmental cooperation do not.

I analyze the actions and motivations of the three great powers involved in the contest for regional leadership, with a particular focus on the role of Japan. In every aspect of financial regionalism, Japan is clearly the preponderant power in East Asia, and thus it should have a decisive impact on which initiatives are actually carried out and how they are arranged. Japan has been constrained in its ability to do so, however, by its need both to integrate with and hedge against the economic and political power of China and the United States. At the same time, Japan's position as a bridge between developing East Asia, on the one hand, and the advanced economies and international financial institutions, on the other, offers it unique opportunities for shaping a system that best meets its needs. As the closest U.S. ally in the region and the region's only state with the ability to help serve as a counterweight to Chinese power over the next quarter century or so, it is the state with the most to gain or lose from the regional economic institutions that are now being created.

Japan's challenge is to remain a leader in East Asian regional cooperation while simultaneously maintaining its close political and security ties with the United States, containing political rivalry with China, and gaining the support of other participating states. China's challenge is almost a mirror image: to support economic institutions that will allow it to continue to grow rapidly while simultaneously reducing Japan's influence in East Asia by isolating it and weakening the web of U.S. bilateral relations in the Asia-Pacific region that threatens to contain its rise as a regional and global power. The United States must contend with both sets of motivations while seeking to maintain its core interests in an open regional economy and positive security relations with as many states as possible. Despite many mutual interests in regional prosperity and economic stability, these conflicting interests raise questions about the long-term feasibility of regional financial cooperation. The process of regional cooperation also carries the potential to curb the long-term global financial dominance of the United States and the dollar.

The Rise of Financial Regionalism

Financial regionalism consists of various endeavors by regional governments to create institutions to promote financial coordination and integration within a given region. In East Asia, moves toward financial regionalism are based primarily in the Association of Southeast Asian Nations, comprising Malaysia, Singapore, Thailand, Indonesia, Philippines, Brunei Darussalam, Vietnam, Laos, Myanmar, and Cambodia, plus China, Japan, and South Korea, generally referred to as ASEAN+3.

There are four major streams of East Asian financial regionalism:

1. Emergency liquidity provision through the Chiang Mai Initiative. CMI significantly increases the amount of money that can be mobilized in the event of a crisis as a supplement to IMF lending.
2. Development of regional bond markets through ASEAN+3's Asian Bond Markets Initiative (ABMI) and the Asian Bond Fund (ABF) of the Executives' Meeting of East Asia-Pacific Central Banks (EMEAP).
3. Improved communication, in the form of surveillance, policy dialogue, informal contacts, and various Track II projects.
4. Currency management. Ideas about regional currency stabilization, and even the eventual development of a regional common currency, have gained attention but remain in early stages of discussion.

Functionally, East Asian financial regionalism seeks to address the lessons of the Asian Financial Crisis of 1997–98 (AFC): that dollar pegs and short-term borrowing in foreign currencies create vulnerability to hot money flows[1] and that it is dangerous to rely on the good will of the IMF and the United States in resolving actual crises.[2] The crux of East Asian financial regionalism is to reduce vulnerability to crisis and to enhance development and growth by strengthening domestic financial markets and creating institutions of regional self-help.

The development of formal institutions is an important aspect of East Asian financial regionalism. This movement coincides with a qualitative shift in regional cooperation away from informal, nonbinding consultative forums toward more substantive, organized activities and organizations. At least potentially, these institutions constitute a challenge to the global financial architecture, which is embodied in the IMF, the Bank for International

---

[1] Ito and Park 2004; McCauley 2003; Yoshino, Kaji, and Asonuma 2005c; Goldstein and Turner 2004; Eichengreen and Hausmann 2005.

[2] As Thailand's minister of finance, Thanong Bidaya, asserted publicly in May 2005: "The U.S. responded passively to the Asian Crisis, compared to the speed and effort which it had responded to the Mexican Crisis. In addition, the IMF conditionality was not appropriate to the crisis-effected countries because of the lack of true understanding of the situation and underlying economic condition. Other forums of cooperation such as APEC [the Asia-Pacific Economic Cooperation forum] had played no significant role in solving the crisis. These lessons reminded us of the importance and necessity of a stronger regional cooperation." "Future of Asia" Conference, sponsored by the *Nihon Keizai Shimbun*, Tokyo, May 25–26, 2005. Text of speeches available at http://www.nni.nikkei.co.jp/FR/NIKKEI/inasia/future/2005/index.html.

Settlements (BIS), and the Group of Seven (G7). Surprisingly, however, East Asian financial regionalism has so far been generally supportive of that system.[3] When looking at its political foundations, though, it is not clear that East Asian regional financial cooperation will forever be nested in that global architecture.

The Rise of China, Strategic Geometry, and the Role of Institutions

U.S.-Japan-China relations are sometimes seen as an Asia-Pacific strategic triangle. Other ways of looking at the strategic geography include Russia or Southeast Asia as key components. No matter what geometry one chooses, however, the core issue is how regional states should deal with the rise of China as an economic, political, and military power. Of course, how to deal with the United States and Japan will be an ongoing concern for other regional governments, but that is a concern that is conditioned by the existence of predictable patterns of behavior and interaction. Change is the greatest challenge to international systems, and the big changes in East Asia now revolve around China.

The rise of China has inspired considerable debate about the capabilities, priorities, and intentions of the Chinese state.[4] While "China threat" analyses have garnered a great deal of publicity over the last decade, the academic consensus is much more cautious about pointing to China as an imminent challenge; indeed, those scholars who have tried to gauge Chinese intentions from actions and official pronouncements have shown convincingly that China is, at least for the moment, a "status quo power" intent on economic development rather than regional hegemony.[5] The problem with such analyses is that current intentions are not necessarily good predictors of long-term behavior.[6] It hardly seems reasonable to expect that China's neighbors will base their longer-term strategies on current Chinese intentions or political priorities. But it may also be the case that there is now an opportunity for them to shape patterns of Chinese interests and regional interactions through institution building and the fostering of interdependence.

The political challenge of the rise of China—for itself as well as its neighbors—is twofold. First, China's continuing and rapid rise in power means that neighboring states must be concerned about how the Chinese

---

[3] Grimes 2006.

[4] See, inter alia, Christensen 2001, 2003; Deng 2006; Friedberg 2005; Jervis 2006; Johnston 2003a, 2004; Lampton 2007; Legro 2007; Mearsheimer 2001, 2006; Medeiros and Fravel 2003; Sato 2003; Shambaugh 2004–05; Sutter 2006; Zheng 2005.

[5] Johnston 2003a; Lampton 2004–05; Medeiros and Fravel 2003; Deng 2006.

[6] Goldstein 2005.

state and economic entities will behave toward them directly. Second, displacement of economic activity toward China will mean greater dependence on it, and thus deeper vulnerability to changes of all sorts in the Chinese economy and politics. (Economically, China's rise will present competitive threats for some firms and economies at some points in time, but it will provide attractive opportunities and shared interests for others. Economic theory, as well as experience elsewhere, suggests that on balance the shift will be welfare enhancing for China's economic partners.)

Both political aspects may be expected to change the preferences of regional states in two ways. First, states will want to encourage those Chinese economic and political interest groups that tend to make it friendlier and more amenable to peaceful compromise over disputes. Second, states should try to avoid excessive political and economic vulnerability to Chinese actions.

From a structural perspective, reducing vulnerability can be accomplished in one (or, preferably, both) of two ways—creating institutions to improve predictability and constrain misbehavior, and maintaining at least the potential for a balancing coalition. Well-functioning institutions serve several roles, including coordination, monitoring, and enforcement. But looked at from the point of view of power, two of their most important functions are to provide a voice for weaker players and to constrain the actions of strong players by getting them to agree to a mutually acceptable set of rules. Southeast Asian governments in particular should be eager to bind China (and Japan, for that matter) to behave in predictable and positive ways.

With regard to balancing, I am not making the counterproductive argument that China must be contained by the United States and its allies.[7] Rather, the emergence of a new, single regional hegemon in the form of China is not in the interests of the rest of the East Asian states, just as unchallenged U.S. hegemony is not—indeed, the whole regionalism project has clearly been aimed, at least partly, at reducing dependence on the United States. At the moment, with China clearly less capable in the region than the United States and its allies, balancing is not even an issue, but the maintenance of a *potential* balancing coalition is a practical response to a situation in flux. Any potential balancing coalition must include both the United States and Japan simply because of their magnitude in economic and military terms.

Although regional institutions will help to constrain the long-run uses of Chinese power (albeit taking its rise as given), they can also contribute to the other imperative of East Asian countries to maintain friendly and

[7]This argument is most closely associated with Mearsheimer 2001, 2006; also, U.S. House of Representatives Select Committee 1999. See Sutter 2006 and Legro 2007 for carefully reasoned arguments for postponing any such confrontation.

mutually beneficial relations with it. Most important, they can contribute to the broader process of regional economic integration, which can help expand common interests and raise the costs of conflict for all participants. Some analysts have argued that the process of international cooperation and dialogue can also change policymakers' perceptions of their countries' national interest to take greater heed of their counterparts' concerns, although I remain skeptical.[8] Of course, much of the task of maintaining friendly relations will depend on ongoing diplomacy and the actions of various nongovernmental actors. However, the development of regional institutions will be an important, perhaps even indispensable, contributor as well.

Moving away from the broad strategic level, we must consider implications for the design and course of financial regionalism. The strategic geometry of East Asia means that financial regionalism will need to focus on (1) promoting financial integration of China into regional and global systems and (2) supporting responsible regulatory and macroeconomic policies in order to prevent transmission of financial crises or price instability, as Chinese financial markets become more open to international flows. In terms of institutional design, an additional necessary factor will be ongoing policy dialogue, not only to improve domestic policies, but also to ensure that regional counterparts are forewarned of policy shifts and that their concerns are taken into consideration by Chinese and Japanese policymakers. Conveniently, given its ongoing need to reassure its counterparts of its positive intentions, all of these points are in the interests of China as well, at least for the time being. Many specific issues remain, however, including ones on which there are real or potential differences between the interests of China, Japan, and the United States.

Japan as Balancer

Japan occupies a unique position in the East Asian political economy—it is the richest and most technologically advanced economy, has the region's deepest financial markets, is the only regional state to play a leading role in global financial and economic regimes, and is the closest U.S. ally outside of Europe. Coupled with its lack of close, stable relations in the region (sometimes provoking the criticism that it is in Asia but not of it), that position offers Japan the opportunity to be a leader in financial regionalism by acting as a balancer and intermediary.[9]

From an economic perspective, Japan is indispensable to financial regionalism in East Asia. It will, for the foreseeable future, be the largest provider

---

[8] Johnston 2003b; Ruggie 1993.
[9] Katada 2002; Grimes 2005; Hayashi 2006, chap. 5.

of funds both for official initiatives and for investment in regional financial markets. Japanese experiences in financial liberalization and currency management offer important lessons (both positive and negative) for many of its regional counterparts. And Japan has institutional power in both global (such as the IMF, BIS, and G7/G8) and regional institutions (such as the Asian Development Bank or ADB) that are unmatched—indeed, not even approached—by any other East Asian government.

Strategically as well, Japan is indispensable. If the South Korean and Southeast Asian governments wish to maintain at least the potential for political balancing against China, they will need to keep the United States engaged. Japan will be a necessary partner in any balancing coalition, both because of its own capabilities and because of the strength and extent of the U.S.-Japan alliance. Although the close relationship with the United States undoubtedly exacerbates regional discomfort with Japan, it is also an important political asset for Japan, even beyond the need for defense of the archipelago.[10] Meanwhile, Japanese analysts are increasingly thinking about China when they analyze opportunities for regionalism, and many have become more cautious in their expectations for regional cooperation.[11] Others see cooperation with China and other East Asian economies as offering an essential counterweight to the power of the United States in international finance and currency issues, or as offering the economic benefits of reducing reliance on the dollar.[12]

A major problem for Japan is its disconnect with other East Asian countries, particularly China and South Korea. The "history problem" (continued resentment of Japan stemming from its military and colonial activities from 1895 to 1945), as well as a host of practical issues such as the perceived closed nature of Japanese firms' subsidiaries in the region and the treatment of East Asian migrant labor in Japan, constitute at the very least a continuing detriment to its image and official relations. Decades of proactive aid policies and nonintervention in other countries' domestic politics have not been sufficient to bridge the divide. Thus, for better or for worse, balancing is Japan's strongest card.

Outline of the Book

The book proceeds as follows. Chapters 1 and 2 lay out the background for the analysis of East Asian financial regionalism. Chapter 1 describes my analytical framework, drawing on the realist political economy literature to

[10]Sutter 2006.
[11]Sano 2005; Watanabe 2005; Rozman 2005; Tamura 2004; Taniguchi 2005.
[12]Utsumi 1999; Kuroda 2005; Sakakibara 2005.

make predictions about the ways in which power considerations will affect regional cooperation. Chapter 2 provides an overview of the development of East Asia as an economic and political region. It addresses the debate over regional definition, the rise of private-sector-led regional economic integration, the various efforts of governments to promote integration through regional cooperation, and the specific challenges of financial regionalism.

Chapters 3, 4, and 5 address the substance of East Asian financial regionalism. Each substantive chapter focuses on a more narrow analysis that highlights the core challenges for Japan and its partners and allows each issue area to be understood in the broader context of great power rivalry. In chapter 3, on emergency liquidity provision, my analysis of the Chiang Mai Initiative and its predecessors based on institutional design makes clear that Japan and China share similar interests in the initiative's decision-making mechanisms but that the current configuration also provides opportunities for China to undercut Japan's regional position. Chapter 4, on currency cooperation, looks both at the longer-term debate about the role of the U.S. dollar within the international monetary system (which massive East Asian dollar reserves are currently helping to sustain) and the economic trade-offs that face East Asian states under various proposed currency regimes. Both chapters 3 and 4 lead back to the question of whether countries can best stabilize their macroeconomic environments through autonomous action, regional cooperation, or reliance on existing international financial institutions such as the IMF and the global financial leadership role of the United States. Chapter 5, on bond market development, analyzes the political and economic costs and benefits to ASEAN+3 countries of market liberalization, as well as the economic incentives for Japanese financial institutions and savers, in order to better understand the opportunities for coalitions in favor of liberalization both between governments and transnationally.

In the concluding chapter I reassess the potential of East Asian financial regionalism to achieve its stated goals and reexamine the opportunities and dangers that it creates for Japan, China, and the United States. Acknowledging the still unsettled nature of regional financial cooperation, I address broad scenarios under which current efforts will contribute to greater or lesser economic stability regionally and globally, and to advantage and disadvantage for the major actors.

1

The Strategic Political Economy
of Financial Regionalism

To analyze the dynamics of financial regionalism and demonstrate the importance of great power politics in shaping it, we need the right tools. In this chapter I clarify the framework for analysis as well as the specific political and economic contexts in which East Asian states are operating. In doing so, I demonstrate how we can apply the realist logic of great power politics—which was, after all, developed in the context of security issues—to the market-driven world of international finance.

Approaches to Understanding Economic Regionalism

Economic integration in East Asia coexists uncomfortably with the reality of continued political rivalries and suspicion. There are at least three ways to look at the interaction of politics and economic function found in economic regionalism. The first, which scholars of international relations identify as "neoliberal institutionalist," is to see the basic problem as one of *managing interdependence.* In this perspective, the creation of regional economic institutions is in the economic interest of all the relevant actors. As in any public goods problem, coordination is difficult and distributional issues are likely to arise. Still, the primary political problem is internal to the coordination issue at hand: How can the interests of participants in integration be satisfied? Broader political rivalries add one more layer of difficulty to a complex coordination problem. As such, they may be seen as something of an annoyance, an obstacle to be overcome along the way to public goods provision. In the end, cooperation is a means of improving the actors' absolute gains.[1] The specifics of national interest, in turn, are determined through states' political processes, which aggregate the interests of domestic political and economic actors with characteristic patterns of weightings, inclusion, and exclusion.[2]

Alternatively, following the realist tradition of international political economy, we can see economic regionalism as a *reflection of political factors*.[3] In this view, the patterns of inclusion and exclusion, as well as particular rules and norms that are embodied in regional cooperative institutions, result from and affect power relations among relevant actors. The process of creating, maintaining, and transforming regional institutions is an inherently political one, defined by differing capacities, preferences, and bargaining strategies. Leading states seek to impose their preferences on their counterparts through the creation of structures of dependence, while weaker states seek to constrain the powerful through binding agreements.[4] Under certain alignments of interests and capacities and beliefs, there is an opportunity for mutually beneficial institutional arrangements.[5] But while mutually beneficial outcomes are possible and certainly desirable, the emphasis of state policies is on relative gains—not only in economic terms, but particularly in terms of political influence and security.

Finally, we can see regionalism as a *reflection of belief systems*. Constructivist writers argue that the menu of available choices is determined not only by interests and power but also by beliefs about what is possible and/ or desirable.[6] Until a dominant discourse of cooperation and shared interests develops, opportunities for cooperative institutions will remain limited. Moreover, the existence of such a dominant discourse or belief system can, in and of itself, create new opportunities for institutional development by providing an interpretive frame by which participants calculate their interests. It is not always clear who must hold a given belief or identity or how best to measure or describe beliefs, identities, and discourses. But one way or another, the constructivist approach demands that we take them seriously.

The neoliberal and realist perspectives can be understood as prescriptive as well as descriptive. After all, there is no guarantee that states will always and everywhere act "rationally," however that may be defined. The central message of realism is that, in a world defined by self-help, failure to deal effectively with relative power shifts will be punished sooner or later, whether in the form of unfavorable rules, political isolation, or—in the extreme—loss

---

[1] Keohane 1984; Axelrod and Keohane 1986.

[2] Ikenberry, Lake, and Mastanduno 1988; Frieden and Rogowski 1996; Garrett and Lange 1996. Pempel 2006 makes this point about East Asian economic regionalism (e.g., 246).

[3] Hirschman 1945 [1969]; Gowa 1994; Strange 1994; Gilpin 1987, 2000, 2001.

[4] Hirschman 1945 [1969]; Krasner 1985.

[5] Stein 1990.

[6] Wendt 1992; Haas 1992; Breslin and Higgott 2000; Johnston 2003b; Blyth 2003.

of territory or sovereignty. For neoliberals, failure to cooperate in areas where economic gains are to be found means loss of opportunity for greater prosperity. (Constructivist arguments are more difficult to characterize in general as descriptive or prescriptive, since interests are determined by understandings.)

In the real world, all three of these dynamics are intermingled, but that does not mean that all are equally important. In this book, I work primarily off of the realist presumptions that power matters, that the long-term security of states trumps the particularistic concerns of even well-connected domestic economic actors, and that states that do not focus on core national interests will in the future find themselves more at the mercy of rivals than they need be. The pursuit of these core national interests is, of course, conditioned by financial globalization, the actions and interests of individual economic actors, and the beliefs of leaders and at least some portion of the citizenry. But the basic story of rivalry, power, and influence takes us a long way toward understanding the opportunities and threats inherent in the movement toward financial regionalism.

Money, Finance, and Power

The political economy of international money has become a fertile field for political scientists, economists, and sociologists who are trying to understand how power and markets interact in an increasingly global financial system. There is a considerable literature on great power rivalry in terms of general international political economy, which can be categorized more broadly as state-centered analysis of financial issues.[7] There is, beyond this, an extraordinarily vast literature on financial globalization, some of which takes a political approach[8] and more of which is functionalist.[9] Moreover, considerable attention has been paid to post–Asian Financial Crisis financial regionalism in East Asia.[10] However, there have been relatively few scholarly works that have made a serious and sustained analysis of great power rivalry in international finance.[11] In this book I seek to close that gap by focusing on regional financial efforts in East Asia.

This is an important gap to fill. Financial regionalism may not become the primary playing field for great power rivalry in East Asia, but it will be

---

[7]Hirschman 1945 [1969]; Gilpin 1987, 2000; Funabashi 1989; Henning 1994; Destler and Henning 1989; Kapstein 1994; Kirshner 2003; Helleiner 1994; Strange 1994.

[8]Andrews, Henning, and Pauly 2002; Pauly 1997; Mittelman 2000; Odell 2000.

[9]Kenen 2001; Eichengreen and Hausmann 2005; Eichengreen 1996, 1999; Goldstein 1998.

[10]Higgott 1998; Kawai 2005; Kuroda 2005; Kondō 2003; Henning 2002; Lincoln 2004; Hayashi 2006; Sohn 2005, 2007.

[11]Exceptions include Kirshner 1995, 2000; Taniguchi 2005; and Andrews 2006.

an important one, and it is an excellent lens through which to analyze that rivalry. Economic activities are by far the major form of interaction among the countries and populations of East Asia, and economic cooperation is the most active aspect of interstate institution building in the region. In addition, the power asymmetries are striking for both their vastness (compare, say, Japan to Laos, or even to ASEAN as a whole) and their unusual nature. For example, China is a developing country that concurrently has the world's second largest GDP on a purchasing power parity basis, as well as the world's largest official foreign exchange reserves. Add to this the predominant maritime power of the United States and the lack of Chinese power projection capability, and it is clear that economic issues are the place to look for the major political currents in the region.

To date, trade and investment have been the focus of most analyses of East Asian economic regionalism.[12] Nonetheless, trade is not the only place to look for understanding the impact of great power relations on economic cooperation. Indeed, Jonathan Kirshner argues that "trade relations will not [be] the best place to look to gauge realist behavioral expectations," since it is too hard to link trade and relative power and because realist predictions are often similar to those derived from other approaches.[13] I would add one other point: trade politics are domestically complex, requiring careful analysis of interest groups' preferences, strength, and connections with the government. In contrast, a significant part of regional financial cooperation is decided and carried out by a limited number of strategically minded actors within governments. For these reasons, I join Kirshner in seeing the monetary and financial spheres as better laboratories for analyzing international-level influences on states' regional strategies.

Drawing from the Realist Tradition

My approach to analyzing East Asian financial regionalism falls into the tradition of realist political economy. But that tradition does not provide a single set of predictions, testable hypotheses, or even untestable hypotheses. Certainly, writers of realist political economy have come up with a number of more or less general causal claims and expectations. But more important than following this or that existing line of literature is the approach, or perspective, itself.[14]

---

[12]Scollay and Gilbert 2001; Stubbs 2002; Meng 2005; Mukōyama 2005; Aggarwal and Urata 2006; Aoki 2006; Baldwin 2007; Solís and Katada 2007.

[13]Kirshner 2003, 288. Kirshner also points out that financial transactions across borders vastly exceed trade in goods and services.

[14]Gilpin (2001) makes essentially the same point in his call for an eclectic approach to the study of international money and finance. This is consistent with his earlier works as well, such as Gilpin 1987.

I draw two main insights from the realist political economy tradition. The first is that most if not all of the processes and choices that lead to the establishment or modification of international economic rules, institutions, and expectations have an important political component, and that the economic choices that states and firms make subsequently have important political impacts. Politics is foreordained when there are multiple actors with varying preferences and capabilities; realist political economy makes clear that rules and their enforcement at the international level reflect the interests of, and depend on choices made by, the strong. Meanwhile, the quantity and quality of economic transactions that occur under a given system have profound implications for states' prosperity and long-run influence and security.

Drawing on this insight, the second insight concerns the types of questions we should be asking and the types of variables on which we should focus. For our purposes, the key questions are: Which states' interests are reflected in economic institutions? And how can power be exerted in them? These questions are based on a general agreement among analysts as to which types of variables should be important: for realists, they are preeminently power, security, alliances, national wealth, and system stability.[15]

Even though international finance may appear at first blush to be purely a game of profit maximization for private actors, and thus to have little or nothing to do with state power politics, the analysis in this book is based on an understanding that power and security are at stake and that it is thus essential to focus on states and their choices. This focus is likely to be controversial on at least two counts. First, it is immediately apparent that states have limited control over markets in an era of financial globalization.[16] Second, in order to make the concepts of state power and preference useful as an analytical lens (and to keep the size of this study manageable), it is necessary to severely truncate analysis of the formation of state preferences in various states, each with its own political system and constellation of economic actors. Some readers will undoubtedly be skeptical of the value of an approach that makes these choices; it is my responsibility here to justify them.

To address the first objection, financial globalization is a market phenomenon inhabited by large numbers of diverse and highly mobile actors engaged in huge numbers of extremely rapid and often massive transactions of great and expanding variety. Moreover, global financial markets have profound economic effects even for those national economies that are only peripherally connected or that try to manage their vulnerability to

[15] Keohane and Nye 1989; Gilpin 1987, 2001.
[16] Strange 1996; Solomon 1999.

investor sentiment through capital controls or other regulation. This much is indisputable, as the ASEAN+3 countries learned in the crisis of 1997–98.

A focus on state action is nonetheless indispensable.[17] Indeed, the difference between regionalization (on which I am not focusing) and regionalism (on which I am) is that regionalism involves the formation of institutions to support and shape regional transactions. The most important of these are created and maintained by states, which alone have the financial wherewithal and motive to lend into financial crises, to regulate financial transactions within and across their borders, and to set monetary and exchange rate policies. Among states, hierarchies of power exist—as seen, for example, in the development of "global standards" in financial regulation and practice that closely track U.S. and UK practice.[18] The global nature of financial markets is both an objective fact with which policymakers must deal and a phenomenon that is subject to changes in state behavior, technology, and other factors. Financial markets are indeed only partially controlled (and controllable) by states, but that does not remove the need to understand state actions as a primary factor in their functioning.

Although financial globalization can be seen as but one of many objective factors that limit states' choices, it also differs from other such factors in important ways. One is the sheer speed and mobility of many of the actors, allowing even microterritories such as the Cayman Islands to create major headaches for regulators in the largest global markets. But international finance is also an area in which rules are made by a small number of powerful states, with the rest choosing either to go along or to be excluded.[19] In this sense, international financial regulation—more than any other area of international political economy—resembles the traditional world of realist politics, in which scholars have concentrated almost exclusively on the actions of great powers. The same point is true of liquidity provision for currency crises, and especially for currency cooperation: the world of global finance is dominated by a small and shrinking number of currencies, with the rest essentially functioning as price takers.[20]

The second objection essentially asks what we mean by national interests. The standard international political economy approach is to look at

[17] Helleiner 1994; Kapstein 1994.

[18] Cohen 1998a; Strange 1994; Kapstein 1994; Helleiner 1994; Singer 2007.

[19] A classic case is the 1988 negotiation of the Basel Accord on capital-adequacy ratios for banks, which began as an agreement between just two key states in global finance—the United States and United Kingdom. See Kapstein 1991; Singer 2007, chap. 4.

[20] Strange 1994; Cohen 1998a. Nonetheless, Cohen in his 1998 book was skeptical about the ability of even the dominant currency states to reap the full rewards of currency dominance. Cohen in his 2006 essay is even more skeptical, arguing that the deterritorialization of currencies and the appearance of currency alternatives will profoundly affect the freedom of action of even the states with the greatest concentration of apparent financial and monetary power.

the structure of economic interests within an economy and to analyze their interrelations with the state.[21] Thus, for example, macroeconomically stable states with large and competitive financial sectors that have close connections with the state policy-making apparatus will, as a result of their composition, prefer open, transparent, and efficient capital markets. This is undoubtedly true, and it is undoubtedly interesting as an object of analysis. But it is by no means the only—or even necessarily the most profitable—way to go about understanding state actions. At one level we can approximate fairly well the national economic interest of states in international finance simply with a broad-brush description of the type just offered. To get that level of understanding of national interest does not really require deep analysis of state-society interactions, interesting though such an analysis might be. But there is a stronger justification for not focusing on the domestic politics of national interest formation: states have interests in long-term security that are not explained fully by who gets rich or how, and these values are also affected by decisions about economic regulation and regional initiatives. In this regard, the contrast between the prevailing political and security conditions in 1950s Europe and contemporary East Asia could not be starker. France and Germany politically committed to mutually beneficial cooperation under the watchful and supportive protection of the United States and under the shadow of an encroaching iron curtain.[22] In East Asia, a rapidly rising China is integral to East Asian economic activity and cooperation, but it is simultaneously the greatest potential security threat to Japan and to U.S. leadership in the region. Whatever else the field of international political economy has to say about East Asian regionalism, it must regard this confluence of rivalry, cooperation, and competition as a central factor in how regional institutions will develop and what their effects will be.

Realist Theories

Turning away from the broad perspective, it is worth examining more closely the conclusions and predictions of realist writers concerning the issues at hand. While I have characterized realist political economy analysis of international financial and monetary issues as relatively undeveloped, there are a number of prominent analyses that either directly address finance or are relevant by extension. Realist analyses of international finance look at various aspects of the relationship between power and capital, including the role of hegemony (both benign and predatory) and the tools of financial statecraft. On only a few points is there anything like a consensus, however. Here, I situate my approach within the larger universe of realist analysis.

[21] Milner 1997; Frieden and Rogowski 1996; Singer 2007.
[22] Chang 2003; Gowa 1994.

Hegemonic Stability Theory

The greatest point of consensus among realist international political economy scholars is that cooperation among states is inherently difficult except where there is a politically preponderant power or hegemon. One reason is that contests over relative gains between the major powers might otherwise wash out potential absolute gains.[23] The other is the problem of free riding.[24] The main realist solution to those concerns can be found under the general rubric of "hegemonic stability theory," which was stimulated by Charles Kindleberger's argument that the provision of international public goods in the absence of world government requires a single leader: "For as far ahead as today's social scientists can see, I think it is necessary to organize the international community—both related to policy and economy alike—on the basis of leadership."[25] For Kindleberger, looking at international trade and finance, that leader would be needed to act as a market for distressed goods (i.e., to provide demand in the face of excess supply) and as lender of last resort; he went so far as to argue in 1981 that "the danger we face is not too much power in the international economy, but too little, not an excess of domination, but a superfluity of would-be free riders."[26]

A weaker version of hegemonic stability theory was envisioned by neoliberal institutionalist writers like Robert Keohane, who agreed that leadership was essential to international cooperation, but whose work focused on seeking ways in which shared leadership might be possible.[27] Even among realist writers, there is some debate over whether hegemony is needed to maintain a system or cooperative regime, although the system's creation is generally agreed to require a single dominant power. Either way, it should be noted that leaders are expected to lead for their own benefit, which may not always match the interests of other participants. As Robert Gilpin summarizes one set of critiques of U.S. leadership in the postwar international economy:

> [Susan] Strange and other critics alleged that such international regimes as those governing trade and monetary affairs had been economically, politically, and ideologically biased in America's favor, that these regimes were put in place by American power, reflected American interests, and were not (as American regime theorists have argued) politically and economically neutral.[28]

[23]Grieco 1988.

[24]Olson 1965; Olson and Zeckhauser 1966.

[25]Kindleberger 1981, 252. The idea was first developed in his 1973 *The World in Depression*. See also Kindleberger 1986. The term "hegemonic stability theory" was coined by Keohane in 1980.

[26]Kindleberger 1981, 253.

[27]Keohane 1984; Axelrod and Keohane 1986; Snidal 1985.

[28]Gilpin 2002, 30. See also Gilpin 1987, and Kindleberger 1981. The temptation of hegemons to exploit their position, especially as their preponderance declined, was seen to make the international system inherently unstable.

Looking at financial issues, Kindleberger emphasized years ago that the world monetary system requires an ongoing source of international liquidity and an effective lender of last resort in the event of payments crises. Despite the existence of the IMF and BIS, realist political economists have argued that neither of those functions can be effectively provided by supranational organizations or multilateral cooperation in the absence of clear leadership. Nonetheless, currency leadership clearly gives the dominant state incentives for exploitation of partners and arbitrary decisions. Going back at least to the 1960s, when French president Charles de Gaulle complained about the "exorbitant privilege" that the United States gained as a result of the use of the dollar as a key currency,[29] the global role of the dollar has created fear and concern as well as reassurance for monetary policymakers around the world. As Treasury Secretary John Connally was alleged to have told his European counterparts in 1971, "The dollar is our currency, but it's your problem."[30] The combination of the dominance of the dollar as an international currency, the size of U.S. financial markets, the importance of U.S. government bond markets as a global benchmark, and the strong U.S. role in global financial institutions such as the IMF and BIS provide the United States with attractive opportunities to exert power and privilege.

On a systemic level, two major issues apply, both related to the U.S. dollar's role as international key currency. First, due to the widespread global use of dollars, the United States benefits from seignorage on a global level, creating value for the government on the order of $11–15 billion per year.[31] Second, and presumably far more important, essentially all U.S. trade and international borrowing is denominated in dollars, not to mention most international trade and borrowing by third countries. Alone among the world's economies, the United States does not face large losses when its currency depreciates, and it does not see fit to maintain substantial foreign currency reserves. (However, it is also difficult to achieve depreciation against the currency of major trading partners, such as China, that choose to peg to the dollar.)[32]

Hegemonic stability theory suggests two implications for regional cooperation. One is that efforts at regional cooperation, like those at the global level, will be easiest to implement if there exists a single clear leader. The development of the European Union appears to weaken that argument, although at least some realists predict that the European Union will become

[29]Volcker and Gyohten 1992, 42–43.

[30]While the original source is obscure, this line has long been widely quoted (with some variations of wording) by reputable sources. See, for example, Eichengreen 1996, 136; Martin Wolf, "Falling Dollar Saga Still Has a Long Way to Go," *FT* December 5, 2006.

[31]Estimates by Jeffrey Frankel and Alan Blinder, quoted in Cohen 1998a, 124.

[32]See, for example, "Beijing Refuses to Yield to U.S. Pressure," *FT,* February 22, 2006, 3.

internally divided and thus less effective over time.[33] Certainly, however, a realist political economy perspective clearly predicts that binding East Asian economic cooperation should be difficult to achieve (or fragile if it does develop) due to the deep competition between Japan and China for leadership.

The second implication is that if the global leader begins to falter or to use its power to the detriment of its less powerful counterparts, the global system is likely to be supplanted by a set of more or less separate regional systems.[34] Regional cooperation would arise as a defensive mechanism as regional powers sought to insulate themselves from either exploitation by the dominant player or system instability.[35] East Asian financial regionalism is driven partly by concerns about vulnerability to global financial flows. Although as of the first decade of the twenty-first century regional trade and financial cooperation remain under the umbrella of the global economic institutions, a standard realist concern is that over time those institutions will need to adapt, that adaptation will be difficult without a clear leader, and that regions will become the default organizing principle of the world economy.[36]

A less pessimistic view is that "defensive regionalism" might create the means for the (re)establishment of a more symmetrical global system. This might be particularly likely in financial and monetary affairs. The reason is twofold. First, the preeminence of the U.S. dollar and financial markets is so large, so established, and so useful to most global financial actors that there may be little appetite on the part of regional rivals in Europe and Asia to actually supplant the dollar as international key currency.[37] Rather, they would be satisfied just with disciplining the more egregious U.S. abuses of its position.[38] Second, an essential aspect of a long-term shift away from dollar dominance would be declining interest in holding dollars, and thus a serious downward pressure on the currency that should evoke an assertive

[33] Kirshner 1999. It has also been argued that Germany created de facto hegemonic leadership in European monetary policy by first creating a subregional following among the Benelux countries (Andrews 2006, 106–7). Even so, serious movement toward a single currency was possible only after the French and Italian states concluded that inflation was their key challenge. European monetary union became possible as a deal in which Germany compromised on collective decision making in exchange for French acquiescence to anti-inflationary policy.

[34] Gilpin 1987; Kirshner 1999.

[35] Realists thus interpret the recent burgeoning of preferential trade agreements (PTAs) firstly as a means of gaining advantage at a time when global leadership is lacking in the Doha Round and secondly as a defensive measure against other countries' PTAs. A useful analogy would be the reciprocal trading agreements of the interwar period. Oye 1993.

[36] Gilpin 2001, 255–60.

[37] Kindleberger 1986. See also McKinnon and Schnabl 2004; Cohen 2007.

[38] Foreign Exchange Commission 1999; Utsumi 1999.

response from U.S. authorities in the form of more conservative fiscal and monetary policies.

States and Markets

All this concern with power and public goods may seem remote from the study of financial markets, which are, after all, populated by huge numbers of private actors trying to make a profit, regardless of the preferences of their home or host governments. Probably the most difficult aspect of international political economy analysis, regardless of which analytical approach one takes, is how to reconcile state power with the "power" of markets.[39]

One viable approach, as noted, is to look at market activity as a constraint on state action. But that is not the only way. An alternative is to try to fully integrate the concept of power into our understanding of markets. Following Susan Strange's pioneering work, we can draw a distinction between "relational power" and "structural power," where the former is power as typically understood (that is, the ability of one actor to force another to change its behavior) and the latter is the ability "to decide how things shall be done, the power to shape frameworks within which states relate to each other, relate to people, or relate to corporate enterprises."[40] At the core of hegemonic power is structural power, and international finance and monetary affairs are the classic examples of the global structural power of the United States.[41]

One aspect of U.S. financial power is the U.S. role within international financial institutions—without U.S. approval, the IMF does not lend to countries in crisis, nor does the World Bank provide development lending. This is only the most visible aspect, and is primarily relational. For Strange, however, the most overwhelming aspect of U.S. power in finance was that other states found themselves with little or no choice but to follow U.S. standards (the key underpinning of "global standards") in one instance after another. In the Basel Accord of 1988, for example, U.S. and UK regulators demonstrated that their power to create and enforce standards extended even into the domestic regulation of the Japanese banking industry, which at that point was widely seen as challenging U.S. banking for world dominance.[42]

More subtly, the no-holds-barred financial liberalization that many observers most closely associate with globalization, and which is so often presented as the triumph of markets over states, was unleashed by U.S. regulators

[39]For attempts to wrestle with this question from various perspectives, see inter alia Helleiner 1994; Blyth 2003; Strange 1994, 1996; Cohen 1998a, 2004; Singer 2007.

[40]Strange 1994, 24–29 (quotation, 25). This recalls Lukes 1974.

[41]Strange 1994; Helleiner 1994, 2000; Cohen 2006; Andrews, Henning, and Pauly 2002.

[42]Various accounts of the 1988 Basel Accord can be found in Ohta 1991; Kapstein 1994; Helleiner 1994; Tadokoro 2001; Singer 2007.

and continues to privilege U.S.-based financial institutions and markets.[43] Although Strange and other analysts of power in international finance stress that markets have severely eroded the power of states to control them, to the extent that control exists it is held by an extraordinarily small group of state actors, with the United States as the preeminent—essentially indispensable—state in all aspects of regulation and governance. As Benjamin Cohen has it, there is a "currency pyramid" with the dollar at the top, the euro a significant tier down, followed by the yen; once one gets past the pound sterling and Swiss franc at yet another big step down there is no more agenda-setting power left in the system.[44]

Another vitally important point is that the dominance of the U.S. dollar means that the United States, alone among debtor nations, borrows in its own currency, leaving counterparties to take the currency risk, which they do willingly. For better or for worse (and Strange made clear that she saw it as the latter),[45] the United States has yet to encounter a hard constraint on fiscal and current account deficits.

Working from a similar point of view, Cohen argues that international monetary power can be divided into the "power to delay" and the "power to deflect" macroeconomic adjustment.[46] The lack of a hard constraint on U.S. deficits is a classic example of the power to delay in action—indeed, Cohen labels the United States a "special case."[47] Another recent example was the ability of Japanese authorities to delay a decisive resolution of a massive nonperforming loan problem for over a decade, secure in the knowledge that there would not be a run on either the currency or Japanese government bonds. The power to deflect costs of adjustment onto other states or entities is given by the asymmetries of the system as well as the specific interests of the states in question. The United States was able to deflect the costs of adjustment from the early 1970s until at least the mid-1990s onto Europe, and especially Japan, the most financially powerful actors in the world economy other than itself, primarily through the use of what C. Randall Henning calls the "exchange-rate weapon."[48]

In the face of such deflection of costs, it seems reasonable for states to try to make themselves less vulnerable—in other words, to insulate themselves from the impacts of U.S. policy through defensive regionalism. Indeed, that is not only the consensus of authors of studies of international monetary

[43]Strange 1986; Wade 1998; Helleiner 2006. Stiglitz 2002 generally agrees with the point but emphasizes the relational power of the United States and the IMF in forcing countries to liberalize.
[44]Cohen 2004, 14–16.
[45]See, for example, Strange 1994, 107–10.
[46]Cohen 2006.
[47]Cohen 2006, 45.
[48]Henning 2006; Hiwatari 1996.

power, it is also apparent both in Europe (where monetary union has by now moved well along the path to providing effective insulation from destructive U.S. policies) and in Japan.[49] As we shall see, East Asian financial regionalism arises at least partially from the incentive to insulate regional economies from the dollar and from U.S. economic policies.

Politics of Hedging, Commitment, and Leverage

As with security issues, application of a realist approach to the study of regional or bilateral cooperation must draw on the concepts of hedging and commitment. Both hedging and commitment are strategies for dealing with the various uncertainties that pervade international relations. Chief among these uncertainties for our purposes are the current and future power interests of other actors, future patterns of economic change, and sources of future political and economic crises. For Japan, for example, uncertainties include the rapidity of the rise of China, the reaction of other regional actors to that rise, preferences of the Chinese and U.S. governments, changes in interdependence, likelihood of entrapment or abandonment in the U.S.-Japan alliance, the possibility of sudden events or miscalculations (such as a hot war between Taiwan and China or aggressive actions by North Korea, or a trade war resulting from a spiral of retaliatory actions between, say, the United States and China), and the origins of the next financial crisis.[50]

Commitment is a means of trying to *reduce* uncertainty by locking oneself and one's partner(s) into a prescribed set of behaviors. Commitment reduces uncertainty about the motivations and future actions of the actors involved, both for each other and—for better or for worse—for outside actors. Military alliances are prototypical commitment strategies, which seek to guarantee an improved balance of threats.[51] International regimes, treaties, and organizations also constitute commitment strategies by those states that participate in them. Alliances are typically understood in the context of balancing or bandwagoning, while regimes and other forms of cooperation are generally meant to reduce some functional or environmental uncertainty. In all cases, credible commitments are ones in which meaningful costs are incurred by states that do not meet their obligations.[52]

[49] Regarding Europe, see, for example, Strange 1994, 109; Henning 2006; Frasher-Rae 2008; on Japan, see Utsumi 1999; Grimes 2003a, 2003b.

[50] Policymakers around the world are acutely aware of the possibility that the next great financial crisis will look very different from previous versions. See, for example, Caprio, Hanson, and Litan 2005, especially the chapter by Goldstein and Wong. As of early 2008, the U.S. subprime crisis threatened financial stability around the globe.

[51] Here, I stick with Walt 1990, which emphasizes balance of threats over balance of power. The difference is that perceptions of threat include beliefs about potential adversaries' intentions as well as the offense-defense posture of their militaries. (The latter is not obviously relevant to the economic issues.)

[52] See Oye 1986, and Axelrod and Keohane 1986.

Hedging, in contrast, is a means by which actors seek to *manage* uncertainty by reducing their vulnerability to changes in their environment via the creation of feasible exit options.[53] Hedging differs from commitment in several ways. Most importantly, it is a contingent strategy, meant to create viable policy alternatives in case the environment or national interests shift in such a way as to make key aspects of national grand strategy counterproductive. Economically, hedging calls for diversification of suppliers, customers, lenders, and borrowers.[54] Politically, hedging also depends on diversifying vulnerabilities. Moreover, by creating viable policy alternatives, it affects the perceptions and thus potentially the actions of other actors in the system—particularly if those alternatives look relatively attractive.

It can be difficult to simultaneously commit and hedge in a single issue area, particularly in issues where relative gains rather than absolute gains dominate. This is less true in economic issues, where absolute gains are more important. Indeed, combining bilateral, regional, and multilateral strategies with regard to trade negotiations has become the rule rather than the exception. More generally, linkage strategies are possible between different economic issues or with political issues.

Finally, both commitment strategies and hedging strategies can be used as leverage to affect the behavior or options of other actors. Threats of tightening an alliance (a strong form of commitment) affect the calculations of potential adversaries, possibly inducing them to step back from confrontational stances.[55] Hedges can provide leverage against actors that might otherwise seek to exert power through asymmetric dependence, whether military (e.g., EU military cooperation as a hedge against U.S. unilateralism) or economic (e.g., access to markets, which the United States used to force changes in Japanese trade policy for much of the postwar period, or to raw materials, in the way that developed nations turned to alternative power sources or oil suppliers after the 1973 OPEC embargo). In this sense, hedging and commitment strategies have both "offensive" and "defensive" implications. Moreover, they often are most effective as a means of signaling intentions and capabilities to potential or actual adversaries or allies.

Financial Statecraft

Realist analyses of "financial statecraft" and "monetary power" bring together the strands of structural power with specific state policies and strategies such as commitment and hedging. Jonathan Kirshner in *Currency and Coercion* argues that there are three main ways in which monetary systems

---

[53] Medeiros 2005–06.

[54] "Hedging" is also used in a much more specific sense in finance. Modern financial hedging can be mind-bogglingly complicated, but at its core it calls for nothing more than that all liabilities be matched by an asset of equal value that has opposite risk characteristics.

[55] Of course, this can also backfire and force the adversary to seek to balance the home country's alliance by forming or strengthening its own countervailing alliance(s).

can be exploited by states to achieve foreign policy ends: currency manipulation, monetary dependence, and systemic disruption.[56] All three are in play in East Asia, at least potentially.

Currency manipulation, which for our purposes means the use of the "exchange-rate weapon,"[57] can be carried out in either a predatory or protective manner, by attacking or supporting the value of the currency of an enemy or ally. Kirshner considers this to be a particularly useful tool due to its "speed, cost, flexibility, and weight."[58] It can be useful against both minor economies and major ones, depending on sensitivity to exchange rate changes, which in turn is a function of domestic politics as well as trade structure, current account position, and reserve holdings.[59] Currency manipulation was in fact practiced by U.S. policymakers for years against Japan, the world's second largest economy, as seen in repeated instances of U.S. officials "talking down the dollar" in order to pressure the Japanese government in economic negotiations.[60] Since 2003 the U.S. government has engaged in rather less effective efforts to force China to revalue against the dollar. In the meantime, the undervaluation of the renminbi (RMB) has contributed to the extraordinary growth in China's foreign currency reserves, adding to a substantial world dollar overhang and significantly complicating political and economic adjustment in both surplus and deficit nations.[61]

Monetary dependence takes several forms, but the key one is "entrapment," in which the interests of the private sector and state are actually transformed by their dependence on another state for their monetary stability.[62] According to Kirshner, states are subject to monetary dependence when they are dependent on a more financially powerful state for maintaining the value of their currency. (More overt uses of monetary dependence, such as threatening withdrawal of support to force concessions in other areas,

[56] Kirshner 1995. See also Andrews 2006. While Steil and Litan 2005 purports to be the first serious study of the subject, it is actually much less systematic than Kirshner's work. Moreover, in terms of its treatment of monetary issues, it is primarily focused on making an argument in favor of dollarization, which is not really very useful in analyzing the political economy of East Asia. It does take seriously the potential of financial tools of statecraft, however. Bracken 2007 also discusses financial statecraft, but with an emphasis on financial sanctions.

[57] Kirshner 1995 and 2006 also discuss threats of expulsion from currency arrangements, which is not relevant for East Asia in the way that it would be for the study of, say, the CFA franc zones in Africa.

[58] Kirshner 1995, 111.

[59] Henning 2006.

[60] Funabashi 1989, especially chap. 7. See also Destler and Henning 1989, 50–53; Volcker and Gyohten 1992, 279–80.

[61] I hasten to add that U.S. macroeconomic policies and consumer preferences have contributed a great deal—probably more than Chinese policies—to complicating global adjustment. See, for example, Cline 2005.

[62] Kirshner 1995, 117–19.

carry greater political costs.) Regional arrangements that seek to stabilize currencies raise the possibility of new regional patterns of monetary dependence, and thus potential entrapment. In this sense, the Chiang Mai Initiative may be seen as a potential source of monetary entrapment of East Asian economies by Japan or (perhaps more likely) a future rising China. It can also be seen very clearly as an effort by the East Asian countries to reduce the region's and their own dependence on the United States and the IMF as lenders of last resort.

The third form of monetary power is "systemic disruption," in which a middle power threatens to create disarray within the monetary system, in the full knowledge that it has no ability to offer an alternative, with the objective of forcing the leading power to change its policies.[63] This provides a counterweight to the seemingly overwhelming power of the key currency country, but it is not an easy strategy or one that can be entered into lightly, as France's president de Gaulle discovered in the 1960s when he tried to pressure the United States by demanding conversion of dollar assets into gold.[64] Nonetheless, Japanese policy debate has been animated for years by the idea that Japan and the European Union together may be able to constrain profligate and externally damaging U.S. fiscal policies, although the call is usually for something more subtle than actual "disruption."[65] In East Asia, the huge dollar reserves of China and Japan provide potential ammunition for both currency manipulation and a threat to other aspects of the dollar's key currency status, such as the dollar denomination of the global commodities trade. I return to this point in chapter 4.

Kirshner has recently argued that the meaning of systemic disruption is in flux. Rather than focusing on second-tier powers, he suggests that the United States itself may have an interest in "strategic disruption"—that is, encouraging a high level of system instability, in order to maintain other states' dependence and perhaps even to maintain access to capital, as crises create a "flight to quality."[66] To quote him at length:

> Awareness of this type of structural power can help explain U.S. efforts to render illegitimate any forms of international capital control and, likewise, its efforts to promote complete and comprehensive domestic financial liberalization abroad in the absence of evidence to support the proposition that such deregulation is optimal from an economic perspective and in the

---

[63] Several authors invoke Thomas Schelling's analogy of a passenger in a lifeboat rocking the boat in a dangerous manner in order to get his way: he cannot take control of steering the boat himself, but he may be able to make the leader nervous enough to accede to his demands. See Schelling 1966, 91; Kirshner 2006, 157; Cooper 2006, 164.

[64] Kirshner 1995, chap. 5; Volcker and Gyohten, 42–43.

[65] See, for example, Utsumi 1999; Volcker and Gyohten 1992, 303–10. Kikkawa 1998 is a not-so-subtle example.

[66] Kirshner 2006, 157.

wake of spectacular and unanticipated disruptions such as the East Asian
financial crisis. For while a world of completely unregulated capital is risky,
it is perhaps the least risky for the United States, given the hegemonic position of the U.S. economy.[67]

Of course, if Kirshner is right, there would seem to be all the more incentive for both the European Union and the East Asian economies to seek to
insulate themselves by means of regional cooperation.

One other tool of financial statecraft that is of potential importance to
East Asian states is capital market sanctions.[68] To the extent that states make
use of dollars as a medium of exchange and for their reserves they may be
more vulnerable to U.S. policies that allow for freezing dollar accounts of
enemies, whether states or subnational criminal or terrorist networks. This
is not a major concern for any of the major ASEAN+3 states at the moment,
but it is a potential one. Certainly, the difficulties of freeing up North Korean funds held in Macao's Banco Delta Asia in 2006, as well as the freezing
of the accounts of various Islamic charities accused of being linked to ter-
rorism, are issues of which states in East Asia are aware.

Applications to Financial Regionalism: Insulation, Liberalization, and Dollar Politics

Having surveyed a variety of writers and approaches, the question remains:
How can we apply the principles of realist political economy to contemporary East Asian financial regionalism? While specific issues call for specific
analyses—and there will be much of that in the chapters that follow—we
can map out several general predictions of the preferences and priorities
of each of the major state actors regarding three major themes: insulation,
liberalization, and dollar politics.

Realist political economy predicts that insulation will be a central motivat-
ing factor in financial regionalism. Japan's experience is particularly instructive, given that it has been on the receiving end over the years of multiple
instances of U.S. use of monetary power. The classic national response to financial vulnerability is imposition of capital controls. For a state like Japan,
however, the preference for insulation is complicated by two factors that
make the insulation dynamic interesting. First, as an advanced and globally
engaged economy, Japan benefits enormously from full integration into the
world financial system. Indeed, despite complex domestic political considerations, the logic of openness has been so overwhelming that Japanese

[67] Kirshner 2006, 157.
[68] See Steil and Litan 2006, chap. 4; Bracken 2007.

markets are now "free, fair, and global."[69] Thus, any Japanese insulation strategy must use international, especially regional, means to reduce economic exposure to unilateral changes in U.S. economic policies.[70] Second, any regional insulation strategy that Japan pursues must deal with Japan's overall political, economic, and security dependence on the United States, on the one hand, and its rivalry with China, on the other. We would therefore expect Japan to be proactive in promoting regional collective action to reduce its vulnerability to the effects of U.S. macroeconomic policies as well as that of the region on which it increasingly depends—and indeed, even to be willing to accept substantial free riding in terms of the costs—but also to do so in a way that does not directly challenge the United States.

Other East Asian states have also had an interest in regional strategies of insulation, although to varying degrees. Those hardest hit by the Asian Financial Crisis, including South Korea and the ASEAN4 (Indonesia, Malaysia, the Philippines, and Thailand), have been particularly sensitized to the need for insulation from financial attack. This is a slightly different emphasis from that of Japan, whose vulnerabilities are much less extreme and whose currency and economic policies have been frequent targets of direct U.S. pressure, but in other ways the dilemma is quite similar. They are economies whose prosperity depends on openness to foreign trade and investment, and therefore they must maintain a relatively high degree of financial openness.[71] As relatively small and vulnerable economies, they can benefit from regional solutions as well—not only from collective action per se, but also from the interest of Japan (and in the future, China) in reducing their vulnerability to speculative attacks by committing resources to reduce regional currency volatility. China, for the moment, has the weakest interest in pursuing a proactive policy of regional insulation, given that its own vulnerability is limited by strict capital controls and a (mostly) dollar-pegged currency. However, it has a vital interest in shaping regional financial cooperation over the longer run, as it opens up financially and develops a larger stake in regional financial stability. It also has a strong incentive not to cede regional leadership to either Japan or the United States. The United States, meanwhile, generally benefits from other states bearing the costs of preventing currency crises but strongly prefers that any regional cooperation be nested within the global financial order and pursued alongside financial liberalization.

[69] This was the motto of Big Bang, the 1998–2001 liberalization of the Japanese financial market. For analysis of the process of financial opening, see especially Vogel 1996; Laurence 2001; Toya 2006.

[70] Grimes 1999, 2003a, 2003b.

[71] Even Malaysia, often cited as an example of financial nationalism, has a substantially open capital account. See, for example, McCauley 2003 and the country capital rules listed on the ASEAN website, http://www.aseansec.org/carh/index.htm.

Since shortly after the Asian Financial Crisis, Japan has in fact pursued a strategy of monetary insulation through regional diversification, initially through attempts at "internationalization of the yen."[72] The key elements of this strategy have been to try to increase the covariance of regional currencies with the yen (thus reducing the impact of shifts in the yen-dollar rate), to provide funds for regional stabilization (most lastingly through the Chiang Mai Initiative), to promote regional financial liberalization and development, and to do so in a way that does not directly threaten U.S. interests or the integrity of the IMF and other global financial institutions (after the initial misstep of the Asian monetary fund proposal in 1997). Financially vulnerable East Asian economies have been enthusiastic participants in those elements of the strategy that reduce their vulnerability and have been willing to accept Japanese leadership, which has come with substantial commitments of financial support. China, which was initially more hesitant, has come to realize the benefits of participating in a regional insulation strategy, while still insisting on its prerogative of having a leadership role.

In terms of liberalization, motives also vary among states. The United States and Japan, with globally or regionally competitive financial institutions as well as a need to either recycle excess savings or to obtain others' excess savings, have a strong interest in promoting financial market development and liberalization. The economically open developing and middle-income states of East Asia (that is, the original ASEAN5 of Indonesia, Malaysia, the Philippines, Singapore, and Thailand plus South Korea and China)[73] have long-term interests in developing more robust and efficient—and thus less vulnerable—financial markets, but their short-term interests vary. We expect to see strong attempts by Japan at the regional level to promote financial liberalization, but with a particular emphasis on market development.[74] Japan also has an interest in locking its East Asian counterparts into a system of market-based rules (i.e., global standards) before China is in a position to set standards. Those counterparts are interested in receiving Japanese and other regional support for market development, but at their own pace. In particular, the primary motivation of insulation from financial volatility pushes against acceptance of a major U.S. role, given the experiences of the 1990s.

[72] Grimes 1999, 2003a, 2003b.

[73] Taiwan is excluded from the list only because it is not a member of ASEAN+3. Similarly, we could add Hong Kong, Australia, and New Zealand as states with strong interests in regional financial liberalization, but they play only a peripheral role, mostly through EMEAP. Taiwan, Hong Kong, Australia, and New Zealand are all members of APEC, as is the United States, but APEC has not been at the center of regional financial cooperation.

[74] While U.S. financial institutions have an interest in East Asian financial market development, the U.S. government's primary interest is in maintaining a constant supply of funding for its own current account deficits and addressing currency valuations. Thus, its primary interest is in financial openness rather than financial development per se.

The final general prediction generated by our analytical framework addresses dollar politics—in other words, acceptance of or resistance to the global role of the U.S. dollar as key currency and to the global role of the United States as financial leader. This is a tricky area. On the one hand, there are many economic advantages to amassing and using dollars for international transactions. On the other hand, both building up dollar reserves and pegging to the dollar increase economic vulnerability to movements in the value of the dollar; moreover, the dominance of the dollar contributes significantly to the global economic leadership role of the United States.

For small economies, it is most practical to maintain at least a partial link to the dollar, while there is also a collective incentive to do more or less what major trading partners and competitors are doing. But the governments of major economies like Japan and China have at least the potential for charting their own paths and making decisions that directly affect the role of the dollar. The United States, of course, prefers to maintain its powers to delay and to deflect economic adjustment, as well as to have the potential to use other tools of financial statecraft such as the exchange rate weapon, monetary dependence, and capital sanctions.

Thus, the issue of dollar politics in East Asian financial regionalism is most relevant to Japan and China. For Japan, the strong interest in insulation against U.S. exchange rate manipulation and adjustment deflection seems to call for a preference for disengaging from the dollar.[75] Indeed, several semiofficial Japanese studies have called for exactly that: creating a counterweight to U.S. unilateralism in macroeconomic policymaking. However, the Japanese government must also consider the political dangers of using the exchange rate weapon directly; moreover, it is a big enough economy that disengagement efforts—for example, diversifying its foreign exchange reserves—could also have the effect of systemic disruption. Thus, an incremental strategy of raising its exposure to East Asia relative to the United States while not staging a direct attack on dollar hegemony is to be expected. For China, the economic incentives for remaining within the dollar sphere, at least for the time being, are much stronger than for Japan, but the long-term political incentives against disruption are weaker.[76] Thus, it appears that the United States and China are in what former U.S. Treasury secretary Lawrence Summers has called a "financial balance of terror," in which there seems to be no first-mover advantage to disruption.[77] If conditions change, however, we should expect to see much more assertive action by China than by Japan.

---

[75] Shimizu 2005, 58–64, makes this explicit, stating that Japan's goal in financial regionalism should be "*doru banare*," or "disengagement from the dollar."

[76] McKinnon and Schnabl 2004.

[77] Summers 2004.

To summarize our general predictions, we should expect to see:

1. Conscious regional efforts to insulate economies from global volatility, and particularly from unilateralist U.S. macroeconomic policies.
2. Japanese promotion of financial market development and liberalization, reflecting global standards and with Japanese financial support. However, Japan does not have the ability to compel liberalization, and other ASEAN+3 participants will prefer self-paced liberalization. Compared to the United States, all participants will have a stronger preference for development than liberalization.
3. Japan will have a particular interest in promoting rule-based financial market development so as to lock China into global standards. The United States, independently and in other venues, will continue to pursue the same outcome.
4. The actions of Japan and China will determine the extent to which the region as a whole disengages from the dollar. Both will prefer to move incrementally in the short-to-medium term, but China will be in a position to move more decisively in the longer term if conditions are advantageous. Only China, therefore, can threaten systemic disruption—a tool of monetary power that is more effective as a threat than in actual use.[78]

Alternative Explanations: Liberal and Constructivist Approaches

So far in this chapter I have laid out in some detail a realist political economy framework of analysis, along with some general predictions that the framework generates for East Asian financial regionalism. But this is not the only, or even the most popular, way of analyzing that phenomenon—most writers on this subject work from either a liberal institutionalist or a constructivist point of view, or in some cases a combination of the two. It is my responsibility to demonstrate the usefulness of this framework; to do so, I must compare its applicability against that of other approaches. I do this more specifically in chapters 3, 4, and 5, but here I offer a general overview of how liberal and constructivist explanations play out in East Asian financial regionalism.[79]

---

[78]Consider the nervous reaction of some market participants in August 2007 to very tenuous claims (subsequently officially denied by the People's Bank of China) that China was threatening to unload its dollars as retaliation for U.S. protectionism. For the article that created the scare, see Ambrose Evans-Pritchard, "China Threatens 'Nuclear Option' of Dollar Sales," *Daily Telegraph,* August 8, 2007.

[79]This will not be a taxonomic exercise. Neither I nor—I assume—most readers have much interest in my placing all the various writings on East Asian regionalism into neat little liberal

Much of the analysis to date about East Asian economic regionalism can be categorized as coming from a liberal approach. While the specific analyses vary, broadly speaking there are two versions. One is an economic discourse on institutional design.[80] This version sees regional economic integration as creating positive gains for states that participate in creating institutions to support further integration. The key questions for these writers are whether benefits are to be achieved through given types of cooperation, and how those ventures should be designed in order to maximize benefits and minimize costs. The other version is political economy analysis of interest groups within states and the effects they may have on policies.[81] In both cases, increasing regional integration among East Asian economies creates opportunities for mutually beneficial multilateral cooperation among governments. Thus, the political questions revolve around collective action problems and how they might be solved. While specific predictions vary, in general they follow a common theme: cooperation may be difficult, but success in the long run will depend on the distribution of costs and benefits. The rise of regional economic integration suggests that in most cases some sort of regional institutional solution is likely to emerge that will facilitate the needs of economic actors.[82]

Constructivist approaches to regionalism begin from the common premise that self-identified regions are not natural units in the sense that they simply exist; rather, they are formed through political and social processes that vary across time and space. Constructivist analyses of East Asian regionalism focus on the development of a more or less widely shared regional identity.[83] A regional identity is seen as driving regionalism in two ways. One is the fellow feeling implied by intersubjectively held beliefs in common membership in a community, which increases the desire to cooperate and lowers feelings of mistrust.[84] The other is in the specific content of the identity, which may shape holders' understanding of both the situation in which they find themselves and the options available for dealing with that situation. Many Japanese advocates of financial cooperation, for example, follow an almost teleological approach in which the ultimate goal of economic cooperation is an Asian Community (*kyōdōtai*) along the lines of the

---

or constructivist pigeonholes. Rather, I focus on the major themes and questions raised by these approaches. I reference a number of specific texts, but this is meant to be illustrative rather than comprehensive.

[80] Kawai 2005; Kawai and Takagi 2005; Asian Development Bank 2004, 2005.

[81] Katada 2001; Hiwatari 2003; Pempel 2006; Singer 2007.

[82] See, for example, Kim 2004, which depends in the main on an interest-based explanation, although it also carefully engages power and constructivist explanations.

[83] I will not attempt to define "identity" in any rigorous manner, although that has been part of the agenda of many constructivist writers. For one such effort, see Lee 2006, 342–44.

[84] See, for example, Ōba 2004, 50–54.

European Union, with the ultimate goal of financial regionalism being a unified currency.[85]

Many such works assume that a pan-Asian identity is in the process of being formed, but they do not seriously address what that identity might be or how it is being created. These are issues that tend to be of greater concern to scholars. For broad populations, this typically involves identi-fication of common cultural tropes, values, or historical purpose—in East Asia, for example, these have included "Asian values," the "ASEAN Way," anticolonialist narratives, or the regional spread of East Asian cultural prod-ucts. Both advocates and analysts see such an identity as developing as a result of conscious decisions of political leaders and processes of functional cooperation,[86] as well as through shared history, such as colonialism, late development, or the experience of the Asian Financial Crisis.[87] A 2004 U.S. National Intelligence Council report goes so far as to claim that "an ex-panded Asian-centric cultural identity may be the most profound effect of a rising Asia."[88]

To get a better handle on how writers put this approach into operation in the study of regionalism, I find it useful to group their explanations along two axes: who holds a given regional identity, and the nature of the identity. Most writing in the constructivist vein works off the assumption that regional identities must be widely shared and intersubjective. However, writers dif-fer regarding how broadly shared that identification must be—for some, a large proportion of the citizens of all the constituent countries must hold a common understanding of being members of a single definable region,[89] while others focus on smaller groups of policy elites.[90] This distinction mat-ters very much in both analytical and predictive terms. Analytically, it is much more practical to focus attention on a relatively small group of elites and to find some fairly homogeneous set of beliefs than to try to do the same for large and diverse populations. Predictions of meaningful change are also more feasible given that it is easier to envisage significant change in beliefs among a small group of experts, advocates, or policy elites who are professionally focused on a given issue than among broader populations. Much of the scholarly work on regionalism has followed this approach.[91]

---

[85] Such works include several written by former policymakers, including Ōnishi 2005; Kuroda 2005; Sakakibara 2005; Kondō 2003. Sakakibara has even come up with a name for the proposed currency—the "Aseana."

[86] Acharya 2000; Johnston 2003b.

[87] Kurlantzick 2006 even sees it as based on an increasingly pan-Asian popular culture, as seen in music and other entertainment. See also the work of the AsiaBarometer project, http://www.asiabarometer.org.

[88] National Intelligence Council 2004, 28. See also Kurlantzick 2007.

[89] Kurlantzick 2006, 2007.

[90] Johnston 2003b; Evans 2005; Lee 2006.

[91] Johnston 2003b; Evans 2005; Lee 2006.

However, "buy-in" from the population at large is presumably a good guarantee that the workings of an epistemic community or policy network will in fact have a lasting effect on regionwide policies.

In terms of content, much of the writing on East Asian regionalism has an air of inevitability—former Singaporean prime minister Lee Kuan Yew has called it "an idea that would not go away."[92] But there is, uncomfortably, a lack of consensus on what the idea actually is or has been, or indeed whether it is positive or defensive in character. In the early 1990s, for example, there was a significant effort to posit East Asia as a natural region, based on a notion of shared "Asian values."[93] An alternative is a defensive consensus, or as Richard Higgott has so memorably put it, a "politics of resentment."[94] Here, the opponent against which the East Asian economies must gather is typically either global capitalism, global institutions intent on imposing free-market policies on any and all economies, or the United States, which is presented either as self-interested in forcing liberalization on its economic partners and rivals or as jealously guarding its hegemony.[95]

One final point that should be made is that not all constructivist interpretations of East Asian regionalism are optimistic about its prospects. Just as writers in this vein see opportunities arising from shared perceptions of identity, so can apparently attractive opportunities be seen as becoming impossible because of mutual mistrust, suspicion, or alienation.[96] In a 2003 article, for example, Shaun Narine wrote, "The political and economic incentives to create an effective regional financial institution are not enough to overcome the historically-defined identities, interests, and regional rivalries that limit institutionalism in East Asia."[97]

There is much more that can and should be said about constructivist approaches to East Asian regionalism, but for now the main point to make is how constructivist arguments and predictions differ from mine. First, their expectations of actors' interests and behavior is based on those actors' understanding of their own preferences and the preferences and intentions of others. Second, in practice, constructivist accounts of regional financial cooperation have often presented such cooperation in a teleological light, with progress expressed as moving toward the common goal of an Asian

[92] Quoted in Evans 2005, 197.
[93] On the Asian values debate, see Chua 2004; Mauzy 1997. Evans (2005) also considers broad-based identities, including not only Asian values but also a cosmopolitan middle-class "identity without exceptionalism" (208–9), although he focuses primarily on policy networks.
[94] Higgott 1998.
[95] Bello 1998; Higgott 1998; Breslin and Higgott 2000 (especially, 339–40); Yu 2003; Lee 2006; Hayashi 2006; Sohn 2005, 2007.
[96] This is an important aspect of Wendt's famous 1992 article, "Anarchy Is What States Make of It."
[97] Narine 2003, 66; Rozman 2005. I should note that I disagree with Narine's assessment of the economic incentives, as chapter 3 makes clear.

community with a shared understanding of state-guided capitalism. Third, the United States is understood to be an outsider in the process (this differs from earlier writings on the Asia-Pacific Economic Cooperation forum)[98] rather than a core player. Finally, political frictions between state actors, particularly Japan and China, are obstacles to be overcome, rather than an intrinsic part of the process.

Methodological Considerations and Cases

Realist political analysis begins from the premise that the overall structure of power and interests and great power rivalry runs through all aspects of international relations. However, those forces are only observable when they are manifested in state actions, which in turn are based on specific opportunities and constraints. The structure of this book, in which each of the substantive chapters addresses a different aspect of financial regionalism, offers methodological benefits while also creating analytical and narrative challenges.

Methodologically, there are two benefits. First, the existence of three functional tracks of regional financial cooperation means that we have meaningful variation across variables. If the power politics approach provides insight into all three tracks, it is much more convincing than if it were applied only to a single, coherent phenomenon. Second, several important variables are held relatively constant across tracks, including participants, power, economic context, and whatever regional identities policymakers might hold.

Analytically, the major challenge in applying a realist political economy approach is clarifying the political interests and options of each major state in each track within financial regionalism, since those tracks differ significantly in terms of the ways in which they affect participating (and some nonparticipating) states. Each substantive chapter isolates the fundamental political issue at play in a single regionalist track in order to apply the power analysis in a nuanced way. To do so, I draw from the standard political economy toolbox as appropriate to the subject at hand. Tools include the principles of institutional design in looking at the Chiang Mai Initiative and its predecessors, analysis of optimum currency areas and sustainability in considering currency issues, and assessment of transaction costs and sequencing in examining bond market initiatives.

In all three cases, regional solutions must also somehow be squared with existing global institutions or standards (which, of course, reflect the power and interests of major world players, particularly the structural power of the United States). The trade-offs between what is gained and what is lost by nesting in or seeking to supplant an existing institution are complex and

---

[98]Funabashi 1995; Ravenhill 2001; Ōba 2004.

not uniform across countries. But analysis of how states approach questions of institutional nesting or the role of the dollar and regional currencies leads us unfailingly back to broader questions about the strategic role of the United States, global IMF and WTO politics, and the economic and political rivalry of Japan and China.

Finally, from the perspective of narrative, each of chapters 3, 4, and 5 seeks to fulfill three somewhat conflicting objectives: providing an accurate description of regional efforts, analyzing the ways in which those efforts achieve or do not achieve functional ends, and demonstrating the power politics that underlie those efforts. Given most readers' unfamiliarity with the specifics of East Asian financial regionalism, it is essential to provide detailed descriptions or relatively involved economic analyses of regional endeavors or specific state actions. In some passages, the broader argument about the role of power is at least temporarily submerged. This is unavoidable, but I have tried to the best of my ability to maintain a consistent tone and a clear relationship between large themes and even microlevel details.

2

The Rise of East Asia as a Region
Progress and Challenges

Having laid out an analytical framework for analyzing the politics of regionalism, I turn now to a close consideration of East Asia as an economic
and political entity. While we should expect great power politics to intrude
into even functional areas of cooperation, it is the market-driven logic of economic competition, integration, and growth that provides both the basic im-
petus for regional cooperation and the negotiating chips that the political
process requires.

To gain a concrete understanding of what is going on in East Asia, we
need to answer some basic questions: What is the logic of "East Asia" as an
economic region? In what sense do the economies of the ASEAN+3 share a
common economic destiny and face common economic challenges? How
might regional cooperation improve their ability to maximize on opportunities while minimizing vulnerabilities? And how have regionalization and
regionalism progressed to date?

Conceptualizing an East Asian Region

ASEAN+3 is the main locus of East Asian financial cooperation, reflecting
an increasing preference among its core states to define their economic
region primarily as East Asia rather than the Asia-Pacific region. Nonetheless, the idea that the ASEAN+3 countries make up a coherent region is
problematic. "East Asia" is a contested concept not only politically but also
economically. Indeed, patterns of economic interaction suggest both a high
level of dependence on outside economies and deep chasms between the

more economically dynamic ASEAN+3 economies on the one hand and Cambodia, Laos, and Myanmar on the other.

There has been considerable debate over the meaning and delineation of regions in general, as well as the East Asian region in particular.[1] One point on which everyone—even hard-headed economists and political economists—agrees is that "regions" are political or social constructions and that their borders are inherently problematic.[2] They are, to borrow Benedict Anderson's famous characterization of nations, "imagined communities."[3] While economic, ethnic, cultural, or religious interchange are relevant to understanding the content and borders of what constitutes a region, they are not determinative, nor is their role or influence consistent over time or across commonly identified actual or potential regions. In the end, a region is defined by political processes from both within and without, whose course and outcome are seldom predictable.

It is possible to expend nearly infinite thought and ink on the philosophical questions raised by the concept of regions, but I will not do so here. Instead, I will review various conceptions of regions and regionalism, discuss how the terms might be most usefully applied to the issues and countries addressed in this book, and make note of some of the potential pitfalls of the concept of regionalism both analytically and for policymakers. It is important to note here that political economists make a clear distinction between "regionalism" and "regionalization." Regionalism refers to interstate efforts to create regional institutions of interdependence, while regionalization is a pattern of increasing concentration of economic and social interaction across national borders within a given region.[4]

Peter Katzenstein argues that there are three main approaches to the delineation of regions: materialist, ideational or critical, and behaviorist.[5] "Materialist" approaches are essentially geopolitical, looking at the physical geography and power projection capabilities of major powers. Critical theories, in contrast, focus on the arbitrary, artificial, and imagined aspects of defining regions. To the extent that the specification of a given region is meaningful, it is socially constructed, politically contested, and subject to rapid change. Behavioral approaches look to patterns of economic, political, and social interaction. Rather than geography, the defining characteristic of a region is actual cooperation or integration. This approach allows,

---

[1] On the general scholarly debate, see Breslin and Higgott 2000, and Hettne 2005. On East Asia, see Katzenstein and Shiraishi 1997; Pempel 2005; Duffield 2003; Berger 2003; Johnston 2003; Rozman 2005; Katzenstein 2005; Watanabe 2005.
[2] Cohen 1998a, 2004; Ravenhill 2001; Pempel 2005.
[3] Anderson 1991.
[4] Frankel and Kahler 1993.
[5] Katzenstein 2005, 6–13.

for example, the inclusion of Greece but not Serbia in "Europe" and the effective exclusion of North Korea and Taiwan from "East Asia."

All of these approaches have their own uses and shortcomings. Recognizing this basic reality, analysts need to define regions according to the problem at hand. Katzenstein combines approaches to create a new vision of regions as an organizing principle for international politics. For him, the regions of the cold war and post–cold war world are a new phenomenon created by simultaneous forces of globalization (bottom-up increases in global interactions) and internationalization (states' management of global interactions through institutions and other means), conditioned all the while by a new American "imperium"—a "conjoining of power that has both territorial and nonterritorial dimensions."[6] Coherent regions are built on the existence of regional powers that are closely associated with the United States, but they are nonetheless porous and thus differ fundamentally from both traditional ideas of insular regional blocs and liberal conceptions of transnationalism or loss of sovereignty in the face of globalization:

> Regions are made porous by both global and international processes and also by a variety of vertical relations linking them to other political units. The world of regions is therefore not simply a territorially bounded system of geoeconomic blocs that extends national mercantilism onto a supranational plain. Nor is it a system that unbundles territorial sovereignty in an era of postnational politics. Porous regions offer both buffers against unwelcome constraints and platforms for exploiting new opportunities.[7]

Katzenstein's conception of a new "world of regions" is thought provoking in its use of regions as a prism for understanding the global system and the nature of U.S. global hegemony. My own goals in defining regions are less ambitious. Like most political economists writing about East Asia, I work from the premise that it is possible to speak meaningfully of a "region" when economic, political, and social interactions are high among constituent parts (whether states or otherwise).[8] The focus on observable patterns of economic and political interaction does not imply a complete dismissal of the "imagined community," or ideational, element that both intuitively and apparently empirically accompanies the recognition of a region.[9]

[6] Katzenstein 2005, 2.

[7] Katzenstein 2005, 22.

[8] Pempel 2005a; Evans 2005; Ravenhill 2001. Cohen 1998a has a similar, albeit nonterritorial, conception of monetary regions, although he uses some of the language of critical theory. Rozman 2005 starts from a behavioralist, or perhaps functionalist, vision of the potential coherence of a Northeast Asian region before explaining its failure on the basis of nationalism and distrust among the nations of the "region."

[9] As noted in chapter 1, it is not always obvious who must hold an identity for it to be widely enough held to be meaningful. Anderson (1991) sees a very broad consensus for the im-

Nonetheless, I see shared economic and political interests as the key to the creation and maintenance of a regional identity, even though self-identification as a region remains an important political support for regionalism. East Asia in particular can be seen as a behaviorally meaningful region despite a rather weak regional identity.

For our purpose of examining the strategic causes and implications of the various moves toward interstate financial cooperation centering on Japan, China and their near neighbors, "East Asia" can be seen as a fairly coherent region based on its high and growing levels of economic interaction. (The same, incidentally, can be said of the Asia-Pacific region.) The *political* region, however, is defined as ASEAN+3, particularly in financial matters, where Taiwan is a peripheral player at best. This identification of "East Asia" as a region is explicitly based on the political efforts of states, albeit in the context of much broader transnational activity by firms, financial institutions, multilateral organizations, scholars, and activists.[10]

For policymakers, conceptions of region are at least as problematic as they are for analysts. They are forced to make decisions about where to allocate their time and energy, where the most advantageous negotiating positions are to be found, and which potential partners to placate or annoy. Obviously, the stakes are much higher in the real world than in the academic world, where misjudgments are likely to cause only heated arguments. For this reason, I take it as essential to follow what states and government officials are actually doing. And in financial regionalism, the main arena is ASEAN+3.

It should be noted that although ASEAN+3 is where the action is in financial regionalism, it too is a bit arbitrary. Brunei, Cambodia, Laos, Myanmar, and Vietnam are peripheral members with limited economic participation, and the exclusion of Taiwan is justified only by political complications. It is also important to recognize that ASEAN+3 is just one grouping of several that center on geographical East Asia, including the Asia-Pacific Economic Cooperation forum (APEC), the Executives' Meeting of East Asia-Pacific Central Banks (EMEAP), the Asia-Europe Meeting (ASEM), the ASEAN Regional Forum (ARF), the Pacific Basin Economic Council (PBEC), and others.

It is, however, relevant in and of itself that essentially all of the groupings that include both China and Japan and that are based on some conception of region have East Asia as their main concern and constituency. At this

---

agined community that is a nation-state. Johnston (2003) in his socialization theory-based analysis of the ASEAN Regional Forum appears to be content with political cooperation based on a shared regional conception among top decision makers. Lee (2006) similarly looks to elite identities in explaining the politics of the 1997 AMF proposal.

[10] See, inter alia, Katzenstein and Shiraishi 1997; Pempel 2005; Duffield 2003; Berger 2003; Johnston 2003; Rozman 2005; Katzenstein 2005; Watanabe 2005.

time, only the United States would be a meaningful addition to the idea of core ASEAN plus China, Japan, and South Korea, but I take its conscious exclusion from ASEAN+3 and the moribund status of APEC as reason to consider it a player in, but not a member of, the East Asian region. Other potential players include India and Australia—indeed, Japanese diplomacy in recent years has called for including them in regional activities,[11] while their inclusion in the East Asia Summit (EAS) appears to have significantly cooled China's interest in using it as a forum for more ambitious political cooperation.[12] In any event, although the borders of "East Asia" may be elastic over time, for the foreseeable future ASEAN+3 is the main arena for regional cooperation.

Two defining characteristics of East Asia as a region have been its economic openness (in Katzenstein's terminology, "porousness") in recent years and its political fragmentation. (The latter hardly seems surprising when we bear in mind the staggering diversity among—and sometimes within—its constituent countries across political, economic, linguistic, cultural, and historical dimensions.)

East Asia as an economic region is striking for its openness. While APEC's motto of "open regionalism" had the feeling of both cliché and public relations gambit when it was coined, it has actually come to be a remarkably apt description of both East Asia and Asia-Pacific as regions. By this, I do not mean to say that East Asian *states* have not deployed protectionist measures, even since the current phase of economic regionalization that began in the 1980s: that would be an obvious falsehood. But open regionalism is an accurate description in at least three important senses. First, there is no history of regionally based preferences or exclusion, unlike in Europe, even though most East Asian economies at one time or another have erected substantial barriers to investment or imports.[13] Despite predictions in previous years that a yen bloc might grow in "Japan's embrace,"[14] U.S. and European firms and financial institutions have entered regional production networks on an equal basis (although they have not necessarily been

---

[11]Some Japanese writers and policymakers go so far as to call for an "axis of democracy" that includes Japan, India, Australia, and the United States. Hisane 2007. Former prime minister Shinzō Abe was particularly associated with calls for such a partnership.

[12]Malik 2005.

[13]The ASEAN free trade area is an obvious exception to this point, but two caveats must be made. First, AFTA did not begin to come into effect until 1999, and its antecedents were both unambitious and limited in scope and effect. Second, even in its current phase, AFTA is not a meaningful obstacle to extraregional actors in the most attractive aspects of trade and investment. (For example, as Baldwin 2007 shows, utilization rates for AFTA preferences are extremely low, while unilateral tariff reductions have been considerable since 1980—see especially, 10–13.) This stands in marked contrast to the practices of the European Union's predecessors from the 1950s through the 1980s.

[14]Hatch and Yamamura 1996; Frankel and Kahler 1993.

accorded national treatment *within* countries).[15] Indeed, China and the ASEAN economies owe much of their growth in the past quarter century to foreign direct investment (FDI) and technology transfers from Western firms as well as Japanese firms. Second, East Asia has been highly dependent on extraregional markets in North America and Europe for its final goods as well as technology inputs. Third, the weakness of financial systems and institutions throughout the region has meant that East Asia has been deeply penetrated by and dependent on global financial institutions, most of which are based in the United States and Europe. These economic attributes are buttressed by persistent suspicions of potential regional leaders (Japan or China for "East Asia," Indonesia in ASEAN) and the continuing role of the United States as a security balancer.

The second defining characteristic of East Asia has been regional fragmentation. By this, I mean not only the diversity of individual country experiences but even more so a lack of centripetal forces or even consultative forums—until recently, there was nothing like an equivalent to the Organization of American States or African Union, let alone something like the European Union, North Atlantic Treaty Organization (NATO), or the Organization for Security Cooperation in Europe. Regional fragmentation has been largely a legacy of European colonialism, the Pacific War, and the cold war. In contrast to its establishment of NATO for the defense of Western Europe, the United States created a hub-and-spokes network of bilateral alliances in Asia in the cold war period.[16] This pattern resulted both from U.S. preferences and from the deep historical animosities that Japan's Pacific War aggression had created among essentially all the countries of Northeast and Southeast Asia. With the Chinese revolution, Japan was the only viable economic leader within non-Communist East Asia; widespread distrust made that impossible and undergirded the hub-and-spokes system.[17] Whether one prefers to use the term "hegemony" or "leadership," no country except for possibly the United States can yet pretend to be the preponderant regional power. If realist political economy can make any prediction at all, it is that this situation should make regional cooperation difficult.[18]

In Southeast Asia, a history of colonial occupation further complcated cooperation, as the newly emerging states not only struggled with self-identification and wrenching societal changes but also had no relevant history of interstate relations with one another. While the establishment of ASEAN in 1967 was a watershed, its main purpose was to dampen conflicts among its original five members so that they could concentrate on

[15]McKendrick, Doner, and Haggard 2000.
[16]Duffield 2003; Katzenstein 2006, 50–60.
[17]Katzenstein 2005, chap. 2.
[18]Stein 1990.

suppressing the Communist threats within (or, in the case of Thailand, from neighboring countries as well). It is not much of an exaggeration to say that ASEAN did so by resolving to brush all conflicts under the carpet except for those that were unavoidable.[19] The political situation of the time, rather than traditional cultural tropes, appears to be the most convincing explanation for the emergence of the so-called ASEAN Way of consensus, incrementalism, and noninterference in domestic affairs.[20]

The end of the cold war in both Southeast Asia and most of Northeast Asia (excepting the Korean Peninsula) raised the possibility of change from the fragmented system that had developed. For the first time, alternatives to U.S.-centric foreign policies began to appear possible, and debate began about the potential for the creation of a new kind of regional cooperation. Nonetheless, although the cold war was over and policymakers began to entertain the possibility of new regionalist opportunities, great power politics had not ended. Concerns over the relative opportunities and threats posed by reliance on Japan, China, and the United States persisted, profoundly affecting the forms and extent of regional cooperation.

Regionalization and Regionalism in East Asia

In the last quarter century, East Asia has seen remarkable increases in regional economic interactions from the perspectives of both trade and financial flows. For much of the period, those increases occurred with minimal formal support at the regional level. Only after the Asian Financial Crisis of 1997–98 did regional governments seek in earnest to establish institutions to promote economic integration and cooperation. Despite the late start, the efforts have been striking in both their vigor and their comprehensiveness. Although East Asia is far less densely populated with institutions of cooperation than the Americas—much less Europe—it appears that states are now taking seriously the project of regionalism. Financial regionalism is one important part of those broader efforts. While it offers a particularly revealing lens through which to view the power politics of economic regionalism, it is important to understand that broader context. It is not feasible or even necessary for our purposes to provide a full-scale description and analysis of these phenomena; the purpose here is simply to provide a general sense of the development and current status of regional integration.[21]

---

[19] See, for example, Kahler 2000, 551.

[20] This at least is my interpretation. See also Katzenstein 2005, 141. There are, of course, a variety of culturalist explanations, as discussed in Dupont 1996.

[21] See Munakata 2006 for perhaps the best comprehensive description. Other excellent resources include Lincoln 2004; Watanabe 2004; Thorbecke and Yoshitomi 2006; Ghosh 2006; Gill and Kharas 2006.

Growing Regional Integration

I start by examining regionalization, where East Asia is distinguished by the impressive speed of the growth of regional economic interdependence, including intraregional trade, investment, division of labor, and financial ties. There has been tremendous growth in trade among the East Asian economies since 1980. The region's trade reflects the broader story of the rise of East Asia as a production and trading center for the global economy. In a twenty-five-year period in which world imports grew an average 7.7 percent per year (250% total), imports of Asian countries grew an average 11.3 percent (over 340% in total).[22] The export story was even more dramatic. Most dramatic of all has been the rise of non-Japan Asia, especially China, as both an importer and exporter since 1990. Growth in trade has accompanied rapid economic growth as well, and East Asian economies have clearly prospered as they have become key players in the global economy.

There have also been substantial increases in intraregional trade (figure 2.1). As a percentage of total trade of the East Asian economies between 1980 and 2005, intraregional trade has increased rapidly from a share of

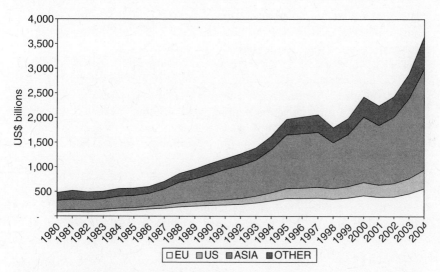

Figure 2.1. ASEAN+3 Trade by Region, 1980–2004.
Source: IMF, *Direction of Trade Statistics.*

[22] IMF *Direction of Trade Statistics,* various years. Confusingly, calculations of intraregional trade include Taiwan and Hong Kong, although they are excluded from most forms of official cooperation.

about one-third to over one half.[23] Japanese policymakers and writers emphasize that East Asian economies have a higher percentage of trade among themselves than do the North American Free Trade Agreement (NAFTA) countries.[24] In short, the trade story shows that the region of the world with the fastest growth in trade and income is seeing its trade grow most quickly intraregionally. This is a powerful demonstration of East Asia's economic regionalization.

Nonetheless, the degree of regionalization of trade is open to debate, particularly if we understand this to mean preference for intraregional trade ("regional bias"). The fact that East Asian trade has grown so much more rapidly than world trade means that virtually all economies now execute more of their trade with East Asia than they did twenty-five years ago. In order to evaluate the argument for greater regional preferences, the standard tool is a "gravity model," which controls for overall growth in trade as well as geographical proximity. Gravity models tell a more equivocal story than the simple statistic of intraregional trade. Indeed, Edward Lincoln argues that the data show that what appears to be regionalization is largely accounted for by the rise of China as a trading state—and that Chinese trade is increasingly oriented toward the United States.[25] Also, East Asian intraregional trade figures are skewed by the inclusion of Hong Kong, much of whose trade (especially with China) is of a purely entrepôt nature. C. H. Kwan has estimated that perhaps two-thirds (around $80 billion in 2005) of China's exports to Hong Kong are in fact destined for the United States.[26]

That said, the issue of regional bias may be a bit beside the point. While it may well be relevant to the argument of whether East Asia is a natural economic area, the fact remains that intraregional trade has increased substantially, creating an incentive for regional governments to create frameworks to lower transaction costs. Moreover, regional firms are clearly increasingly dependent on suppliers and consumers within the region, and are likely to concentrate more of their resources on servicing regional needs. Again, however, the fundamentally political nature of defining a "region" is apparent. In particular, the choice of the ASEAN+3 as the primary venue for regional cooperation demonstrates deliberate choices to exclude the United States and to respect the organizational integrity of ASEAN, regardless of

[23] Munakata 2006, 46–48.

[24] See, for example, Munakata 2006, 46–51; Watanabe 2004, 7–9. This is also universal in ASEAN+3 briefing materials provided by the Japanese government.

[25] Lincoln 2004, chap. 3.

[26] Cited in Thorbecke and Yoshitomi 2006, 13. It is also worth noting another reason why straightforward comparison of ASEAN+3 to NAFTA is problematic: the number of economies chosen is so different. Adding more Latin American countries to the NAFTA intraregional numbers would have a noticeable effect. Conversely, the designation of East Asia as a region is arbitrary—adding the United States to the East Asia total would substantially increase the intraregional share, while dropping many of the ASEAN economies would not make an appreciable difference.

the relative economic roles in East Asia of the economies of the United States and ASEAN's least developed members.

The lack of significant regional bias does, however, confirm that East Asia is a porous economic region—or to put it another way, that the APEC oxymoron of "open regionalism" is an apt description of the actual state of affairs.[27] Fundamentally, patterns of trade in East Asia suggest a regional division of labor for production of products that are purchased in their final form in the advanced economies of Japan, the United States, and Europe.[28] The role of extraregional economies as locations of final demand reinforces the implausibility of an East Asian regional economic bloc, at least in the sense in which the term "bloc" has traditionally been used.

The active participation of East Asia in the world economy is shown also by financial flows, particularly in the form of foreign direct investment. FDI into East Asia's developing and middle-income countries, particularly China, dwarfs flows into other economies at similar levels of development. While data are less reliable for FDI than for trade, they are at least as dramatic. Indeed, China actually surpassed the United States as the world's most popular destination for FDI in 2003 and was number three in the world for 2004 and 2005—a remarkable fact, given that both FDI and capital flows in general into China remain highly regulated.[29] By 2003, 57 percent of FDI into East Asian economies came from within the region, with about two-thirds of China's inbound FDI allegedly coming from East Asia.[30]

There is some doubt as to the scale of East Asian FDI into China due to the practice of "round-tripping." Round-tripping occurs when domestic Chinese economic actors illegally move money out of the country, then bring it back in (primarily from Hong Kong) in order to take advantage of special benefits and protections that are afforded to foreign investors under Chinese law. Most estimates of total round-tripping range from 20 to 30 percent of Hong Kong's FDI into China, but others are as high as 50 percent.[31] One way or another, however, it is clear that intraregional FDI has expanded enormously.

Regional Division of Labor

Together, the data on trade and FDI reflect a central truth of East Asian economic activity: an increasingly articulated regional division of labor.[32]

---

[27] Katzenstein 2005 makes this point strongly.

[28] Bernard and Ravenhill 1995; Thorbecke and Yoshitomi 2006.

[29] UNCTAD 2006.

[30] Gill and Kharas 2006, 45. It is not clear how the authors address issues of investment from Hong Kong into China, including round-tripping. It is likely that the two-thirds figure is a considerable overestimate.

[31] Xiao 2004.

[32] On regional production networks, see among others Peng 2000; Bernard and Ravenhill 1995; Nelson 2003; Thorbecke and Yoshitomi 2006; Gill and Khadras 2006, chap. 2; Fukao, Ishido, and Ito 2003; Aoki 2006, chap. 5.

While a great deal of trade and investment, particularly investment by small and medium-sized enterprises (SMEs) from within the region, can best be understood as a pure flight to comparative advantage, multinational firms have created a new pattern. Beginning in the 1980s, Japanese and Western multinationals began to introduce regional strategies of production in East Asia.[33] Firms and their suppliers would manufacture components of varying sophistication in different countries, according to comparative advantage and specific cost structures. Japanese firms in particular have developed a pattern of vertical intra-industry trade that has become ubiquitous in East Asia.[34] Over time, these regional production strategies have led to a vibrant trade in components among the economies of East Asia, as well as significant increases in intraregional and extraregional FDI (figures 2.2, 2.3).[35] However, it is important to note that a significant proportion of final demand for such regionally produced manufactures is still from the developed economies of North America and to a lesser extent Europe.[36]

Supporting that growth in economic transactions, governments in the region have significantly lowered barriers to trade and investment.[37] Although these changes have often been selective, and in some cases even grudging, the long-term result has been impressive indeed. China is only the most dramatic example, transforming itself in two decades from a minor trader and marginal FDI destination to being the world's third-largest trader and destination for FDI. Although these figures are undoubtedly skewed by the way that Taiwanese and Hong Kong investment and trade are counted (in particular, the significant amount of presumed round-tripping investment), there is no mistaking the importance of this transformation. In South Korea and ASEAN the governments have significantly reduced the barriers to trade and investment, although the numbers there are less dramatic due to their higher initial participation in the global economy and the relative allure of China for many foreign investors.

For the most part, barriers to trade and investment were removed unilaterally or in response to commitments made through the General Agreement on Tariffs and Trade (GATT) and the World Trade Organization (WTO).[38] A partial exception has been in ASEAN, where (mostly ineffectual) regional

---

[33] Hatch and Yamamura 1996; Bernard and Ravenhill 1995; McKendrick, Doner, and Haggard 2000; Nelson 2003; Aoki 2006, chap. 3.

[34] Ernst 1994; Fukao, Ishido, and Ito 2003; Ito and Fukao 2003; Koike 2004.

[35] Thorbecke and Yoshitomi 2006.

[36] Thorbecke and Yoshitomi 2006, fig. 13. The other major markets are Japan and Hong Kong. (As noted, most of the latter is accounted for by Chinese-assembled goods that are transshipped to the same final markets.) Thus, even if "East Asia" is increasingly a meaningful region in terms of production, when one looks at final demand, Kohsaka's 1996 point about Asia-Pacific being a more relevant economic region still holds.

[37] Baldwin 2007, 6–12.

[38] Baldwin 2007, 6–12.

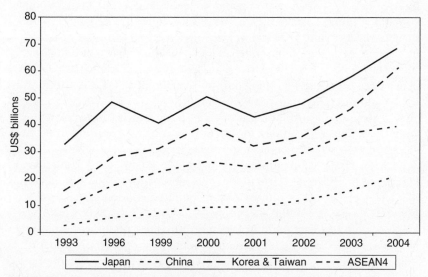

Figure 2.2. Intermediate Goods Exports to East Asia by Source, 1992–2005.
Source: Thorbecke and Yoshitomi 2006.

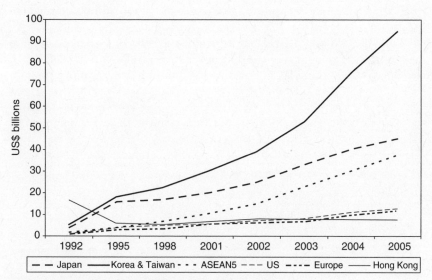

Figure 2.3. China's Imports for Processing by Source, 1992–2005.
Source: Thorbecke and Yoshitomi 2006.

trade preferences have been ongoing since the late 1970s.[39] Despite limited regional institutional backing, self-interest prompted key ASEAN economies such as Malaysia and Thailand to open up strategically to make themselves more attractive to high value-added manufacturing, such as automobiles, consumer electronics, semiconductors, and computer hard drives.[40]

A similar story can be told about investment policies. Every economy in East Asia other than Singapore and Hong Kong maintained strict scrutiny (if not always strict formal regulation) of inward direct investment in the early 1980s. But by the 1990s, most had substantially liberalized investment rules and in many cases created a broad array of positive incentives, at least for certain kinds of investment.[41] Particularly notable were reductions in barriers to wholly owned subsidiaries and ownership (or long-term leasing) of land, as well as streamlining or actual elimination of approval processes. A two-level self-reinforcing process began to unfold by the late 1980s. Regionally, it was evident that the fastest-growing economies were those that had most significantly reduced their barriers to trade and investments (at least in key sectors), drawing the interest of relative laggards like the Philippines and China. Within liberalizing economies, economic coalitions that benefited from openness became richer and stronger politically, creating support for maintaining or even furthering policies of openness.[42] In most of the dynamic economies of East Asia (i.e., Japan, South Korea, Taiwan, and the ASEAN5), liberalization of policies toward inward FDI was accompanied by liberalization of other capital flows. While this openness led to vulnerability for dollar-pegged currencies during the Asian Financial Crisis, it also had the effect of supporting regional capital formation and regional production networks.

Thus, the 1980s and 1990s saw a generic move by East Asian economies toward greater openness in support of regional production networks and, by extension, in support of regional trade and investment more broadly. Nonetheless, other than the limited efforts of ASEAN in trade, and to a much lesser extent in even less consequential initiatives such as designation of "growth triangles," none of it was accomplished in the context of regional agreements. Instead, the key was *individual* responses by East Asian governments.[43] To be sure, there was significant rhetorical and sometimes

[39] Narongchai and Stifel 1994.

[40] Munakata 2006, chap. 3; Bowie and Unger 1997; McKendrick, Doner, and Haggard 2000.

[41] I am not including the transitional economies of Vietnam, Laos, Myanmar, and Cambodia, which did not enter ASEAN until 1995, 1997, 1997, and 1998, respectively. We have, however, seen significant liberalization even in these countries (with the exception of Myanmar), with Vietnam beginning as early as 1986.

[42] See, for example, Bowie and Unger 1997. For analysis of such a self-reinforcing cycle as a generic phenomenon, see Frieden and Rogowski 1996, and Garrett and Lange 1996.

[43] Baldwin 2007, especially 10–11.

technical support for these efforts by global and regional bodies such as the IMF, the Asian Development Bank, and the WTO as well as trading partners inside and outside the region. But regionally, informal institutionalism reigned.[44]

In sum, economic regionalization in East Asia is real and has been dramatic in its growth. Nonetheless, it is also a complicated and confusing situation. Regional production networks have transformed regional economies and integrated them closely together. At the same time, East Asian regionalization can be understood as a microcosm of globalization. North American and European firms and financial institutions are deeply involved in developing and supporting integration of economic transactions of all sorts, and they are both major markets and major suppliers of high value-added components and intellectual property. Looked at without the assumption that East Asia is a natural region, the role of Japanese firms and financial institutions appears much more like that of their North American and European competitors (albeit with the caveat that balance of imports and exports are almost opposite) than like that of their East Asian counterparts.

The Emergence of Regional Institutions

East Asian economic regionalization has been much less supported by formal regional institutions than in Europe or even the Americas. Katzenstein argues that preferences for informal networks among East Asian economic elites help to explain why institution building has so lagged increasing economic integration. He writes that "Asian states seek to ride markets that are evolving in broader networks," rather than creating formal rule-based structures.[45] Gilbert Rozman, on the other hand, suggests that institutionalized regional cooperation in Northeast Asia has been "stunted" by societal mistrust and unresolved historical enmities.[46] In contrast, I focus on states' interests and the regional strategic situation rather than on culture or trust.

Compared to its level of economic interactions, East Asia is thinly institutionalized in terms of coverage, density, and capabilities of regional organizations. But this does not mean that East Asia has been wholly without regional economic and political institutions. Current efforts at regional cooperation did not appear out of thin air but have been built on existing (albeit often weak) arrangements and agreements—although the Asian

[44]Katzenstein and Shiraishi 1997; Peng 2000; Bernard and Ravenhill 1995; Kahler 2000.
[45]Katzenstein 2005, 43. See also Katzenstein 1997; Pempel 2006, 245.
[46]Rozman 2005. On Japan's "history problem," see Berger 2007.

Financial Crisis emerges as a critical juncture in the development of regional institutions.[47]

In addition to the relative dearth of regional interstate organizations, East Asian regionalism has been marked by its lack of legalism.[48] With the major exception of the Asian Development Bank, whose lending function makes attention to contracts and voting and formal evaluation procedures essential, until the 1990s the institutions of regionalism were either state-based forums with minimal procedure or organizational backing, such as ASEAN, or nonofficial consultative bodies such as the Pacific Economic Cooperation Conference (PECC) and the Pacific Basic Economic Council (PBEC).

ASEAN and Related Efforts

ASEAN occupies a special place in the universe of cooperative institutions in East Asia. Aside from the ADB (which is but one year older, having been established in 1966) it is the longest-lived among them and expresses a coherent view of its region. ASEAN is characterized procedurally by norms of consensus and nonintervention in domestic affairs, as well as a preference for nonbinding agreements and minimal autonomous monitoring capability.[49] Nonetheless, even prior to the agreement to create an ASEAN free trade area (AFTA) in 1992, its members did undertake a variety of cooperative projects aimed at promoting economic cooperation and integration, including the ASEAN preferential trade arrangement in 1977, ASEAN industrial projects in 1980, ASEAN industrial complementation in 1981, ASEAN industrial joint ventures in 1983, and brand-to-brand complementation in 1988.[50] None of these schemes was very successful in terms of increasing economic integration or even in terms of securing wholehearted cooperation from the participants. On the security front, ASEAN added to its existing ministerial meetings additional consultative practices in the form of the Post-Ministerial Conference (1977) and the ASEAN Regional Forum (ARF, established in 1994), which brought in the foreign and defense ministers, respectively, of outside powers with interests in the region, known as "dialogue partners."[51] ASEAN did commit to a formal security agreement, the Treaty of Amity and Cooperation in Southeast Asia (TAC) in 1976, but it had no mechanisms for enforcement, nor any obvious effect.

Not until the 1992 agreement to form AFTA did the ASEAN states create an institution with clear rules and decision-making procedures. In practice,

---

[47]Calder and Ye 2004; Higgott 1998; Lee 2006; Sakakibara 2005.

[48]See, among many others, Kahler 2000; Katzenstein and Shiraishi 1997; and Katzenstein 2005.

[49]Weatherbee 2005, chap. 4; Katzenstein 2005, 36.

[50]See Weatherbee 2005, chap. 7. Official documents on all ASEAN agreements and projects can be found at http://www.aseansec.org.

[51]Weatherbee, chap. 4.

AFTA has also been characterized by a gradualist approach that valorizes voluntary compliance, but it is also clearly a departure from past practice.[52] The 1990s saw greater ASEAN efforts at instituting clearer procedures and rules more generally as well—for example, the 1992 ASEAN Declaration on the South China Sea led eventually to the 2002 Declaration of Parties on Conduct in the South China Sea, in which China joined ASEAN members in pledging to act in a cooperative and nonbelligerent way in that disputed area. (This has not been entirely successful, as seen in a Chinese naval attack on a Vietnamese fishing vessel as recently as July 2007.)[53] ASEAN also agreed in 2005 to create an ASEAN Charter that would codify expectations regarding member states' political systems and protection of human rights; agreement on the charter was announced in December 2007, but uncertainties about ratification and ambiguities regarding specifics appeared to suggest that the charter would be more of a rhetorical exercise than an enforceable binding agreement.

East Asia vs. Asia-Pacific

East Asia as a whole has been even less institutionalized than Southeast Asia. The first official consultative group that included all the states of East Asia was in fact APEC, which was based on a model of Pacific-Rim regionalism and included among its founding members the United States and Australia. In reaction, in 1990 Malaysian prime minister Mahathir bin Mohamad called for an East Asia Economic Group (EAEG) that would include the ASEAN states (of which there were then six), plus China, Japan, and South Korea and specifically exclude the United States and Australia.[54] The original proposal appeared to be for a trade bloc and was immediately unattractive to Japan, which was already deeply concerned about losing access to U.S. markets and thus not inclined to anger U.S. policymakers. The following year, Mahathir repackaged the idea as an East Asia Economic Caucus (EAEC) with a more ambiguous purpose; this too was a nonstarter, although the EAEC reconstituted as a consultative caucus within APEC in 1994, later serving as the basis for the ASEAN+3.[55] Other official regional forums based around East Asia formed in the 1990s as well, including functionalist ones such as the Executives' Meeting of the East Asia-Pacific Central Banks and cross-regional ones such as the Asia-Europe Meeting.[56] These too were consultative or purely functional institutions, with minimal structural,

---

[52] Kahler 2000.

[53] On the code of conduct, see Weatherbee 2005, chap. 5. The July 2007 attack was reported in "Chinese Navy Fires at Vietnamese Fishing Vessel, Injuring Five," *BBC Monitoring Asia Pacific,* July 21, 2007.

[54] Milne and Mauzy 1999, 128–30, provides a good account.

[55] Funabashi 1995, chap. 11; Ravenhill 2001, chap. 3.

[56] ASEM is perhaps best known for sponsoring the Kobe Research Project in 2001–02. For more on ASEM, see Yeo 2003, and Kaiser 2004. Little if anything has been written on EMEAP as an organization. Both ASEM and EMEAP have rather informative websites, however.

rule-making, or enforcement capabilities. Nonetheless, by the early 1990s, competitive definition of the "region" was underway.

Supporting the hopes of advocates of Asia-Pacific regionalism, before the late 1980s the main cooperative regional institutions other than ASEAN in which East Asian states participated were unofficial Asia-Pacific–based consultative venues like PECC and PBEC, both formed in 1967. While PBEC can be understood as a transnational business association, it was PECC that proved to be the basis for the 1989 establishment of APEC. PECC was set up as a council of national committees based in various Asia-Pacific countries (plus PBEC and the academically oriented Pacific Trade and Development Forum, or PAFTAD). The national committees in turn are made up members from government, business, and academia, who participate as individuals rather than as representatives of their government or other employer. These consultative venues contributed to effective exchange of information and to greater familiarity among policymakers and interested parties, but they had no official role in structuring economic transactions or political decisions. Nonetheless, the general orientation of PBEC's, PAFTAD's, and PECC's businesspeople and academic economists favored liberalization of trade and investment as well as greater official cooperation and transparency.

Building on the unofficial discussions and various task force activities in PECC, in addition to Australian concerns about being left out of East Asian growth and Japanese fears of future U.S. protectionism, the Asia-Pacific Economic Cooperation forum was created in 1989.[57] APEC was the first official multilateral, East Asia–wide or Asia-Pacific cooperative institution other than the ADB—a striking reminder of the lack of institutionalization relative to Europe, the North Atlantic, the Americas, or even Africa and the Middle East. APEC was given the mission of providing formal backing to the work of previous unofficial or semiofficial ventures such as PECC and PBEC, and pushing forward the already accelerating economic integration and liberalization among the capitalist economies of the Asia-Pacific.[58] But like the existing intergovernmental and unofficial regional economic institutions, APEC was created as a consultative body with no secretariat (until 1993, now small and minimally funded) and no binding rules. John Ravenhill summarizes its governing principles as follows:

- Ambiguous obligations
- Voluntary and unilateral commitments
- Reciprocity not assured
- No mechanisms for resolving disputes
- Limited monitoring mainly through non-APEC institutions

[57] See Ravenhill 2001 on the history of APEC.
[58] Soesastro 1994.

- Ambiguity on open regionalism
- Disagreement whether APEC agreements should be applied on a MFN [Most Favored Nation] basis to all WTO members[59]

To these principles, we can add the principle of keeping the key economies on both sides of the Pacific at least rhetorically committed to economic openness. Other than that, APEC's specification of membership criteria and organizational structure were rather loose.

APEC's major role in the 1990s proved to be exhortatory, although the United States did try to use it as a vehicle for promoting liberalization in Japan and other Asian economies. With a stated goal of fostering economic integration and openness in East Asia, its calls for "open regionalism" and the 1995 Bogor Declaration trumpeting an APEC free trade area by 2020 (2010 for developed members) were widely publicized.[60] But despite high hopes and ambitious rhetoric, APEC has never acted as more than a facilitator of economic policy decisions, with its greatest successes to be found in functionalist cooperation, such as harmonization of product categories, technical assistance to developing country members in adapting domestic rules to conform with WTO agreements, and the like. The limits of APEC were made strikingly obvious with the failure of the 1996–98 Early Voluntary Sectoral Liberalization (EVSL) negotiations. As Ravenhill puts it, the EVSL was a "double blow to APEC," confirming U.S. perceptions of it as an ineffective venue and alienating the Japanese government.[61]

The EVSL debacle and the Asian Financial Crisis delivered a symbolic coup de grâce to U.S. efforts to make APEC a vehicle for anything more than discussion and facilitation. At some level, APEC's declarations and rhetoric may have supported or even persuaded (at least at the margin) some policymakers and public opinion leaders regarding the general desirability of openness as a means of taking advantage of globalization.[62] But as a regional organization, it lacked the tools to ensure the advancement of its agenda (as embodied in the rhetoric of its communiqués and the efforts of the Eminent Persons Group).[63] Once the Asian Financial Crisis hit, APEC largely

[59] Ravenhill 2001, 164, table 4.1.

[60] Ravenhill 2001 is probably the best political economy account of APEC.

[61] Ravenhill 2001, 180–85 (quotation, 206). Most observers agree that EVSL failed due to the resistance of the Japanese government. Ironically, the Japanese Ministry of Economy, Trade, and Industry is currently pushing a project to reinvigorate APEC as a venue for trade liberalization, with one goal being to be able to announce by 2010 that Japan has fulfilled its Bogor obligation.

[62] Kim 2000 provides an excellent and nuanced overview of the ways in which East Asian governments sought to benefit from or protect themselves from globalization.

[63] The Eminent Persons Group, a key driver of APEC efforts during its brief lifespan from 1992 to 1995, was replaced by the less ambitious APEC Business Advisory Council, which has been far more quiescent.

lost its credibility even as an agenda-setter, despite the membership of three of the world's largest economies and trading nations. Even formal exhortations at the APEC Summit meetings from 2003 to 2007 for "re-energizing" the Doha Development Agenda have not led to actual new cooperation among APEC governments in those negotiations, although they may have had some symbolic significance.[64]

The Rise of East Asian Regionalism

By the late 1990s, the institutional infrastructure of East Asian regionalism remained quite limited. Given the weakness of APEC, the limited functional scope of the ADB and EMEAP, and the outright failure of Prime Minister Mahathir's attempt to create an exclusive East Asian bloc, the most articulated official-level regional cooperation was that which revolved around ASEAN. And ASEAN itself was weak in organizational terms, as a result of member states' determination to cling to consensus and voluntary action (the so-called ASEAN Way) as the basic principles of ASEAN cooperation.[65] ASEAN-centered efforts included intra-ASEAN initiatives such as the ASEAN free trade area (AFTA) and ASEAN investment area. They also included forums such as the ASEAN Regional Forum and the Post-Ministerial Conference, which invited outside representatives to discuss matters of significance to Southeast Asia.[66] This tradition, weak as it was, provided the rationale for the creation of the ASEAN+3 over the course of 1997–99.

In the fall of 1997 events were moving rapidly in East Asia. The financial crisis was ongoing, and indeed spreading. Meanwhile, a proposal by the Japanese government to create an Asian monetary fund had been shot down by U.S., IMF, and Chinese opposition in September.[67] At the initiative of the U.S. Treasury and under the auspices of APEC, the Manila Framework Group, consisting of senior central bankers and finance ministry officials from Australia, Brunei Darussalam, Canada, China, Hong Kong, Indonesia, Japan, Korea, Malaysia, New Zealand, the Philippines, Singapore, Thailand, and the United States, had its first meeting in November. The Manila Framework was meant specifically to address financial crises through surveillance, technical assistance, and if necessary by contributing to bailouts.[68] But as if to hedge their bets, the ASEAN+3 heads of state met for the first

---

[64]Even APEC's own list of "key milestones" shows that substantively the forum has been reduced to almost entirely technocratic cooperation since the EVSL episode. See www.apecsec.org.sg/apec/about_apec/history.html, accessed October 2, 2006.

[65]Kahler 2000 provides an excellent analysis of the logic behind choices of legalistic and informal (e.g., ASEAN Way) styles of regional organization.

[66]Narine 1997.

[67]Katada 2004, 185–88.

[68]Hayashi 2006, 93–95.

time only a month later on the occasion of the second ASEAN informal summit in December. Although that initial meeting was dubbed as informal, by 1999 the third ASEAN+3 heads of state meeting declared itself formally to the world, issuing a joint communiqué.

ASEAN+3 has been characterized as the reappearance of Mahathir's 1990 East Asian Economic Group proposal. Certainly, the membership is approximately the same (although ASEAN itself had expanded by four since the original proposal). Mahathir had originally mooted the EAEG as trading bloc. When that proved a nonstarter, he called instead for an East Asian Economic Caucus, which he pitched as a consultative group.[69] Despite the lack of traction that the EAEC concept achieved when announced in 1991, Malaysia's Asian neighbors at least paid lip service to it, creating an informal caucus within APEC in 1994. Moreover, the Asian half of Asia-Europe Meeting was, at least in terms of membership, the EAEC all over again.

There is some irony to the fact that a group whose time had never come (EAEC) and that existed within a group whose time had passed by 1997 (APEC) provided the minimal organizational basis for the move toward East Asia–only regional cooperation in the post-AFC world. But the ASEAN+3 must be understood not just as a grouping of East Asian countries but also as a group centered on ASEAN.

Regardless of whether the ASEAN basis was due to historical accident or political calculation, it has had a variety of effects on the shape and parameters of ASEAN+3 economic cooperation. At the most basic level, it has made the development of ASEAN+3 regional cooperation relatively seamless—ministerial and summit meetings follow the rhythm of the already established ASEAN calendar, and the ongoing practice of ASEAN post-ministerial meetings and ARF has made the addition of a "+3" meeting unexceptional, and therefore not symbolically threatening to the United States and Australia in the way that the EAEG proposal was.

The ASEAN basis also has created some peculiar aspects of regional cooperation. Most obviously, the membership necessarily includes all ASEAN members, including Brunei, Cambodia, Laos, Myanmar, and Vietnam, which have little in common with the core members when it comes to economy and finance. (This point is explicitly recognized in the Chiang Mai Initiative, which does not include those economies; elsewhere, it suggests differential paces.) A second artifact of the ASEAN basis of cooperation is the organization of activities. Rather than having a single rotating chair, the ASEAN+3 has cochairs—one from ASEAN, following the rotating chairmanship of ASEAN itself, and the other from the +3. This arrangement leads to several effects, both functional and dysfunctional. On the one hand, it ensures that

[69] Milne and Mauzy 1999, 129–31.

one of the +3 countries—the most economically and politically powerful in the group—always has a role in agenda setting. It also encourages "buy-in" by the ASEAN members. On the other hand, negative effects arise. First, the differences in capability among cochairs can be staggering, as demonstrated most dramatically by the cochairmanship of Laos and Japan in 2005. Such a divergence in capability and interests makes effective agenda setting and follow-through a more difficult chore. Following the ASEAN cycle also presents political challenges, such as when Myanmar was set to take over the ASEAN chairmanship in 2006, much to the embarrassment of Japan (not to mention Myanmar's other ASEAN partners). As it turned out, Myanmar waived its chairmanship for that year.[70]

But probably the most important effect of the ASEAN basis of the ASEAN+3 has been the de facto adoption of ASEAN procedures and decision making. ASEAN has been organized loosely, with a minimum of rules, a small secretariat, and—most famously—the guiding principles of consensus, noninterference in members' domestic affairs, and voluntary compliance.[71] While this mode of cooperation has sometimes been lauded as an alternative to excessive legalism, I agree with Donald Weatherbee, who has written: "It is not a problem-solving mechanism. It is a conflict avoidance system."[72] The ASEAN Way is reasonably well-suited to an organization whose original purpose was to shelve potential conflicts and disagreements so as to allow member states to concentrate on their very real domestic challenges, but it does not create the kind of confidence about the future environment that is the main potential benefit of economic institutions. This has been a problem for ASEAN itself in the case of AFTA; it is a considerable problem for ASEAN+3 in creating effective economic cooperation. As we shall see, the Chiang Mai Initiative deals with this weakness by sticking with a network of bilateral agreements that do not require a joint ASEAN+3 decision (despite lip service to the concept of reserve pooling), while the bond market initiatives address it simply by setting vague goals and allowing for self-paced reforms. Neither solution is promising for more legalistic cooperation, such as preferential trade agreements, or for more ambitious ventures, such as macroeconomic or exchange rate policy coordination.

In 2004, building on the 2002 final report of ASEAN+3's East Asia Study Group,[73] the Malaysian and Chinese governments proposed to expand ASEAN+3 cooperation beyond discussion of economic matters by creating

[70] Suzuki (2004) analyzes at length the role of "chairmanship" in ASEAN and ASEAN+3 as an organizing principle. She argues that the chair's informal agenda setting constitutes a de facto mode of organization.

[71] This is often termed the ASEAN Way, with the central tenets of *musjawarah* (consultation) and *mufakat* (consensus).

[72] Weatherbee 2005, 121.

[73] East Asia Study Group 2002, 5–6.

a new East Asia Summit. The original proposal called for no specific agenda or even membership but was quickly opposed by the United States based on a concern of being excluded from regional cooperation—former deputy secretary of state Richard Armitage, for example, was quoted as saying, "My view is this is a thinly veiled way to make the point that the United States is not totally welcome in Asia. I think that's a real mistake."[74] Japanese policymakers worried too, apparently because of fears that it might become a regional tool for Chinese domination. They called for the inclusion of Australia, India, and New Zealand in addition to the ASEAN+3. Much bickering ensued, but Japan's vision of an ASEAN+3+3 membership did prevail.[75] However, the Chinese government decided to deemphasize the East Asia Summit in favor of ASEAN+3, and the three summits held as of the end of 2007 have had no practical accomplishments to speak of.[76]

Trade Agreements and the Problem of Bilateral vs. Regional Cooperation

So far, I have discussed regional cooperation in the context of multilateral efforts based on competing notions of East Asia and the Asia-Pacific region. But a comprehensive picture of economic cooperation requires a recognition that most official economic cooperation under either conception of the region is actually carried out on a bilateral basis. To understand the relationship between regional ambitions and rampant bilateralism, we need to look at trade arrangements.

Trade cooperation significantly complicates the picture of East Asian economic regionalism. It has become almost a cliché to pose the "bloc(k)" questions of whether regional cooperation will lead to exclusionary regional blocs, or whether a web of overlapping preferential trade agreements[77] will constitute a building block or stumbling block to regional trade creation.[78] These are actually important questions, although the latter is beyond the scope of this book. (With regard to the former, it is difficult to imagine

---

74 "No Invitation in Sight for Washington," *Straits Times*, May 14, 2005.

75 "An Asian Union? Not Yet," *International Herald Tribune*, December 17, 2005.

76 Other than Malik 2005, there is not much published on the East Asia Summit outside of newspapers and magazines. The chairman's statements and summit declarations are available at the ASEAN website http://www.aseansec.org.

77 I use the term "preferential trade agreement" instead of free trade agreement because few if any bilateral or minilateral trade agreements involving East Asian economies are really based on free, as opposed to preferential, trade. To a considerable extent, the widespread use of the term "free trade agreement" or Japan's favored "economic partnership agreement" is a public relations gesture that objective analysts should avoid buying into.

78 Bhagwati (1991) coined the terms "building block" vs. "stumbling block." Their rhetorical overuse since then should not be held against Bhagwati, nor should it obscure the usefulness of the concept. See Baldwin 2006 and 2007 for applications to East Asia.

the construction of an exclusive East Asian trading bloc in any reasonable timeframe in the absence of some major, devastating political or economic event.) But the *political* question is how comfortably bilateral and regional cooperation can fit together without one undermining the other. An additional complication comes from the fact that many of the PTAs involving East Asian economies have been cross-regional.[79] Key extraregional PTA partners have included the United States, India, and Australia, among others.

As has been widely noted, East Asia was slow to move toward PTAs. With the exception of AFTA, there were no PTAs at all involving East Asian economies until Japan and Singapore agreed to negotiate their economic partnership agreement in 2000. Since then there has been a burgeoning of East Asian trade agreements concluded, under negotiation, or under study—over one hundred as of fall 2007 (table 2.1). Most involved an extraregional partner. Moreover, almost all were bilateral or, if cross-regional, involved only one East Asian economy. (The exceptions were mostly ASEAN+1 arrangements.) Clearly, trade cooperation in East Asia has not followed an ASEAN+3 path, regardless of rhetoric calling for an Asian Economic Community to parallel the European Union or the U.S. proposal for a free trade area in the Asia-Pacific region.[80]

The bilateral basis of trade cooperation contrasts visibly with the regional basis of financial cooperation. There are apparently a number of sound reasons for this—for example, Saori Katada and Mireya Solís argue that trade and finance vary along the dimensions of domestic constituencies in key countries, the level of convergence or divergence of interest between Japan and China, and the role of U.S. private and public actors.[81] Also, bilateral trade agreements produce private goods, due to the fact that gains from trade are divisible. In contrast, financial stability has the quality of a public good—neighboring country A benefits from the financial stability of country B even if A does not commit any resources to that cause. (Of course, country B has the greatest incentive to avoid financial instability. But the point is that all of B's major economic partners and rivals are affected by financial instability and have a collective incentive to prevent or manage B's instability, although they have individual incentives to free ride.) Moreover, currency crises are apt to spread to neighboring economies that are either closely linked or structurally similar to the economy where the crisis originated. In the increasingly regionalized economic environment of East Asia,

---

[79] Solís and Katada 2007. A full list of PTAs involving ADB members can be found at http://aric.adb.org/FTAbyCountryAll.php.

[80] East Asia Vision Group 2001; East Asia Study Group 2002. On the free trade area of the Asia-Pacific proposal, see PECC's informative webpage http://www.pecc.org/ftaap/.

[81] Katada and Solís, forthcoming.

TABLE 2.1.
Preferential Trade Agreements Involving East Asian Economies (as of October 2007)

Under implementation	Signed	Under negotiation	Proposed/under study
ASEAN Free Trade Area	Japan–Brunei	ASEAN–Australia– New Zealand	Australia–Japan
ASEAN–China	Japan–Philippines	ASEAN–EU	Australia–Korea
ASEAN–Korea	Japan–Chile	ASEAN–India	China–India
Asia–Pacific Trade Agreement	Group of Eight	ASEAN–Japan	China–Japan–Korea
China–Chile	Japan–Thailand	Canada–Singapore	China–Korea
China–Hong Kong	Taiwan–El Salvador– Honduras	China–Australia	China–Peru
China–Macao	Taiwan–Nicaragua	China–GCC	China–South Africa
China–Pakistan	Korea–U.S.	China–Iceland	East Asia Free Trade Area
China–Thailand		China–S. African Customs Union	India–Indonesia
EFTA–Singapore		China–Singapore	Indonesia–EFTA
India–Singapore		India–Korea	Japan–Canada
Japan–Malaysia		India–Thailand	Korea–MERCOSUR
Japan–Mexico		Japan–Australia	Korea–South Africa
Japan–Singapore		Japan–GCC	Korea–Thailand
Korea–Chile		Japan–India	Malaysia–India
Korea–EFTA		Japan–Indonesia	Malaysia–Korea
Korea–Singapore		Japan–Korea	New Zealand–Korea
Laos–Thailand		Japan–Switzerland	New Zealand–Mexico
New Zealand– Singapore		Japan–Vietnam	Pakistan–Philippines
Singapore–Australia		Korea–Canada	Pakistan–Thailand
Singapore–Jordan		Korea–EU	Shanghai Coopera- tion Organization
Singapore–Panama		Korea–Mexico	Singapore–Bahrain
Taiwan–Guatemala		Malaysia–Australia	Singapore–Sri Lanka
Taiwan–Panama		Malaysia–Chile	Singapore–United Arab Emirates
Thailand–Australia		Malaysia–New Zealand	Thailand–Chile
Thailand–New Zealand		Malaysia–Pakistan	Thailand– MERCOSUR
Trans–Pacific		New Zealand–China	U.S.–Brunei
U.S.–Singapore		New Zealand– Hong Kong	U.S.–Indonesia
		Pacific ACP–EC	U.S.–Philippines
		Pakistan–Indonesia	U.S.–Taiwan
		Pakistan–Singapore	
		Singapore–Egypt	
		Singapore–Kuwait	
		Singapore–Mexico	
		Singapore–Peru	
		Singapore–Qatar	
		Taiwan–Dominican Republic	
		Taiwan–Paraguay	
		Thailand–Bahrain	
		Thailand–EFTA	
		Thailand–Peru	
		U.S.–Malaysia	
		U.S.–Thailand	

Source: Asian Development Bank, Asian Regional Integration Center.

financial stability is indeed a regional issue, and thus it makes sense that attempts to institutionalize cooperation have been regional in nature.

But, while it is understandable why finance and trade cooperation have followed differing tracks, the political question remains of whether trade bilateralism undermines broader economic regionalism. The extensive cross-regionalism of East Asian economies' trade agreements and the often inconsistent coverage and rules of origin (ROOs) that they adopt suggest a highly open regionalism, on the one hand, and the difficulty of using bilaterals as building blocks for regional agreements, on the other.[82] This is likely to be true even of the ASEAN+1 agreements that are being considered with China, Japan, and Korea, which would presumably be the most efficient avenue to an ASEAN+3 FTA.

Several overlapping pictures emerge in looking at East Asian economies' trade agreements. Economically, despite the spaghetti-bowl aspects and messiness of the web of bilaterals, that web reflects the fact that regionalization is an Asia-Pacific, and not just an East Asian, phenomenon. Politically, there has clearly developed a contest for securing PTAs, which Thomas Moore has characterized as "competing to cooperate."[83] The contestants include all of the major players in the Asia-Pacific, including not only China, Japan, and the United States but also Singapore, Australia, New Zealand, Thailand, Malaysia, and India.

To understand this competition, it is essential to bear in mind that PTAs are a form of institutionalized international cooperation. Institutional arrangements are fundamentally meant to force participants to commit to mutually advantageous courses of action while also excluding nonparticipants. Significant advantage can be gained by first movers, who can then set advantageous conditions for other states to join.[84] This dynamic expresses itself in at least three ways in East Asian countries' PTAs: locking in access, locking in rules, and linkage strategies. For smaller and extraregional economies, access is particularly important. Smaller economies (such as Singapore) also have particular interest in moving quickly and widely in order not to encounter more difficult conditions when and if the time comes for enlargement of a particular agreement.

For the major players, the same points can be made, but because they have more leverage, standard-setting and rules of entry are the paramount issues of economic advantage. Fundamentally, the major players are playing against each other, not just (or even primarily, in many cases) their actual counterparts in any given negotiation. For the United States, the

---

[82]Baldwin 2007 provides a good summary of the ROOs problem. Manchin and Pelkmans-Balaoing 2007 offers an in-depth examination of the transaction costs associated with ROOs in East Asian PTAs.

[83]Moore 2004, 121–23; 2006.

[84]Oye (1993) has shown this convincingly in the case of the interwar period, which is a particularly apt laboratory for examining these dynamics.

main political thrust of its PTA strategy with East Asian economies is to maintain its role as a key regional player. Japanese and Chinese negotiators must also worry about exclusion, despite the happy rhetoric of regionalism. Japanese negotiators fear Chinese hardball tactics if they are forced to enter existing Chinese arrangements. Moreover, they argue that Chinese agreements' ROOs, coverage of goods and services, and treatment of intellectual property, and the like are inferior both to international standards and to those of Japan's own PTAs, raising the concern that regional free trade will be highly attenuated and disadvantageous for Japan.[85]

China's concerns are the mirror image of Japan's, but ironically China's status as a developing country gives it three advantages over Japan in these bargaining situations. First, unlike Japan, it is not strictly bound by WTO rules demanding complete openness on "substantially all" trade, which allows it to conclude agreements more quickly and without raising difficult political issues for its partners. Second, as a rich country, Japan typically has to give more to its PTA partners than does China; although many analysts complain that Japan has not been willing to make major concessions on issues like agriculture and immigration that would be of greatest benefit to partners like Thailand and the Philippines, it is also true that Japan has engaged in major side payments in the expanded context of economic partnership agreements (EPAs).[86] Third, China is better able to justify hard bargaining with Japan than the other way around, based on the residual assumptions about trade with developing countries, as contained most formally in the Generalized System of Preferences (GSP).[87]

Meanwhile, all the major powers are involved in an influence game. PTAs and EPAs are meaningful not only in economic terms (whether seen as a bargaining game between the actual participants or a contest among major powers to establish first-mover advantage). They also link to broader political objectives. To some extent, this can be understood in terms of willingness to cooperate on related or even unrelated issues. More intriguing is the possibility that bilateral or ASEAN+1 agreements can create politically useful dependencies. As Thomas Moore writes, citing the quintessential work of realist political economy:

> China's engagement of ASEAN countries fits well with the classic realist explanation of Germany's trading relations with its smaller European neighbors

[85]Personal interviews with officials of Japan's Ministry of Trade, Economy and Industry (METI) and Ministry of Finance (MOF).

[86]In the case of the Japan-Philippines EPA, for example, Japan offered to accept a limited number of Philippine nurses. Most Japanese EPAs also include provisions for technical assistance of various sorts. For full documentation on Japan's EPAs, see http://www.mofa.go.jp/policy/economy/fta/index.html.

[87]Indeed, as of early 2008, China remains on Japan's GSP list. See the Ministry of Foreign Affairs (MOFA) website http://www.mofa.go.jp/policy/economy/gsp/benef.html.

between the First and Second World Wars, as set forth by Albert Hirschman in his landmark book *National Power and the Structure of Foreign Trade.* In Hirschman's account, Germany sought to increase its political leverage by offering favourable trade arrangements to its smaller neighbors. Rather than try to dominate by extracting economic concessions from weaker parties, Germany sought to increase its political influence by purposely accepting asymmetric economic relations. From this perspective, contemporary China would be seen as cultivating interdependence with smaller countries such as its ASEAN partners, not as a separate end or primarily for economic purposes, but as a means of enhancing its political power.[88]

East Asian economies have indeed been growing increasingly dependent on the Chinese economy. China is now South Korea's largest trading partner and largest destination of outward FDI, and the Taiwan economy is almost unimaginable now without taking into account the webs of mutual interest across the Taiwan Strait. Meanwhile, in continental Southeast Asia, Chinese trade, aid, and investment are beginning to integrate the developing economies of Myanmar, Laos, and Cambodia into a periphery of southern China.[89] More well-to-do Southeast Asian economies like Thailand, Malaysia, and Singapore are less dependent (and their PTA overtures toward Japan and the United States suggest that they plan to stay that way), but they too are bound into the regional production networks that increasingly center on China. Japan's economic influence remains important, but it is understood to be declining, never again to inspire fears of Hirschman-like asymmetrical dominance.[90]

Financial Vulnerability and Financial Regionalism in East Asia

The challenges of regional cooperation in finance differ fundamentally from those facing trade policymakers. As noted, there is a public goods aspect to preventing and containing currency crises that has no clear parallel in the contemporary global trading system. Unlike trade-oriented regionalism, which seeks to accelerate an ongoing process of growing interdependence, the core rationale of financial regionalism is to reduce East Asian economies' vulnerability to crises as well as to promote integration in the

[88] Moore 2007, 42–43.

[89] This process was first described to me by a METI official in 2002, although most Western analysts only become aware of it several years later.

[90] Hatch and Yamamura 1996 was a key text that warned against the possibility of a de facto Japanese sphere of economic influence in East Asia. Lincoln 2004 demonstrates fairly convincingly the relative retreat of Japanese economic preponderance in the region.

interest of economic growth. Thus, while trade regionalism can be largely boiled down to interest-group politics and cost-benefit analysis, financial regionalism in some ways more closely resembles security regionalism, including that vulnerabilities can be exposed in sudden catastrophic episodes. Before closing this chapter, it is essential to map out the key financial vulnerabilities of East Asian economies and some of the resulting challenges for financial regionalism.

Vulnerability and Opportunity: The Effects of Financial Globalization in East Asia

The ASEAN+3 governments are profoundly familiar with the concept of financial vulnerability, having experienced the Asian Financial Crisis of 1997–98. The AFC was a formative moment in the development of financial regionalism in East Asia. It laid bare the vulnerabilities of small open economies in a globalized financial system, as well as the lack of a guarantee of sympathetic and effective response from international financial institutions dominated by other regions. East Asian economies other than Japan, and perhaps China, have thus found themselves subject to the demands and whims of global financial markets to an extent that became unnerving after 1997.[91] This vulnerability appears in the three interrelated areas of currency management, capital market development, and emergency liquidity availability.

Currency management issues have been a major concern for all the countries in the region—even Japan, whose yen has been one of the world's three major currencies for over three decades.[92] The basic problem facing all of the main ASEAN+3 players has been their dependence on foreign capital and goods markets in which the currencies of other economies dominate.[93] There are two issues. First, the bulk of the trade and external debt of all of the developing and middle-income economies of the region is foreign currency–denominated, mostly in U.S. dollars. Second, economists

[91] Even in Japan, the world's largest net creditor, policymakers and media continue to express a deep sense of vulnerability to currency values and capital movement. Grimes 1999, 2003a, 2003b.

[92] On Japan's currency angst, see McKinnon and Ohno 1997; Kikkawa 1998; Oka 1996; Hayami 1995; Grimes 1999, 2003a, 2003b.

[93] Japan differs from its East Asian neighbors in both degree and type of dependence. Japan has a uniquely low ratio of trade to GDP among Asian economies, but its need to recycle its immense current account surpluses persists. The dollar denomination of much of its foreign capital and debt holdings—not to mention its political dependence on the United States—keeps it concerned about yen-dollar exchange rates. Unlike some of its neighbors, however, Japanese economic actors have tended to worry more about yen appreciation than depreciation. Also, there is no danger of a currency crash of the sort seen in the AFC, as its domestic debt is yen denominated and overwhelmingly held by Japanese institutions and savers.

agree that it is impossible to simultaneously maintain open capital markets, monetary policy flexibility, and a given currency value. Small economies with thinly traded currencies naturally have difficulty managing even two of these. In the 1980s and 1990s, most of the East Asian capitalist economies significantly eased capital restrictions as they became both increasingly difficult to maintain and a drag on other economic activities, including trade and foreign direct investment.[94] This created more pressure on authorities to stabilize their economies through currency and monetary policies; essentially all of capitalist East Asia other than Japan chose an implicit or explicit dollar peg as one of the bases of their macroeconomic stabilization policy, which in turn contributed to the onset and spread of the Asian Financial Crisis.

Currency Mismatches and Management

With regard to debt denomination, it has become clear that a currency mismatch—that is, unhedged denomination of debt in foreign currencies— automatically creates the potential for macroeconomic vulnerability to shifts in currency values.[95] The logic is simple. If the home currency depreciates relative to the currency in which debt is denominated, then the effective burden of the debt increases. The problem arises in particular when the revenues of the debtor government or corporation are earned in the home currency rather than the currency of the debt. The extent of actual vulnerability depends on the level of foreign currency–denominated debt relative to GDP, exports, and foreign exchange reserves and the maturity profile of that debt. When a payments crisis occurs, the difficulties of paying back foreign-denominated debt created by a significant depreciation are aggravated by the likelihood of further depreciations caused by creditors' and investors' unwillingness to provide further capital when repayment is in question. Both theoretically and in practice, this can create a downward spiral in currency values leading to an actual crisis.[96] Indeed, this is precisely what happened in the AFC. Unfortunately for developing and middle-income economies, it is typically difficult for them to obtain capital internationally by financing themselves with local currency bonds. Economists have termed this apparent trap "original sin."[97] One of the major concerns

---

[94]Chinn and Ito 2006.

[95]See Goldstein and Turner 2004 and the essays in Eichengreen and Hausmann 2005 for more extensive economic analysis.

[96]Radelet and Sachs 1998.

[97]Eichengreen, Hausmann, and Panizza 2003. Goldstein and Turner (2004) strenuously contest the usefulness of the notion of "original sin." They argue that the causes of excessive foreign currency borrowing are to be found in poor domestic policies rather than in international financial markets. However, the basic challenge of currency mismatch is of central concern to both approaches.

of East Asian financial regionalism is to address this aspect of exchange market vulnerability.

In response to the second problem, which Benjamin J. Cohen has dubbed the "unholy trinity,"[98] one of the primary responses of the East Asian economies has been to tie their currencies to the dollar, whether formally or informally.[99] Pegging to the dollar had both positive and negative effects. On the positive side, developing countries like Thailand were able to borrow the credibility of U.S. monetary policy in the 1980s and 1990s in order to keep domestic inflation under control, maintain a predictable local-currency value of their dollar-denominated international debt payments, and attract foreign investors who felt reassured that their investments would not evaporate as a result of depreciation.[100] On the negative side, international creditors and investors as well as local borrowers were lulled into a false sense of security regarding the likelihood of devaluation, leading to excessive short-term dollar-denominated foreign borrowing. When monetary policymakers proved unable to effectively manage the impact of excessive capital inflows, depreciation was sudden and its effects catastrophic.

Economists affiliated with the U.S. Treasury and IMF argued that the 1997 crisis demonstrated the nonviability of any currency regime other than pure floating or a true currency board (the "two-corner solution").[101] The Japanese government, on the other hand, immediately began pushing for currency-basket systems.[102] Japanese policymakers dismissed claims that a pure float would be in the interests of a small economy, and instead argued that the economies of East Asia would best be served by stabilizing their currencies against a weighted basket of currencies of their major trading and financial partners.[103] (As I have argued elsewhere, Japan's currency-basket advocacy has also tied in with efforts to insulate the *Japanese* economy.)[104] In fact, most East Asian governments reestablished soft pegs against the dollar.

By 2006 there appeared to have been some movement away from the dollar as the sole target of currency management among East Asian economies. This could be seen practically in econometric evidence that showed slightly lower correlations between East Asian currencies and the dollar, as well as nominally in the summer 2005 announcements by Chinese and

[98] Cohen 1993, 1998a, 2004.

[99] McKinnon and Schnabl 2004.

[100] McKinnon and Schnabl (2004) argue that this condition continued to hold even after the financial crisis.

[101] On the persistence of this interpretation, see, for example, Geithner 2007.

[102] Grimes 2003a, 2003b; Hayashi 2006, 77–80.

[103] Optimal weighting formulas are a topic of continuing debate. For recent scholarly investigations of this question, see Kwan 2001; Goldstein 2002; Yoshino, Kaji, and Asonuma 2005b, 2005c.

[104] Grimes 2003a, 2003b.

Malaysian authorities that they would be moving to currency-basket systems (although until mid-2007 there was little practical change in the behavior of either currency). Nonetheless, a significant debate persists over the appropriateness and sustainability of soft-dollar pegging by current account–surplus economies in East Asia; while conventional analysis sees it as dangerous and unsustainable, an influential minority of scholars argue that it will remain rational at least into the medium term.[105] I address this debate in chapter 4.

Capital Market Development

Capital market development is associated with the debt denomination issue noted above. It has been widely observed that finance in the East Asian economies has been dominated by banks and that financial markets have lagged in comparison. The level of dominance has changed considerably in the last quarter century, particularly in Japan, Singapore, and South Korea, but stock and bond markets remain much less accessible as a means of financing than in the United States, United Kingdom, or even many Continental European economies. In the aftermath of the AFC, several governments in East Asia, including Japan, Thailand, Malaysia, and South Korea, have agreed that better local-currency debt markets are essential to preventing currency mismatches. The logic is that excess savings at home have been exported overseas and then lent back to finance domestic needs in the form of foreign currency–denominated debt. If better investment opportunities existed at home, according to this analysis, there would be less need for exposure to that kind of currency risk.[106] Thus, one of the major goals of financial regionalism has been to improve the functioning of domestic bond markets in East Asia, although these efforts have been made under the rubric of the creation of a unified regional bond market.

A closely related issue is capital controls. Considerable capital liberalization preceded and set the stage for the Asian Financial Crisis, as small financial markets like Thailand's were unable to handle massive movements of money across their borders.[107] Japanese policymakers entered the debate soon after the crisis with statements supportive of the reimposition of capital controls.[108] They argued that several of the crisis economies had lowered barriers to short-term capital movement before the necessary institutions,

---

[105] Dooley, Folkerts-Landau, and Garber 2003; McKinnon and Schnabl 2004; and Rose 2006 are among the major works that show a lack of concern regarding continued East Asian dollar pegging.

[106] Ito and Park 2004; IIMA 2002. While I concentrate here on currency mismatch, maturity mismatch was also a major problem, as discussed in chapter 5. The combination of currency and maturity mismatch is known as the "double mismatch" problem.

[107] Radelet and Sachs 1998.

[108] Grimes 2003b, 188.

rules, and practices had been put into effect.[109] Advocacy of capital controls has become less pronounced as regional efforts have increasingly focused on local-currency bond market development, since capital controls can hinder or even prevent foreign participation in local markets. (The problem is all the more obvious in discussions of creating a truly *regional* bond market.) Policymakers now emphasize the importance of incremental and well-planned liberalization.[110]

Foreign Exchange Reserves

A final aspect of financial vulnerability in East Asia is the concern about sufficiency of foreign reserves in the event of a currency crisis. Governments and central banks that have not fully abandoned their currency management to a pure float must draw on foreign exchange reserves to respond to a depreciation that they consider to be excessive. If their own reserves are insufficient, then they must seek to borrow reserves, either from other states or from the International Monetary Fund. In 1997 many East Asian economies realized the limits of existing arrangements when their own reserves proved insufficient to defend their currencies. While the Philippines and Singapore accepted significant market-driven depreciation, the problems facing Thailand, Indonesia, and South Korea were so severe that they were forced to turn to the IMF for support, where they immediately faced two problems. First, their quotas at the IMF were far too small to allow them to draw adequate funds, forcing large-scale negotiations to create packages to obtain dollar reserves from other international financial institutions and a variety of other countries. Second, the IMF appeared ill-equipped to deal with the nature of the AFC and imposed onerous, and in some cases counterproductive, conditions on them.[111]

The 1997–98 crisis highlighted the financial vulnerability of the open East Asian economies and left an indelible mark on regional financial policymakers. It also significantly eroded regional policymakers' confidence that the IMF and the United States had their best interests at heart, while demonstrating the willingness of Japan to support its neighbors in their time of need. Regional solutions to global financial pressures, which were unthinkable (or at least unthought of) until the crisis hit, became a major focus of the East Asian states' efforts to reduce vulnerability. Even Japan and China, the economies least vulnerable to attack, continued to feel a

[109] Other arguments can also be made in favor of capital controls under specific conditions. For example, under a fixed exchange rate regime, there is a potential collective action problem in which individual firms overborrow abroad, to the detriment of the economy as a whole. See also Wade 1998.

[110] See, for example, Hayashi 2006, 66–70; Aramaki 2006; Hu 2007.

[111] For two of the many criticisms of the IMF's actions in the crisis, see Yoshitomi and Ohno 1999, and Stiglitz 2002, chap. 4.

deep vulnerability that fuels their regional strategies. The political stage had been set for East Asian financial regionalism.

Financial Regionalism

Financial regionalism builds on existing patterns of regional cooperation, but it also differs from both past and concurrent efforts in important ways. Although chapters 3, 4, and 5 go into great detail on the subject, it is important first to make some general points about East Asian financial regionalism.

First, the role of the Asian Financial Crisis in shaping regional efforts must not be minimized.[112] Contemporary financial regionalism is built on economic and political analyses of what happened in 1997–98. Policymakers and populations in the region either directly experienced or closely observed how quickly financial reversals could lead to free-falling currencies, implosion of financial systems, and economic devastation. That experience has created great motivation to find measures to prevent a repeat. As I have written elsewhere, "The main lessons that governments in the region have drawn from that episode are that dollar pegs and short-term borrowing in foreign currencies are very dangerous, and that little support can be expected from the IMF and the United States in the event of a crisis."[113] Whatever else the East Asian economies want from financial regionalism, their minimum expectation is that it will protect against the need for excessive short-term borrowing in dollars and that it will not depend on an effective and sympathetic response from the United States and the IMF in the event of a crisis. One result is that the United States is unlikely to be invited into any aspect of financial regionalism as a participant—although, ironically, East Asian financial regionalism has been complementary to the existing global financial order, rather than mounting a challenge.[114]

An additional economic rationale for financial regionalism can be found in the need to support the regional production networks described earlier in this chapter. While PTAs and trade facilitation efforts are obvious means of supporting production networks, regional financial cooperation can play several important support roles as well. Improvement of local-currency bond markets, for example, would improve the ability of Japanese, U.S., and other firms and financial institutions operating throughout East Asia to raise funds efficiently and to hedge their costs, revenues, and investments to reduce instability in their business environments.[115] Meanwhile, efforts to

[112] Higgott 1998; Katada 2001; Calder and Ye 2004; Hamilton-Hart 2006.
[113] Grimes 2006, 356–57.
[114] Grimes 2006.
[115] I am grateful to Martin Schulz for clarifying this point for me.

prevent currency crises also reduce instability in the business environment. It is because of the regional nature of production networks that regional solutions are attractive.[116]

Nonetheless, regional financial integration and regional financial cooperation operate in the shadow of financial globalization. With more or less open financial markets (other than China and the least-developed ASEAN countries) and large-scale participation by global financial institutions and multinationals, the East Asian economies are, unavoidably, financially integrated into the global economy. Moreover, even where financial cooperation has the ultimate goal of insulating the economies in question from abrupt movements of hot money, the means that the East Asian economies have available to do so as a region actually require greater liberalization (at least over time), inevitably leading to even greater integration into global finance.[117] Thus,. financial regionalism and financial globalization exist in an uneasy embrace.

Meanwhile, just as with PTAs, in financial regionalism states seek to lock their counterparts into rules that they consider attractive. In the case of financial regionalism, it is vitally important for Japan to force China into a liberal model of economic behavior before China is economically powerful enough to ignore the preferences of its economic partners or even to dictate rules that will give it economic advantages against them. Japanese financial institutions want easy access to and exit from Chinese financial markets, even as Japanese policymakers wish to ensure that China's leaders will manage the economy in such a way that will not be destabilizing for its neighbors. China, meanwhile, does not have the power to set rules or dictate others' behavior yet, so it has an incentive to avoid being locked in by regional agreements. However, it is also in a position where it must gain the confidence of regional and global financial institutions, which constantly pushes it in a generally liberal direction. Thus, both Japan and China face interesting dilemmas in moving forward with financial regionalism.

Finally, it is important to bear in mind that there is nothing inherent in the key elements of East Asian financial regionalism as it has evolved— that is, emergency liquidity provision, local-currency bond market development, regional surveillance, and currency cooperation—that requires them to be pursued simultaneously. In other words, they are not necessarily a "package deal," although there are synergies and overlaps among them that make a package deal both intellectually and strategically coherent. However, Japanese policymakers clearly see them as a package, even though it is not obvious that their ASEAN+3 counterparts agree whole-heartedly with

---

[116]Katada and Solís, forthcoming.
[117]This is analogous to the Japanese dilemma discussed in Grimes 2003a, 2003b.

that approach. In this book, I treat financial regionalism as a single effort both because of the coherence and symbiosis of the elements and because of the political salience of Japan's decision to push it as such. But, because other East Asian governments have not necessarily accepted the necessity of a unified approach to financial regionalism, their opportunities for political maneuvering increase.

3

Lending into Crises
The Chiang Mai Initiative

East Asian financial regionalism was forged in the crucible of the Asian Financial Crisis, as one high-growth economy after another fell victim to severe currency depreciation and credit crunches. Many observers both inside and outside the region attributed the worst of the effects to the slowness, inappropriate design, and punitive nature of the IMF response. So it is not surprising that one of the core elements of financial regionalism has been the effort to create arrangements for emergency liquidity provision—in other words, funding to bail out regional economies caught in currency crises. This is the goal of the ASEAN+3's Chiang Mai Initiative.

The rationale for a regional liquidity scheme is based on two lessons drawn from the 1997 crisis. The first is that speculative attacks on the currencies of Thailand and other AFC economies were successful because those economies' foreign exchange reserves were insufficient to cover capital outflows. The second is that the existing international financial architecture, which depended on IMF-led bailouts with strict conditions attached, was not effective in rapidly addressing the crisis at the lowest possible cost; rather, the IMF efforts were understood throughout East Asia to have been too slow in the making and to have been filled with inappropriate and excessively strict conditions. The downward spiral of currency depreciation and capital flight in the weeks required to negotiate standby agreements caused significant damage; this damage was aggravated, goes the critique, by IMF conditions that caused unnecessary hardship for those in crisis economies and made it difficult to earn or otherwise obtain the foreign exchange needed for the economies to function. The Chiang Mai Initiative thus aims to provide massive amounts of liquidity in a timely fashion to stem those effects if a crisis does arise. It is also meant to dissuade investors from mounting speculative attacks in the first place or from running for the exits when currencies begin to drop.

Although liquidity provision is an economic function, politics pervades any bailout of an economy suffering from a currency crisis. Efforts to create formal arrangements to provide crisis liquidity are even more inherently political, as they explicitly involve questions about international decision making, membership, monitoring, and enforcement—not to mention, large sums of public money. Since the onset of the Asian Financial Crisis in 1997, Japan has been a leader in proposing and carrying out measures to resolve and prevent currency crises: indeed, to a considerable extent, we can say that when it comes to regional crisis management, Japan proposes and other states (including the United States) react.[1] These ongoing efforts have created a variety of political and economic opportunities and vulnerabilities for all of the states involved, although in this chapter I put a particular spotlight on Japan, given its role as agenda-setter.

Political Stakes in the Chiang Mai Initiative

At one level the issue of liquidity provision is a classic public goods problem: in an integrated region, a currency crisis in any economy or set of economies creates costs for all. Moreover, the existing institutional arrangements failed in minimizing those costs in the AFC and were ineffective in preventing the initial crisis and its spread. This failure led to calls for a regional solution. But creating new institutions is no easy matter. Multilateral commitments or regimes, as well as the distribution of costs and benefits they create, are subject to the differing interests and preferences of the participants; without a clear leader, it is difficult to create a structure that satisfies all the participants and ensures their ongoing cooperation.

In the case of post-AFC East Asia, the design issue is made relatively easier by the common economic interests of Japan and China, which are the most likely major providers of liquidity in the system as well as the most politically powerful. But to fully understand the politics of Chiang Mai, we need also to consider the broader political contestation among Japan, China, and the United States, as well as regional power issues. This is primarily an issue of structural power. Drawing on the theoretical discussion in chapter 1, the key issues on which to focus are opportunities to advance or reduce monetary dependence, which states or organizations set the rules and make the decisions that affect financial stability within East Asia, and patterns of hedging

[1] See, for example, Hayashi 2006, chap. 5.

and commitment. Complicating matters is the need to ensure that any regional arrangements be effective at both providing support for currencies in crisis and minimizing moral hazard. These dynamics operate at both global and regional levels, with the IMF as a major foil for ASEAN+3 efforts.

The key political dynamic at the global level is that the establishment of any regional institution of emergency liquidity provision may reduce the dependence of regional economies on the crisis management services of the IMF and at least potentially constitutes an alternative source of support. It should reduce regional vulnerability to globalized finance, but at the same time, it raises the possibility of regional standards of economic management or financial regulation that do not fully parallel "global standards." Standard-setting is the sine qua non of structural power.[2] Given that the global financial architecture and international financial institutions reflect to a considerable degree the preferences of the United States and U.S.-based financial actors, regional efforts can have the effect of undermining one of the bases of U.S. structural power.

The establishment of regional arrangements is not a direct or immediate attack on global standards and institutions. It does, however, raise the *possibility* of partially decoupling from the system if that becomes politically or economically attractive. In other words, regional crisis management constitutes a regional hedge against actions by the IMF or the United States that are perceived as problematic.[3] This fits into a longer-term desire on the part of Japanese and other East Asian economic policymakers to reduce monetary dependence on the United States. Ironically, for the smaller participants in CMI, especially the ASEAN economies, it can also be understood as partially transforming their existing dependence on the global, or U.S.-dominated, system to dependence on Japan and China. In other words, there is the potential for monetary entrapment within these regional arrangements. But that may still be attractive, both as a means of diversification of risk and if they expect to have more influence over Japanese and Chinese economic decision making than over that of the United States and the IMF.

A regional hedge also constitutes a tool for regional leverage. In the 1997–98 crisis, East Asian governments including Japan (the second largest quota-holder in the IMF) expressed deep frustration about their inability to shape IMF conditions to reflect their own understanding of the crisis.[4] The implicit threat of rejecting IMF conditions in favor of regional ones will undoubtedly be a factor in future bailouts in East Asia; and the more credible

[2] Lukes 1974; Strange 1994.
[3] Katada 2004; Sohn 2007.
[4] Hayashi 2006, 77–80. For a sampling of Japanese voices on the subject, see Katada 2001, 260, n. 44 and 45.

the threat (i.e., the more attractive the purely regional solution to regional states), the greater will be ASEAN+3 influence on the shape of those bailouts.

Within East Asia as well, there are important political forces at work; it is misleading to think only of "regional" interests. The central political problem in all regional efforts is the political contest between Japan and China for leadership. The economic interests of Japan and China in regional crisis management are actually very similar: both are likely creditors with strong interests in regional stability and the ability to commit large sums of money to the task. Nonetheless, both must be on the lookout for opportunities on the part of the other to use such arrangements for relative advantage. To a considerable extent, Japan has been the source of ideas and initiatives concerning financial regionalism, especially regional crisis management. The Chinese government has been suspicious of those initiatives at least partly for that reason, as seen in its rejection of Japan's ambitious proposal for an Asian monetary fund in 1997.[5] The reluctance of the Chinese government to cede leadership has contributed to the more incremental approach to regional crisis management since that time.

Another dimension of regional politics concerns followership, or how South Korea and the ASEAN states respond to initiatives. This may not appear to be a major issue, since any regional crisis management arrangements will increase the amount of funds available to lend into a currency crisis. The ASEAN4 countries in particular should be willing to accept almost anything that does not increase their vulnerability or obligate them to accept additional conditionality. But there are at least three complicating factors. First, regional crisis management unavoidably calls for crisis decision making that is rapid, conclusive, and enforceable—in other words, very unlike the existing ASEAN and ASEAN+3 processes, which valorize consensus and nonbinding agreements. The existing processes provide advantages to smaller powers in that they prevent their being coerced by stronger states. While they may be willing to accept crisis decision making in the actual event of a currency crisis, they should worry a great deal about whether that would create a precedent that affects other aspects of ASEAN+3 decision making, thus disadvantaging them and displacing ASEAN from its unofficial centrality in East Asian regionalism. Second, they potentially face considerable uncertainty as to how Japan and China will prefer to deal with crises; thus, they may worry about whether a regional arrangement will actually subject them to additional political pressures. With their approval essential to any regional arrangement, the small powers should be looking for provisions that constrain the exercise of power by the regional leaders. Finally, after the experience of the Asian Financial Crisis, East Asian governments

[5] Bowles 2002, 255–58.

have understandably embraced the principle of self-help, particularly in the form of maintaining high levels of foreign exchange reserves. This reduces the immediate importance of regional arrangements; however, it also gives some breathing room for the establishment and improvement of rules and procedures.

Before moving on to an examination of the Chiang Mai Initiative and its predecessors, it is important to note that contests for power and influence are conditioned by the basic constraints of market expectations, institutional dynamics, and the potential for moral hazard. The key functional issue in creating an institution to provide crisis liquidity is how to manage the trade-off between minimizing the negative effects of a currency crisis and the possibility of introducing moral hazard. Once a crisis is underway, it is generally in most participants' interests to provide foreign exchange rapidly and in adequate amounts to stem capital flight. However, if policymakers expect that funds will be provided in a crisis without onerous conditions, moral hazard necessarily arises.[6] By reducing the expected penalty for economic mismanagement, the institution may lead to more crises than would otherwise have occurred and therefore to worse long-run outcomes for both crisis and donor economies. Conversely, if financial market participants doubt the effectiveness of regional arrangements, then they will have an added incentive to attack apparently vulnerable currencies.

From Asian Monetary Fund to Chiang Mai Initiative: Institutionalizing a Regional Response

Although the Asian Financial Crisis did not lead to the worldwide economic meltdown that some observers feared, it proved to be a transformative event in other ways. In the crisis countries, important political and economic changes ensued.[7] And the basic legitimacy of the global financial system, as embodied in the International Monetary Fund, was called into question across the ideological spectrum.[8]

In the United States, some conservative economists argued that the problem had been caused by moral hazard created by past policies of the IMF.[9] By bailing out debtor countries whose governments had mismanaged their economies, the IMF had significantly reduced the downside risk of economic

[6]For a concise justification of this statement, see Kenen 2001, 51–52.

[7]Haggard 2000; Hamilton-Hart 2002, chap. 7.

[8]Progressive critiques include, among others, Stiglitz 2002; Wade and Veneroso 1998; Sakakibara 1998; while conservative critiques include Calomiris 1998; Schulz, Simon, and Wriston 1998; IFIAC 2000 (the "Meltzer Report").

[9]Calomiris 1998; Schulz, Simon, and Wriston 1998; IFIAC 2000. See Kenen 2001, chap. 3 ("Myths and Metaphors") for a summary and critique of conservative attacks on the IMF.

irresponsibility for both debtor countries and their private sector creditors. Opposed to this emphasis on systemic moral hazard and domestic mismanagement, Japanese policymakers immediately focused on the problem of excessive and premature capital liberalization.[10] By lowering their barriers to capital movements, developing countries had opened themselves to the possibility of unmanageably large inflows or outflows that could play havoc with exchange rates and monetary policy. As Eisuke Sakakibara described the "crisis of global capitalism," global capital flows had grown to be too big and too rapid for any country—particularly a small economy with a thinly traded currency—to defend itself from a sudden loss of confidence.[11] Thus, the AFC was almost entirely a liquidity crisis that should have been solved by rapidly providing large amounts of money with minimal conditions.

Although differences of interpretation go part way toward explaining the different actions by donor economies during the crisis, the actual rescue packages for Thailand, Indonesia, and South Korea can be read as a failure of collective action as well. In particular, from Asian vantage points it appeared that the United States had decided to free ride in the provision of a self-evident international public good. This was especially true of the Thai package, to which the U.S. government pledged no assistance at all; however, even in the Indonesian and (to a lesser extent) Korean packages, the U.S contribution was stingier than that of Japan. While some level of U.S. support was forthcoming in the form of its acquiescence to IMF, World Bank, and Asian Development Bank contributions, once the solution stepped outside of established institutional arrangements, the United States was—for whatever reason—unwilling to pull its weight. (The real reasons were various and included a Congressional injunction against presidential use of the Exchange Stabilization Fund following the 1994–95 Mexican peso crisis.)[12] The U.S. response created an opening for Japan to take on an unaccustomed leadership role that could advance a strategy of regional insulation from currency fluctuations and contribute to ongoing efforts to hedge against excessive political-economic dependence on (and thus vulnerability to) the United States.[13]

The Asian Monetary Fund Proposal

The Japanese government quickly took the regional initiative with its Asian monetary fund proposal, which was first put forward to its East Asian partners in August 1997 and publicly unveiled in September. The plan called

[10]Sakakibara 1998, 26–28; Kuroda 2005, 176–81; Hayashi 2006, 66–70.
[11]Sakakibara 1998, 38–43, 84–85.
[12]Katada 2001, 175.
[13]Lee 2006; Katada 2001, 175–77.

for a large regional pool of available foreign exchange reserves (reported as starting at $100 billion) that could be mobilized quickly to provide short-term financing for an East Asian country facing a currency crisis. Unlike IMF packages, AMF funds would not carry strict conditionality. And the AMF would restrict its efforts to East Asia.[14] Given Japan's economic interpretation of the crisis and the apparent political reality of a lack of U.S. willingness to contribute to an international public good outside its own Latin American backyard, the original Asian monetary fund proposal appeared to make perfect sense.

Each of these elements addressed a key part of the Japanese analysis. First, the sheer scale of the Asian Financial Crisis called for the availability of a vast pool of reserves—much larger than the IMF could provide—that could be tapped in the event of a recurrence. Second, the belief in East Asia that the AFC was a pure liquidity crisis meant that deflationary policy conditions (an IMF staple) would be counterproductive. It also meant that funds would indeed be provided on a purely short-term basis—just until investor confidence returned—so that much more flexible institutional arrangements than those found in the IMF would be sufficient. Third, the restriction of beneficiaries to East Asia made sense in terms of both logic and interests. Regarding economic and political interest, Japan's strong involvement with the East Asian economies made the development of a regionally restricted solution a rational goal.[15] Economically, only the East Asian developing and middle-income countries met the criteria for being victims of pure liquidity crises.[16] Finally, the AMF proposal intentionally excluded the United States and IMF, reflecting a preference for insulating East Asia and Japan itself from a perceived U.S. agenda of liberalization and globalization that primarily benefited American commercial interests and American structural power.[17]

An Asian monetary fund would have streamlined and made more automatic the process through which East Asian states would determine their

[14]Neither the institutional design nor the specific procedures were clearly defined. This can be explained partly by the fact that further negotiation was expected before finalizing arrangements, but it also appears to have been partly because of only perfunctory preparation of the plan within the Japanese government.

[15]Katada 2001 emphasizes the private good characteristic (for Japan as a whole) of regional monetary stability, but it can also be read as a club good for East Asian economies generally. In either case, the main point is the (partial) excludability of the benefit to countries outside the region and nonrivalrous access to the benefit within the region.

[16]Yoshitomi and Ohno 1999. These criteria include low (or nonexistent) budget deficits; relatively low inflation; high exports; and openness to foreign capital, ownership, and technology.

[17]This can be understood from a constructivist perspective as well as a realist one that emphasizes insulation. For example, Lee 2006 argues that Japan sought to support an East Asian model of economic and financial management against the universalistic demands of U.S.-led financial globalization.

contribution to future crises. But the proposal left open many important questions, including decision making in the new organization and criteria for assistance. As important, it did not address the political reality of differing interests among Japan, China, and the United States. Largely due to U.S. and IMF—as well as Chinese—resistance, the AMF proposal died quickly.[18]

The Manila Framework and the New Miyazawa Initiative

Despite their success at blocking the AMF proposal, U.S. policymakers were aware that their actions were perceived as an attack (or at least an affront) by many East Asian economies, and thus politically damaging. They quickly moved forward with an alternative plan for regional arrangements to supplement the IMF's role. The short-lived result of these efforts was the Manila Framework Group, which was established late in 1997 and which petered out by 2004. Well before its formal demise, the group had lost its role in crisis management, leaving only its surveillance function intact.[19]

The Manila Framework committed a subset of the APEC economies— notably including the United States, Japan, China, Australia, and the crisis economies—to mutual surveillance. In exchange, the members from developing countries would have access to an expanded pool of IMF funds. This new framework met the U.S. preference for keeping matters within the existing global framework, thus limiting both moral hazard and the possibility of exclusionary capital controls. Japan's acquiescence was secured by the promise of additional funds for crisis economies (which would not be the sole or even primary responsibility of Japan) and by the prospect of establishing a new set of standards for surveillance that would be more applicable to East Asian economies.[20]

[18]For one account of China's public opposition, see "China Cautious on Proposed Asian Monetary Fund," *Agence France-Press,* November 18, 1997.

[19]Meeting participants were finance ministry and central bank deputies. The twelfth and final meeting of the Manila Framework Group was held Nov. 30–Dec. 1, 2004, in Yogyakarta, Indonesia. The last communiqué, which can be found on the Japanese Ministry of Finance website, http://www.mof.go.jp/english/if/if037.htm, was at the eighth meeting, which was held in Beijing on March 28–29, 2001. The group was phased out at the behest of the U.S. Treasury, due to senior officials' concerns about the proliferation of often overlapping multilateral meetings. Personal communication with former U.S. Treasury undersecretary John Taylor.

[20]Yoshitomi and Ohno 1999 called explicitly for more appropriate standards. The ASEM's Kobe Research Project (IIMA 2002a) notes efforts to create an early warning system (EWS) model, but it is not clear how effective that has been, despite the creation of financial monitoring software called Vulnerability Indicators and Early Warning System (VIEWS) that has been distributed to ASEAN+3 members. ADB 2007; see also ADB 2005a, 2005b, 2007. Similarly, Japanese participants in Chiang Mai Initiative policy dialogue report that discussions in ASEAN+3 follow the same economic fundamentals as the IMF would—indeed, regional IMF representatives now brief participants at the beginning of ASEAN+3 finance ministers' meetings. Personal interviews, summer 2005, fall 2006.

Institutionally, three aspects of the Manila Framework were notable: First, it did not formally commit its members to provide any liquidity at all to crisis economies. Second, and somewhat contradictorily, it was premised on the possibility of preconditionality for the East Asian economies that would lead to more rapid access to greater amounts of IMF funds with fewer conditions.[21] Third, it created an ongoing mechanism to coordinate voluntary contributions to multilateral bailouts.

At the same time that Japan was engaged in the neoliberal, Asia-Pacific–based approach to regional surveillance constituted by the Manila Framework, it also embarked in 1998 on a far more proactive—and expensive—policy initiative known as the New Miyazawa Initiative, whose regional focus was exclusively East Asian.[22] The initiative lent money from a pool of funds officially valued at $30 billion, earmarked evenly between short-term uses and medium- to long-term uses. The short-term funds included $5 billion that was committed to the Asian Currency Crisis Support Facility that Japan created within the ADB. Another prominent feature of the initiative was credit guarantees to ensure that the governments of countries in crisis could borrow money on international markets. In the actual event, much of the money did not need to be used, but it is notable that the first government to receive an official bond guarantee under the initiative was Malaysia, which had symbolically thumbed its nose at the IMF by imposing capital controls in 1997 and 1998 instead of negotiating a standby agreement. As then Japanese vice minister of finance for international affairs Eisuke Sakakibara stated later:

> Malaysia had been the target of international criticism after it announced on Sept. 2 [1998] unilateral restrictions on the outflow of capital that inflicted huge losses on many U.S. and European financial institutions. Malaysia, however, was important to Japan, and Tokyo was not necessarily opposed to the control on capital outflows to avert a crisis. It was, therefore, unthinkable to exclude Malaysia from the list of recipients of the New Miyazawa Plan.[23]

[21] Preconditionality means that economies would be able to prequalify for access to funds in a crisis, based on their adherence to specific economic standards or conditions. This contrasts with the standard IMF procedure of negotiating provision of funds in exchange for meeting strict conditions once a crisis has occurred. The IMF did set up a lending facility based on preconditionality called the Contingent Credit Line in 1999 in response to Japanese and others' concerns after the AFC, but no potential crisis economies actually signed up. It was discontinued in 2003.

[22] There is little analysis available on the New Miyazawa Initiative in the English-language literature, aside from Katada 2001, 183–86, and Hayashi 2006, 99–102. However, in Japan, officials and outside analysts set great store by its successes. For the most complete and rigorous evaluation available, see the Japanese Ministry of Finance's 269-page external review (IIMA 2002b).

[23] Sakakibara 1999, 1. He states that he made a deal with Deputy Treasury Secretary Lawrence Summers, whereby Japan would support U.S. policy in the Brazil crisis in exchange for the United States not objecting to Japan's support of Malaysia.

Another notable feature, which was to return in the CMI, was the establishment of one-way swap lines with South Korea ($5 billion) and Malaysia ($2.5 billion) to augment their foreign currency reserves.[24] While the New Miyazawa Initiative was a unilateral initiative that was at partial cross-purposes with the Manila Framework approach, its swap lines were to provide a conceptual and practical bridge between the AMF concept and the Chiang Mai Initiative.

Meanwhile, there was the beginning of a partial convergence of Japanese and U.S. economic interpretations of both the 1997 crisis and concerns about moral hazard. The concept of preconditionality was becoming more attractive to Japanese policymakers as they began to revise their understanding of the causes of the crisis and their assessment of the willingness of the governments of crisis economies to carry out painful but necessary policy changes based on moral suasion rather than fear of IMF conditionality.[25] As awareness began to grow inside Japan of the possibility that massive short-term provision of liquidity might not be enough to prevent a future financial crisis, policymakers became increasingly focused on building in mechanisms that would prevent Japan's regional benevolence from becoming large-scale, long-term charity. By 1999, although the Miyazawa Initiative demonstrated the continued willingness of Japan to commit real money to regional financial stability, some Japanese policymakers were focusing on ways in which regional arrangements could borrow credibility from third-party actors, whether the IMF or, as in the case of the Manila Framework, the U.S. Treasury.[26]

Although small, the Miyazawa swap lines offered a practical means of providing funds to crisis economies; the next step was to expand them into a regional network while following the Manila Framework path of third-party monitoring and certification. Any plausible third-party guarantor would be politically problematic, however, so an additional challenge was to avoid a repeat of excessive dependence on the IMF and United States. As for the Manila Framework, Japanese officials admit that by 2001 or so it was a pro forma exercise, but they believed they could not pull the plug because it was a U.S. initiative. By 2004 even senior U.S. Treasury officials had grown tired of the effort, and it was discontinued.[27]

[24]These lines existed in parallel with Japan's CMI commitments until 2006, when the Korean line was combined with the Japan-Korea CMI line. The Malaysian Miyazawa line still coexists with the Japan-Malaysia CMI line.

[25]I have made this argument previously in Grimes 2002. See also Amyx 2002 and 2003c.

[26]I base this statement on private conversations with a variety of players inside and outside the Japanese government at that time. See also Amyx 2004c, 214–16.

[27]Personal interviews with Japanese participants and personal communication with John Taylor, former undersecretary for international affairs of the U.S. Treasury. The U.S. position was that it was helpful during the crisis period, but it "was phased out as part of a reform to streamline the number of international meetings which had been growing so rapidly."

The Chiang Mai Initiative, announced by the finance ministers of the ASEAN+3 countries in May 2000, addressed several of the issues that previous efforts had been unable to resolve. In place of the awkward coexistence of the Manila Framework's principle of preconditionality and the Miyazawa Initiative's emphasis on provision of liquidity without new conditions, CMI proposed to lock in large-scale multilateral financing while borrowing credibility from the IMF. Moreover, although it left some room open for expansion of membership, it decisively defined financial regionalism on an ASEAN+3 rather than an Asia-Pacific basis.

Economically, the Chiang Mai Initiative created credible conditions that only those states that followed responsible policies would receive funds in the event of a currency crisis. Those conditions could at least potentially be made more appropriate to the conditions of the East Asian economies by developing a regional surveillance mechanism through ASEAN+3.

It also addressed the political calculus. Whatever else the AMF may have been—and in my analysis, it was a hastily and poorly constructed concept that would have contributed to regional financial instability—it constituted a direct challenge to the authority of the IMF and the structural power of the United States.[28] But Japan was in no position to buck global standards and act as a leader for East Asia in the absence of support from both its greatest regional rival (China) and its closest global ally (the United States). Moreover, Japanese policymakers had not properly thought through the issue of Japan's political exposure—and thus costs—if it were to be in a position of responsibility for approving or disapproving fund provision. Practically speaking, there could be no decision-making process in a regional organization that would simultaneously be effective in avoiding internal rivalries between Japan and China, credible in addressing moral hazard, and reassuring to the United States.

The Chiang Mai Initiative effectively delegated decision making to the IMF, which had the beneficial effects to Japan of reducing its own political exposure and increasing the credibility of the provision of liquidity in a crisis. By doing so, it abandoned the direct challenge to U.S. structural power and thus alienation of its indispensable ally. But the Chiang Mai Initiative should not be understood as simply perpetuating dependence on the IMF or the United States. In fact, it both furthers Japan's objectives of regional insulation and creates the institutional basis for a more credible challenge to IMF management in the next regional crisis.[29] Thus, it increases ASEAN+3 states' leverage over the IMF by creating a credible threat of regional exit from the global regime, and it does so without exposing Japan to the political risks of a direct challenge to the United States or the

[28] Higgott 1998; Bowles 2002; Lee 2006.
[29] Katada 2004.

need to work cooperatively with China to formulate a concerted response to the next crisis.

The Chiang Mai Initiative in Detail

The ASEAN+3 finance ministers announced their decision to create the Chiang Mai Initiative in May 2000, and it was fully in place by the end of 2003. Since then it has more than doubled in size and undergone several modifications.

The central element of CMI is a network of bilateral swap agreements (BSAs) among participants that commit China, Japan, and Korea to support ASEAN5 economies and one another in the event of a currency crisis. BSAs allow crisis countries to borrow predetermined amounts of their counterparts' reserves for ninety days (renewable up to two years) to supplement their own foreign reserves (figure 3.1). In addition to the BSAs, ASEAN countries participate in a multilateral swap agreement known as the ASEAN Swap Arrangement (ASA). Since the amount of money involved in ASA is relatively small (totaling $2 billion, with only a fraction of that available to any one country), the rest of this discussion focuses on BSAs.[30]

In a typical CMI swap, the crisis country would borrow U.S. dollars from its CMI counterparts (including the ASA for ASEAN members), in exchange for which the crisis country would transfer an equivalent amount of its own currency to the lenders for the duration of the swap.[31] If less than the maximum swap amount is drawn, all lenders would provide an identical proportion of their agreed swap lines.[32] At the end of the swap period, the crisis country is required to return the dollars with interest (set at the IMF

[30]The exact provisions of ASA are somewhat opaque. The most recent public document regarding how much foreign exchange a crisis economy can access is from 1992, when the ASA totaled only $200 million, and I have yet to find a U.S., Japanese, or IMF official who can provide more up-to-date information. In 1992 the maximum amount available was $80 million for one country, with no single country required to provide more than $40 million. If those ratios still hold, the maximum a single ASEAN state could now draw would be $800 million. "Fifth Supplementary Agreement to the Memorandum of Understanding on ASEAN Swap Arrangement, 19 September 1992." http://www.aseansec.org/6305.htm.

[31]A small number of BSAs do not involve U.S. dollars. As of fall 2007, they were the China-Japan, China-Korea, China-Philippines, and Japan-Korea BSAs, all of which are local-currency swaps. But the basic story is the same in all cases.

[32]For example, as of fall 2007, the Philippines had BSAs with China ($2 billion), Japan ($6 billion), and South Korea ($1.5 billion) in addition to its access to ASA funds (which for the sake of clarity I assume to be $800 million, as noted above). If it drew one-half of the maximum (approximately $5 billion), the swaps would be carried out as $1 billion from China, $3 billion from Japan, $750 million from South Korea, and $400 million from ASA. (ASA swaps are divided among the participating lenders—in principle, that means equal contributions from the other nine ASEAN members, but in the event that more than one member is experiencing balance of payments difficulties there may be fewer contributors or some contributors may not be willing to offer the same amount of funds.) The original 1976

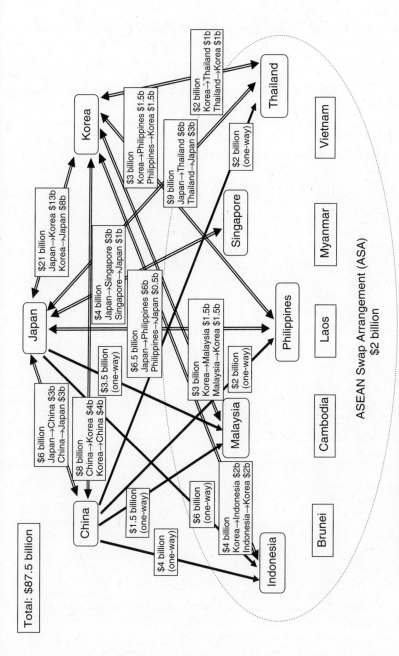

Total: $87.5 billion

$6 billion
Japan→China $3b
China→Japan $3b

$8 billion
China→Korea $4b
Korea→China $4b

$1.5 billion
(one-way)

$6 billion
(one-way)

$4 billion
Korea→Indonesia $2b
Indonesia→Korea $2b

$4 billion
(one-way)

$3.5 billion
(one-way)

$3 billion
Korea→Malaysia $1.5b
Malaysia→Korea $1.5b

$2 billion
(one-way)

$6.5 billion
Japan→Philippines $6b
Philippines→Japan $0.5b

$4 billion
Japan→Singapore $3b
Singapore→Japan $1b

$21 billion
Japan→Korea $13b
Korea→Japan $8b

$3 billion
Korea→Philippines $1.5b
Philippines→Korea $1.5b

$9 billion
Japan→Thailand $6b
Thailand→Japan $3b

$2 billion
Korea→Thailand $1b
Thailand→Korea $1b

$2 billion
(one-way)

Brunei   Cambodia   Laos   Myanmar   Vietnam

China   Japan   Korea   Malaysia   Philippines   Singapore   Thailand   Indonesia

ASEAN Swap Arrangement (ASA)
$2 billion

1. One-way arrows denote one-way swaps; two-way arrows denote two-way swaps.
2. This figure does not distinguish between dollar-based and dollar-equivalent local-currency BSAs.
3. Malaysia-Japan BSA includes New Miyazawa swap ($2.5 billion).
4. Total includes all BSAs (including New Miyazawa) plus ASA.
5. Japan-China BSA is local-currency swap between central banks; $6 billion of Japan-Korea ($3 billion each way) is local-currency
   central bank swap agreement.

Figure 3.1. Chiang Mai Initiative Bilateral Swap Network (as of October 2007).
Source: Ministry of Finance of Japan.

drawing rate),[33] in exchange for the return of its own currency. If a member country experiences a currency crisis, it can draw on these funds rapidly during the period in which it is negotiating an IMF standby agreement. CMI functions purely on a request basis, and in principle it carries no policy conditions for borrowers.[34]

Despite the general characterization of CMI as a swap network, it should be understood that the agreements themselves were not uniform as of early 2008. Initially, many of the BSAs were one-way—in other words, one party was obligated to provide hard currency (usually dollars) to the other but not vice versa. Following the 2005 Istanbul agreement of the ASEAN+3 finance ministers, all BSAs were supposed to be transformed into two-way agreements, although as of early 2008, six of sixteen were still one-way, including Japan's BSAs with Malaysia and Indonesia and all of China's BSAs with ASEAN states. As a further complication, two-way agreements, while reciprocal in principle, are often asymmetric. For example, Japan has committed considerably more than its CMI counterparts in all of its BSAs other than Japan–China. The reason for this is simple: developing economies (particularly the ASEAN economies) are not in a position to commit significant portions of their foreign exchange reserves to their regional partners, whether for prudential or legal reasons.[35] In most cases, the parties pledge

---

ASEAN Swap Agreement and some of the subsequent renewals and modifications are available online at http://www.aseansec.org/6321.htm.

[33] Use of the IMF rate has been an irritation to the CMI's ASEAN members, for two reasons. First, they dislike the symbolism. Second, they are concerned that the IMF rate is excessively high. This is not an unreasonable objection. The IMF drawing rate is calculated based on actual costs of funds plus IMF overhead. The demand for IMF lending has been falling in recent years and its overhead has not been, so the rate is substantially higher than the financing costs of CMI lender governments and central banks. The potential creditors, such as Japan and China, argue that designation of the IMF rate reflects the risk they are taking, is simpler than negotiating some CMI-specific or country-specific formula, is typical of actual bailouts, and reflects the fact that CMI is meant to be complementary to IMF. When I suggested in 2005 to a MOF official that a fifth reason might be the utility of a penalty rate, he quickly denied it. I remain unconvinced.

[34] In fact, since full release of BSAs depends on good-faith negotiations with the IMF, IMF conditions can be seen for practical purposes as CMI conditions as well. If IMF certification of good-faith negotiations is not obtained, crisis countries can request up to 20% of their BSA lines, but in that case there is no requirement for the counterparty to provide those funds. This creates de facto conditionality.

[35] I was told by a Japanese official in 2005 that as a matter of national pride, Prime Minister Thaksin of Thailand had insisted on making all Thailand's post-Istanbul agreements symmetrical. My source stated that this was significantly complicating negotiations for renewal of their BSA. The BSA that was completed in 2005 was indeed symmetrical, obligating both parties to provide $3 billion in case of crisis. Interestingly, after the removal of Thaksin, the Japan-Thailand BSA was renegotiated, with the 2007 agreement stipulating a $3 billion Thai obligation as opposed to a $6 billion Japanese obligation. "Agreement of the Third Bilateral Swap Arrangement between Japan and Thailand under the Chiang Mai Initiative," joint press statement by the Japanese and Thai ministries of finance, the Bank of Japan, and the

to provide U.S. dollars to crisis economies. An exception is China, which has insisted on the use of only local currencies in several of its agreements, although the sums are calculated as a dollar equivalent. In principle, the participants have committed to a shift at some future point to purely local-currency swaps, but this has not yet occurred, nor does it seem very practical other than for Japan, whose yen is widely traded in exchange markets. In the extreme, the distinction appears nonsensical, as can be illustrated with the example of China, whose currency is nonconvertible. If China were to provide its pledged $1 billion worth of RMB to the Philippines in the event of a crisis, those RMB would immediately need to be exchanged *through the People's Bank of China itself* for dollars with which to intervene in currency markets on behalf of the peso.

In terms of overall magnitude, CMI appears comparable in funding to the failed Japanese proposal for an Asian monetary fund in 1997, with the sum of all the commitments under the swap arrangements now well exceeding $80 billion.[36] In fact, references to total amounts under CMI are misleading for two reasons: (1) no potential crisis country has access to the total or even half of the total, and (2) two-way agreements are double counted (e.g., the Japan-China BSA is labeled as $6 billion, but in fact each country has pledged the other $3 billion). Nonetheless, countries facing a speculative attack, even without having an actual IMF standby agreement in effect or having to negotiate with third parties, will have funds available to them under the CMI in amounts that easily dwarf their IMF quotas. The Philippines, for example, has access to $9.5 billion through CMI (not including ASA funds), or about seven times its IMF quota of SDR 880 million (approximately $1.3 billion).

Decision Rules and Conditions

While the AMF proposal was presented as a means of providing funds rapidly with minimal conditions, that is not the case for the Chiang Mai Initiative. CMI makes use of two forms of conditionality and a process of

Bank of Thailand, July 10, 2007. http://www.mof.go.jp/english/if/070710press_release.pdf, accessed August 17, 2007.

[36] Confusingly, the CMI figures include local-currency "peacetime bilateral swap arrangements" equivalent to $6 billion apiece that the Bank of Japan has concluded with its counterparts in China and Korea to provide emergency liquidity in a non–currency crisis emergencies, such as a terrorist attack or a natural disaster. In Japan's BSAs with ASEAN governments, it is the Japanese Ministry of Finance that is the contracting party. The fact that Japan's swap agreements with China and Korea are under the jurisdiction of the Bank of Japan instead of MOF is the reason why they are yen based instead of dollar based. For details of the respective roles of MOF and the BOJ in currency management, see Grimes 2001, chap. 3.

multilateral surveillance in an effort to reduce the problem of moral hazard.[37] The most important of these is the IMF link, which dictates that only 20 percent of funds (originally 10%) can be released without the approval of the IMF.[38] This does not mean that an IMF agreement must have already been reached—only that the IMF certifies that the crisis country is negotiating a standby agreement in good faith. Thus, instead of the one-month lag typically involved in preparing and agreeing on an IMF plan, funds can be released in days. While CMI allows for rapid and massive provision of emergency liquidity, the IMF link provides conditionality for CMI funds and eliminates the need for CMI creditor states to decide whether to release funds and under what conditions.

Clearly, a great deal of decision-making authority has been delegated to the IMF. But there is also a less publicized aspect of enforcement. In fact, as of early 2008, it had not been acknowledged publicly by any of the participating governments:[39] the BSAs contain performance criteria that function as preconditions for release of CMI funds. Preconditions are meant to ensure that economies do not fall into crises and that if they do it is not their fault. The existence of performance criteria is important because it demonstrates that creditor governments are indeed concerned about moral hazard, despite rhetoric to the contrary.

The exact content of these performance criteria varies from agreement to agreement. Japan's original BSAs typically stipulated minimum levels of foreign exchange reserves.[40] In most cases, the stipulated level of reserves was designated as a number of months' worth (usually three or four) of imports, but some of the earlier agreements had absolute levels. (It should be noted that ASEAN+3 countries' foreign exchange reserves as of mid-2006 were much higher than three to four months' worth of imports. They ranged from nearly 15% of GDP for Indonesia to over 100% of GDP for Singapore.) In the 2005–07 renegotiation of BSAs, Japanese negotiators

---

[37] Many of the specifics of how CMI works have not been laid out clearly in public documents. For that reason, I have relied on extensive interviews and discussions with Japanese, U.S., and international officials to obtain and confirm details.

[38] The ASEAN+3 finance ministers' 2005 Istanbul agreement [para. 6(II)] alludes to "other disciplined conditions" in addition to the IMF link. Interestingly, the Japan-China BSA does not include the IMF link.

[39] As far as I know, Grimes 2006, 361, is the first place that the existence of these preconditions has been published in any language. I was informed of it by several interviewees in Japan, but only one gave me permission to publish, albeit without indicating the interviewee's name or position. It appears not to have been known even to key Japanese advisory council participants or to the U.S. Treasury prior to the summer of 2005. The admission to me may have been meant as an intentional indirect leak of a reassuring fact to U.S. Treasury officials, or perhaps it was assumed that the lengthiness of the academic publishing schedule would mean that the information would already be public before I got it published.

[40] I have been told that there are additional conditions, but specifics were not made available to me and there is no obvious way to confirm what they may be.

sought to convert all the agreements that had absolute levels to ones that reflected actual import needs. At least as of 2005, the foreign exchange reserve requirements were not standardized among CMI swap agreements, although one cryptic part of the Istanbul agreement appeared to call for such standardization.[41] Indeed, the varying performance criteria are formally maintained as secrets even within ASEAN+3 in order to prevent stigmatization of states that must meet tougher conditions, but they are apparently a very open secret among participants. Performance criteria are an obstacle (albeit a minor one) to true multilateralization of CMI, since there is no uniformity of basic conditions.

Surveillance

The third mechanism meant to avert moral hazard is a process of multilateral surveillance known formally as "economic review and policy dialogue" (ERPD).[42] ASEAN+3's policy dialogue constitutes the first serious experiment with multilateral surveillance among the East Asian economies, and in this sense it qualifies as a milestone in the development of regional institutions.[43] Surveillance is a necessary (albeit not sufficient) condition for effective international macroeconomic policy coordination, although this appears to be jumping the gun a bit in the East Asian context. But economic review and policy dialogue can be useful for less ambitious purposes as well. By improving transparency, it can reduce surprises for regional policymakers. It also improves channels of communication, which can be crucial in times of crisis—indeed, one of the most common themes I have come across when discussing the Asian Financial Crisis with policymakers has been that when the crisis hit they did not even know whom to call in other East Asian finance ministries and central banks to discuss what was going on and what the regional implications might be. In a sense, East Asian financial policy networks in 1997 could be seen as an IMF-based version of the U.S. hub-and-spokes alliance system in East Asia. That clearly is no longer the case.

There appears to be unanimity of opinion among Japanese policymakers and close observers that the development of surveillance is of central importance to the development of CMI and of ASEAN+3 financial development

[41] Paragraph 6(II) of the Istanbul agreement calls for "clear-defining of the swap activation process."

[42] Kuroda and Kawai 2003, 13–18, although somewhat out of date, provides a picture of the development of surveillance in the ASEAN+3 as well as more minor surveillance efforts such as those of EMEAP.

[43] I am grateful to several participants in my November 14, 2006, author's conference in Tokyo, especially Toyoo Gyohten, for impressing upon me the importance of surveillance despite the lack of an enforcement mechanism.

more generally.[44] Since 2004, when a decision was made to unify the over-all ASEAN+3 policy dialogue with that of the Chiang Mai Initiative, ERPD has been the main venue for regional macroeconomic and financial surveillance. Formal economic review and policy dialogue occurs in the context of the annual meetings of the ASEAN+3 finance ministers, as well as the semiannual meetings of deputy finance ministers and deputy central bank governors. In early years, policy dialogue was fairly loosely structured, but this has changed over time.[45] Currently, the ADB governor leads off the finance ministers' meeting, which coincides with the annual meeting of the Asian Development Bank, with a discussion of regional conditions and challenges at the ministers' meeting; at other meetings, a senior ADB official contributes. Over time, it is said that there has been a move away from an emphasis on country presentations toward shorter, more regionally oriented presentations framing substantive discussions.[46] Since December 2005, IMF representatives have also had a role at meetings, serving not only as a reference on individual countries (presumably the IMF's forte, given the thoroughness of IMF Article IV surveillance) but also giving a perspective on regional issues and the ongoing discussions led by the IMF on global imbalances. Finally, the 2006 Hyderabad agreement formally called for the inclusion of outside experts in policy dialogue, in the form of a new Group of Experts and a Technical Working Group on Economic and Financial Monitoring. These are in addition to the ADB's ASEAN Surveillance Process efforts and research projects chartered annually since 2003 by the ASEAN+3 and carried out by think tanks and other research groups based in member countries. Practically speaking, surveillance is an ongoing process, with economic conditions an important point of discussion in the working-level meetings that typically meet every two to three months, as well as in communications that occur between meetings or when significant developments arise.[47]

In the specific context of Chiang Mai, surveillance is meant to prevent countries from following policies that might invite speculative attacks on the currency. Surveillance provides no *formal* enforcement mechanism beyond

[44]I base this on at least two dozen interviews and discussions in 2005 and 2006, as well as a variety of Japanese and ASEAN+3 briefing documents. See also Kuroda and Kawai 2003; Girardin 2004; Kawai 2005; Kawai and Takagi 2005.

[45]There is relatively little documentary evidence on ASEAN+3 surveillance, aside from brief mentions in ASEAN+3 finance ministers' statements on the Japanese Ministry of Finance webpage (with more detail in Japanese than in English). Most of the specifics noted here, such as they are, come from personal interviews and communications with working-level participants in 2005–07. See also Kuroda and Kawai 2003, 10–16; Ogawa and Kawasaki 2006, 60. The ADB has been involved in trying to improve the quality of regional surveillance—see ADB 2005, 2007.

[46]Again, I am relying on personal communications, as meeting minutes are not available.

[47]Personal interviews with participants in 2005 and 2006.

peer pressure and nonbinding informal cautions. However, participants note an informal sort of gentlemen's agreement: if the representative of a given CMI participant economy (country A) does not make clear his government's disapproval of country B's economic policy, then country A is morally obligated not to reject country B's requests for non–IMF-linked funds on the basis of economic mismanagement.

Obviously, this is a fairly weak mechanism, being essentially norm driven. Aside from the informal nature of this norm, how release of nonlinked funds would work out in practice is actually rather unclear. Although it is often presumed by observers that the 20 percent of CMI swaps not subject to the IMF link would be automatically provided in toto and without conditions to a crisis country, in fact there is no such provision. Nonlinked funds are provided at the discretion of each potential lender government and in principle could have conditions attached.[48] If, for example, an ASEAN participant in CMI were to experience a currency crisis and chose to request nonlinked funds from China, Japan, and South Korea, there is no specific commitment to provide funds at all, nor is there any guarantee that all three of the potential lender governments would have the same response or demand the same conditions.

Even if the gentlemen's agreement were to hold and there had been no prior warning by its counterparts in the context of regional surveillance, the crisis country government still could not be sure that CMI funds would be provided. That is because it would not necessarily be in the interests of either the lender or the crisis country to release them.[49] First, if there were a real crisis, foreign exchange equivalent to 20 percent of existing BSAs would not be sufficient to make a real difference. Second, it is hard to imagine that requests for nonlinked funds would remain secret. To market participants, that would be like blood in the water for sharks: an admission of crisis, but a rejection of IMF conditionality. This would presumably invite redoubled capital flight and speculative attack. For lender governments, it would be highly unattractive either to lend clearly insufficient funds into a crisis or to deny them, despite the gentlemen's agreement. The most likely response from the major creditor governments of Japan, China, and Korea would be informal and concerted pressure on the crisis country government to start negotiating with the IMF. But whether that would be effective is unpredictable. This is a basic flaw in the CMI system from an operational point of view. Although such a situation is unlikely to occur, given that all the participants understand these points, the possibility remains a concern for all of them.[50]

[48] Personal interviews with working-level participants, 2005 and 2006.
[49] Personal interviews.
[50] My interviews with Japanese Ministry of Finance officials associated with regional financial efforts make it clear that they are acutely aware of this flaw.

Development of the Chiang Mai Initiative

The Chiang Mai Initiative has evolved considerably since the official announcement in May 2000. Many observers were initially skeptical of its potential, based on what appeared to be a slow start: it took over three years to complete the full network of BSAs, and even then the amounts were relatively small, there was no consistency among agreements, and the role of the IMF remained in dispute. At the time that CMI guidelines were announced in May 2001, the participants had mandated a review once three years had elapsed. But the finance ministers' actual announcement in May 2004 confirmed the views of many skeptics—as one observer wrote soon after:

> [The review] provided an explicit opportunity for member nations to revisit the idea of an AMF and consider ways to eliminate the current weaknesses in the CMI arrangements. Yet the joint statement by the ASEAN+3 finance ministers issued on 15 May 2004 merely affirmed agreement to "undertake further review of the CMI to explore ways of enhancing its effectiveness" and to establish a working group to conduct this review. In doing so, the group's finance ministers postponed further discussion on the issue of multilateralisation, IMF linkage or fund size until the next ASEAN+3 Finance Ministers Meeting in 2005.[51]

As it turned out, however, the 2004 statement did indeed initiate a two-year-long process of reexamination.

The Istanbul and Hyderabad Agreements

The main results of that reexamination appeared one year later in the ASEAN+3 finance ministers' Istanbul agreement on the Chiang Mai Initiative in May 2005.[52] Additional changes were approved in Hyderabad in 2006, representing the end of the mandated review, but those were more minor. (The potentially more important changes agreed at Kyoto in 2007 are discussed below.) While the finance ministers did not fundamentally change the substance of the initiative, they did agree to several significant decisions regarding the size, rules, and administration of the initiative, which became the basis for renegotiation of existing or expiring BSAs, a process that for Japan lasted until July 2007, when it completed a second revision of its BSA with Thailand. (Since the Chiang Mai Initiative is not based on a truly multilateral swap network, ASEAN+3 ministers' agreements are

---

[51] Amyx 2004b, 7.

[52] The annual meeting of ASEAN+3 finance ministers takes place alongside the ADB's annual meeting, which was held in Istanbul in 2005, in Hyderabad in 2006, and in Kyoto in 2007. The texts of the communiqués can be found at http://www.mof.go.jp/english/if/as3_050504.htm, http://www.mof.go.jp/english/if/as3_060504.htm, and http://www.mof.go.jp/english/if/as3_070505.htm.

not reflected in any given BSA unless the two contracting parties agree to incorporate the changes.)

The most important decision at Istanbul was to approve a doubling of the size of bilateral swap arrangements. While the magnitude of the swap lines would still be insufficient to resolve a crisis of the order of the AFC, by the end of 2007 Chiang Mai swap totals looked like "real money." As a supplement to the already substantial foreign exchange reserves of individual ASEAN+3 countries, they could be expected to have a meaningful impact on currency stability in the region.

Second, the agreement mandated the reduction of the IMF link from 90 to 80 percent of the funds committed. This decision reflected a compromise between ASEAN countries such as Thailand and Malaysia that wanted it to be reduced to 50 percent or even eliminated and the more cautious creditor countries like China and Japan that were content to leave it at 90 percent.[53] The limited shift to which the finance ministers agreed reflected the interests of creditor countries in limiting their exposure, but the fact that the change happened at all also reflected the continued deep-seated resentment of countries that suffered in the Asian Financial Crisis toward the IMF. Interestingly, while ASEAN governments, particularly Thailand and Malaysia, have been publicly in favor of reducing the IMF link much more aggressively, the more likely potential borrower countries of Indonesia and the Philippines have shown less passion for eliminating it. The logic appears to be that the IMF link reduces uncertainty about the availability of funds in a crisis and that speculators would likely be less willing to try to test regional arrangements if they are backed by the credibility of the IMF.[54]

Istanbul also mandated some moves toward multilateralization of networks, such as designating a "coordinating country" whose central bank will aggregate funds and manage swaps in case of an emergency, instead of relying purely on bilateral action. While not publicized, a coordinating country has in fact been designated for each potential crisis country in advance. The one formal requirement is that the coordinating country have a BSA with the crisis country. In other words, ASEAN countries cannot act as CMI coordinators for other ASEAN countries because their financial commitment is in the form of the multilateral ASEAN Swap Arrangement. The ASA, however, has a similar system in place, so in effect, there would be two coordinating central banks if an ASEAN country were to activate CMI. The Hyderabad agreement added minor enhancements to the changes already

---

[53]According to one MOF official with direct knowledge of the discussions, Japan and Korea argued for keeping the percentage of nonlinked funds low, while ASEAN participants called for significant reduction of the IMF link, and Chinese participants stayed on the sidelines. The official suggested that this was due to confusion and bureaucratic politics within China. It is also consistent with leaving Japan to take the unpopular position.

[54]Interviewees were reluctant to go on record about country differences in negotiations.

made in Istanbul. These included some improvements in the means by which funds would be disbursed in a crisis, as well as the establishment of the Group of Experts and Technical Working Group on Economic and Financial Monitoring to improve surveillance.

Finally, the Istanbul agreement established a roadmap divided into three stages for development of the Chiang Mai Initiative.[55] The first stage, beginning in May 2000, was the establishment of CMI and completion of the BSA network. In that stage, CMI was explicitly "supplementary to the global facility [IMF]" and had "no link to regional surveillance." The second stage, beginning after the Istanbul meeting in May 2005, called for "integration of ASEAN+3 surveillance," "introduction of collective decision-making," expansion and standardization of the BSAs and BSA network, and greater effectiveness and discipline. Under the heading "future regional cooperation" (date unspecified) was the agenda of "enhanced surveillance," "multilateralization," "utilization of local currencies," and "intra-regional exchange rate stability." At least in principle, the ASEAN+3 members were committing themselves to enhancing internal decision making and de-linking from the U.S. dollar, problematic though both goals are likely to be. This decision was in line with the broader rhetoric of advancing toward an Asian economic community, giving support to identity-based analyses of regional cooperation.

Kyoto Agreement

At the 2007 ASEAN+3 finance ministers' meeting in Kyoto, the finance ministers announced what appeared to be a major change in the structure of the Chiang Mai Initiative—an agreement to form a reserve pooling arrangement.[56] The term "reserve pooling" implies that states turn over all or part of their foreign exchange reserves to a regional body that manages them and makes them available automatically in the event of a crisis. In fact, most actual instances do not fit that model, and the ASEAN+3 proposal is no exception. Before discussing this innovation further, it is useful to consider the entirety of the finance ministers' statement about it:

> We noted the substantial progress made in the activities of the new Task-force on CMI Multilateralisation. Proceeding with a step-by-step approach, we unanimously agreed in principle that a self-managed reserve pooling arrangement governed by a single contractual agreement is an appropriate form of multilateralisation. We recognised the consensus reached as a

[55] MOF briefing paper entitled "Enhancement of Chiang Mai Initiative (CMI)—2nd Stage" (mimeo, undated, received by author in May 2005). See also Nemoto 2003, which in some ways foreshadowed the Istanbul agreement.

[56] "ASEAN+3 Agree to Cash Swap Scheme: Countries to Pool Reserves for Stability," *Daily Yomiuri,* May 6, 2007, 1.

significant achievement towards an advanced framework of regional liquid-ity support mechanism. We instructed the Deputies to carry out further in-depth studies on the key elements of the multilateralisation of the CMI including surveillance, reserve eligibility, size of commitment, borrowing quota and activation mechanism. Meanwhile, we reiterated our commit-ment to maintain the two core objectives of the CMI, i.e., (i) to address short-term liquidity difficulties in the region and (ii) to supplement the ex-isting international financial arrangements.[57]

As the statement makes clear, the Kyoto meeting produced only an agree-ment to agree, with no action to be taken until there has been significant additional study. Even if the agreed "reserve pooling" does come about, it will not look like the ideal-type. Indeed, the confusingly worded formula-tion of "a self-managed reserve pooling arrangement governed by a single contractual agreement" actually means that each state will continue to man-age its own reserves but there will be a governing agreement regarding the circumstances under which funds will be released.[58] Moreover, that govern-ing agreement has not yet been created. In other words, as of early 2008, there had been no change as a result of the Kyoto agreement. However, participants saw the agreement as important because they believed that a formal precommitment of funds to regional crisis management would re-duce the likelihood that a government might choose not to release funds into a crisis.[59]

All that can meaningfully be said of the Kyoto agreement is that the ASEAN+3 finance ministers remain formally committed to multilateraliza-tion of the swap network; however, without some sort of picture of how decisions will be made, under what circumstances funds can be drawn on, and how much each state can access, we cannot even know what type of commitment is envisioned, much less how realistic it is. Thus, even after Kyoto, the core features of the "reserve pooling" arrangement remained in question, including crisis decision making, harmonization of agreements, and conditions for potential borrowers.

According to the Kyoto joint statement, another major focus of discus-sions was the improvement of surveillance. The Group of Experts and the Technical Working Group have apparently made some reports to the fi-nance ministers, but these had not been made public as of early 2008. Thus, what improved surveillance actually means remains unclear, although there

---

[57]Paragraph 6 of the "Joint Ministerial Statement of the 10th ASEAN+3 Finance Ministers' Meeting," May 5, 2007.

[58]The point about noncollective fund management is clearer in the Japanese version. http://www.mof.go.jp/jouhou/kokkin/as3_190505.htm.

[59]Personal interview with Hiroshi Watanabe, former Japanese vice minister of finance for international affairs, September 16, 2007.

have been efforts managed by the ADB to develop software solutions to give developing country members better ability to assess financial vulnerability.[60] Thus, it is hard to see the Kyoto statement as constituting any kind of major change.

In the end, the key substantive issues are how far the IMF link is going to be reduced and what would happen if a country actually asked for activation of the nonlinked funds. Put simply, a true ASEAN+3 decision-making system for times of crisis does not exist, thus making the IMF link all the more necessary. As we shall see, this condition is likely to hold.

Borrowing Credibility: The Relationship of CMI and IMF

Before we can meaningfully explore the great power politics of the Chiang Mai Initiative, it is first necessary to understand its level of effectiveness and how it affects the economic interests of participants.[61] Thus, we examine issues of institutional design and the bargaining process between potential lender and borrower states.[62] In doing so, it makes sense to focus on the interests of China and Japan, which are the major potential creditors in the CMI arrangement. Given the nature of emergency liquidity provision (i.e., much higher downside risks for borrowers than for creditors and much greater discretion for holders of funds than demanders of funds), institutional design should more closely reflect the interests of likely major creditors than those of potential borrowers.

The design of the Chiang Mai Initiative can best be understood as an effort by likely creditors to borrow credibility at minimal cost.[63] This perspective allows us to clarify Japanese and Chinese interests in terms of monitoring, enforcement, and decision-making mechanisms. Based on this analysis, we can better understand how CMI fits into the emerging strategic landscape of the East Asian and global political economies.

---

[60]ADB 2005, 2007. Japanese MOF officials whom I interviewed in 2006 remained skeptical about its effectiveness in predicting crises.

[61]This section draws heavily on Grimes 2002.

[62]While the AMF proposal and Chiang Mai Initiative have so far not been heavily studied by political scientists (despite exceptions such as Katada 2001; Henning 2002; Grimes 2003a, 2003b, 2006; Amyx 2004; Sohn 2005, 2007; Hayashi 2006; Lee 2006), a great deal has been written on the institutions that underlie the global financial system. Also, the rational-choice institutionalist literature (Hall and Taylor 1996; North 1990; Aggarwal, 1998) has a great deal to say about both institutional design and states' preferences, which can help us to understand the halting process of Asian regional monetary arrangements. (For one influential synthesis, see Koremenos, Lipson, and Snidal 2001.)

[63]This idea is developed at length in Grimes 2002. See also Grimes 2006.

Coordination and Public Goods

The core problem in any discussion of finance or money is that a stable system of exchange constitutes a public good, and hence is liable to be underprovided.[64] Coordination problems arise at two levels: agreement and enforcement. In analyzing the Chiang Mai Initiative, the key design issue is how to set up a credible means of enforcement. In most if not all regimes, effective enforcement of regime norms and rules rests on punishment.[65] In some cases, an international organization may itself be capable of punishing noncooperation (for example, the IMF can withhold assistance to states whose macroeconomic policies are seen as irresponsible),[66] but in general, member states of a regime will be left to sanction members that do not fulfill their obligations. This is most practical when there is a clear leader and when rules and their applicability to a given situation are also clear.[67] Crisis management is particularly difficult, since the stakes are high, decision time is short, and decisions must often be made on the basis of incomplete or ambiguous information.

Credibility, Delegation, and Nesting

Enforcement is ultimately a question of credibility, which is always a potential problem in strategic interactions.[68] In international monetary issues, the credibility problem typically appears in one of two ways. First, a government or central bank of a crisis country might choose not to carry out mandated reforms once international financial institutions and/or other governments have given aid to end the original crisis. Second, donors might choose to bail out an economy even though the government has clearly not lived up to agreed-upon conditions. Whatever the reason, the result is a loss of credibility on the part of donors and the introduction of moral hazard.[69] The

[64] Kapstein 1994; Gilpin 1987; Katada 2001; Cohen 1998a.

[65] This view of the necessity of enforcement holds for both realist and neoliberal analyses. See Keohane 1984; Oye 1986; Stein 1990; Kahler 2000; Koremenos, Lipson, and Snidal 2001. For opposing constructivist viewpoints that emphasize norm-driven behavior and socialization of members, see Ruggie 1993; Wendt 2001; and Johnston 2003b. Young 1989 argues that both are typical of states' behavior within regimes (see especially, 72–77).

[66] Stone 2002.

[67] Snidal 1985 argues that small groups of players ("k-groups") can substitute effectively for a single leader in some cases.

[68] Axelrod 1984; Alt, Calvert, and Humes 1988. Mercer 1996 provides a fairly devastating critique of strong deterministic claims about how reputations are created, based on psychological models of framing. Press 2005 argues that credibility is important but that it depends not on past actions (that is, how counterparts interpret an actor's identity and intentions) but on capabilities and interests.

[69] Stone 2002 highlights political considerations in looking at the former Soviet republics and Eastern Europe.

challenge for institutional design is to create a credible threat that the costs to noncooperation exceed the benefits.[70]

One method of making enforcement more credible is delegation to an autonomous body. Delegation has several potential benefits, including reduction of oversight costs, availability of expertise, and—not least—plausible deniability or blame avoidance. For example, the IMF, World Bank, and regional development banks provide a pool of expertise that generally follows the interests of their dominant members, but without forcing those member states to make political judgments in every case.[71]

Delegation of unpleasant tasks to international organizations allows states to avoid making enforcement decisions, and thus being blamed by governments (or citizens) of countries that perceive themselves to be harmed by those decisions. As long as the organization is enforcing rules that a donor state generally favors, the state benefits by not having to make enforcement decisions on its own. This is presumably particularly true of second-tier powers that have influence but not hegemonic power within the organization (and thus are less likely to be blamed for its actions). Moreover, having the organization as a gatekeeper leaves open the possibility of being more generous when a state's other interests, such as bilateral political relations or the interests of the domestic banking industry, are at stake. Only if a donor state determines that the organization's rules or actual decisions systematically impose large private costs on it or that they reduce the international public good they are meant to maintain will that state seek to drop out or form an alternative.[72] However, the credible threat of undermining or exiting from an organization due to disputes over governance may change the power relations within the existing organization and lead to changes that will advantage the member or members that made the threat.[73]

The creation of a new institution can lead to political disputes among member states of the existing institution if memberships of the old and new institutions are not identical, or if the new institution is formed to remedy the perceived shortcomings of existing institutions. This was clearly in play with the AMF proposal, as well as with CMI. Founders of new international organizations must decide how the new organization will relate to the old

[70]Methods include linkage strategies, specific assets, legalism, limited bilateralization (such as through the WTO dispute-settlement understanding), and extending the length of cooperation. Axelrod and Keohane 1986; Keohane 1984; Oye 1986; Snidal 1985; Aggarwal 1998a, 1998b; Kahler 2000; Koremenos, Lipson, and Snidal 2001.

[71]This is a simplistic picture, but it is sufficient for this discussion. For an extensive analysis, see Woods 2006.

[72]A more likely tactic for most second-tier powers will be voice rather than exit, of course, and there may well be enough like-minded states for that voice to be effective.

[73]Lipscy 2006.

one(s)—in other words, whether to "nest" within or be subordinate to the existing organizations.[74]

The Chiang Mai Initiative and the IMF: Moral Hazard, Delegation, Threat of Exit

Whether and how nesting should occur is complex.[75] But fundamentally, we can boil it down to a single question: How can dominant states design institutions that will provide maximum credibility in achieving a given goal but at minimum cost?

The Chiang Mai Initiative and its various predecessors, including the Asian monetary fund proposal, the Manila Framework, and the New Miyazawa Initiative, have been proposed as institutions of both crisis *prevention* and crisis *resolution*. As noted, Japanese policymakers and economists understood the Asian Financial Crisis to be essentially a liquidity crisis resulting from the fickleness of financial globalization rather than a fundamental crisis resulting from inappropriate policies in crisis economies.[76] Thus, they emphasized that regional arrangements should be based on the assumption that crisis resolution depends on rapid, large-scale provision of liquidity without onerous conditions. In principle, in a pure liquidity crisis, this approach to crisis resolution would be essentially costless, since funds would be paid back on schedule and there would be minimal disruption of regional economies. Crisis prevention at this level is also a simple story: since international investors will be reassured that they will not be damaged by a runaway crisis, they will not withdraw their holdings in a panicked rush to the exits. (Alternatively, ill-intentioned speculators will know that they cannot profit from a panic and will not bet their money on causing one.) In a pure liquidity crisis, prevention and resolution are two sides of the same coin.

The basic story is complicated, however, by the possibility that governments will follow policies that increase their vulnerability to attack if they know they will be bailed out. Access to emergency liquidity without strict conditions in and of itself creates a moral hazard. Regardless of whether or not the AFC economies brought the crisis upon themselves in 1997—and I do not believe they did—a regional institution that would bail them out could easily create an incentive to do so in the future. As Peter Kenen writes, "Conditionality is forward looking, not backward looking. It is concerned

[74]Aggarwal 1998a.

[75]The various essays in Aggarwal 1998 show this clearly. See particularly Aggarwal 1998b; Cohen 1998b.

[76]Foreign Exchange Commission 1999; Nihon Keizai Chōsakai 1998; IIMA 1999; Grimes 2003b; Lee 2006.

with sustainability rather than culpability."[77] Thus, the problem for Japan and China, as East Asia's largest potential providers of funds and the countries in the region least likely to draw on funds to resolve a currency crisis, is how to create both credibility that funds will be provided when a crisis strikes (thus addressing liquidity concerns) *and* credibility that governments that misbehave will *not* be bailed out (thus addressing moral hazard concerns).[78]

Complicating matters further is that Japan, and to a lesser extent China, risk incurring significant political costs if they are blamed for a refusal to provide funds to an economy in crisis, even if the crisis were to have resulted from economic mismanagement.[79] This concern arises for two reasons. First, gaining a reputation for not bailing out mismanaged economies may be politically costly, in that it will likely require refusals to bail out actual economies in actual crises. Second, the reputation of an organization with a small number of members reflects much more directly on individual (especially dominant) members. Japan, as the East Asian state with the largest economy, most developed financial system, and second-highest level of foreign exchange reserves, would necessarily be a dominant player in ASEAN+3 financial cooperation even if it were not a primary driver in institutional design (which, of course, it is). Moreover, those same attributes, as well as its deep economic interests in the economic stability and prosperity of the region, make Japan the state that would be under the greatest international and domestic pressure to commit massive resources in the event of a failure of regional or global attempts at resolution. Quite simply, Japan cannot avoid the economic or political costs of failure at either level and must seek to structure emergency liquidity provisions in such a way as to minimize the likelihood that failure will occur. This story is largely true for China as well, giving the two states rather similar economic interests regarding institutional design.

A relatively easy way to accomplish the two goals of mitigating moral hazard and establishing plausible deniability would be to delegate crisis resolution to a credibly autonomous third party. The problem is that the only viable candidate would be the IMF, which has established and credibility

[77]Kenen 2001, 52.

[78]It might be argued that some of the regional multilateral development banks deal effectively with just this issue of enforcement and blame avoidance, but in fact theirs is a much easier problem to solve. The multilateral development banks lend money on an ongoing basis and are able to solve problems of political confrontation by maintaining relatively constant lending shares to each client. (Gradual changes over time can, of course, lead to large-scale shifts in lending shares.) In contrast, CMI is by its nature meant to be used as little as possible. Even though proportions are set, crisis avoidance rather than loan disbursal is its main criterion for success.

[79]This is especially important for Japan, given its tenuous postcolonial or postoccupation status with many East Asian states. See, e.g., Berger 2007.

expertise and which is not perceived by potential recipient countries to be under the control of Japan (much less China).[80] This would essentially make CMI into an Asian version of the General Arrangements to Borrow (GAB) and its successor, the New Arrangements to Borrow (NAB), which were established by wealthy states to provide back-up funding to the IMF. However, becoming an adjunct to the IMF appears to go against the whole point of regional arrangements. Especially given the post-AFC changes in IMF rules and procedures (in particular the effective elimination of lending limits based on quotas),[81] as well as expectations under the Manila Framework (which was still active at the time CMI was announced) about negotiating second lines of defense, the only plausible reason for creating a regional initiative was to inject the possibility of more regional judgment into how money is used.

The political genius of CMI is to borrow credibility from the IMF (and thus not politically challenge U.S. structural power), while simultaneously creating a viable, if not ideal, exit strategy.[82] In other words, this is a regional hedge that provides leverage against the IMF and United States in times of crisis. Actually creating a regional alternative to the IMF would be costly and very likely noncredible to markets, and it would surely imperil the U.S.-Japan strategic relationship. China too prefers not to antagonize its global partners during its peaceful rise. Moreover, de-linking from the IMF would call for a level of strategic cooperation between Japan and China that is hard to imagine at this point. The ambiguity of the hedge allows use of IMF credibility, while also creating uncertainty about future intentions and thus limiting IMF and U.S. latitude in East Asian crisis management.

Issues for Follower States

For potential borrower economies, the current arrangements might seem less attractive. But due to the inherent asymmetries in vulnerability between likely borrower and lender economies, as well as the difference in sheer scale of economy and foreign exchange reserves, the smaller powers are essentially in a position either to accept or reject deals that work for the big powers. The current configuration of the Chiang Mai Initiative expands the pool of committed funds available in the event of a crisis and streamlines the process by which they can be obtained, without adding any meaningful

[80] There are some doubts about IMF capabilities, as Stone 2002 and others have argued. But the IMF does appear to enjoy considerable credibility in East Asia in the sense that states work hard to avoid borrowing from it (and in recent years have paid their obligations early when they have had to borrow).

[81] I refer here to the Supplemental Reserve Facility. See IMF 2003 for details.

[82] See Cohen 1998b for an imperfect historical parallel in the form of the OECD's financial support fund proposal.

commitments for potentially vulnerable economies or—so far—exposing them to additional pressure from Japan and China. It also creates regional leverage on the IMF to impose less restrictive conditions. Therefore, although they may prefer more truly regional solutions with less conditionality, they have no reason to reject the existing CMI arrangements.

At the same time, governments whose economies were hit by the 1997–98 crisis are not taking any more chances than they need to by relying simply on CMI funds (and thus potential monetary entrapment by Japan or China); rather, as discussed further in chapter 4, they have been involved in a massive buildup of reserves, part of which can be understood as an expensive hedge against CMI failure and dependence on the global financial institutions. Despite the considerable economic costs of maintaining such high reserves, they are at least partly an investment in reducing monetary dependence. Even if the Chiang Mai Initiative were to evolve into a true reserve pooling arrangement at its current level, members might well continue this strategy of self-help.

Effects on Broader ASEAN+3 Cooperation

Another issue for follower states is how CMI decision making links to the broader picture of ASEAN+3 cooperation. Currently, CMI crisis decision making is defined by the IMF link. Meanwhile, noncrisis decision making in CMI and other areas of ASEAN+3 cooperation is on a consensus basis.[83] This builds on the basic ASEAN principles of consensus and nonintervention, also known as the ASEAN Way. A reasonable case can be made for maintaining these principles within CMI during noncrisis periods—after all, this is a small and potentially fractious group of states characterized by rivalry between potential leaders and conflicted interests among followers, a situation that calls for maximum buy-in by members. Although consensus may make for slower progress than other alternatives, the trade-off is for harmony, which regional states seem to value.

But in the face of a currency crisis, decision making by consensus is dysfunctional. On the one hand, it raises the possibility of paralysis if a minority of members (or even one member) opposes a given action. On the other hand, it may create intense pressures on dissenting states for consensus. In either case, it is easy to imagine political tensions between member states spilling over into economic crisis management if it were not for the existence of the IMF link. Sino-Japanese disagreements would be the most difficult to manage if they were to arise, not only because of their broader salience for regional peace and stability, but also due to the central role of the two states in crisis management.

[83] Suzuki 2004.

While various voting systems could contribute to clearer and more timely decisions,[84] none of them would be attractive to the ASEAN states as a precedent for other areas of cooperation. Any formal voting procedure would run the risk of creating or reinforcing cleavages among members, as would the process of assigning voting shares or veto privileges. The Kyoto reserve pooling agreement does presuppose weighted voting, but there is as yet no agreement on how it would work in terms of weights, veto rights, or supermajorities.[85] This appears likely to be a major sticking point in achieving even the limited nature of reserve pooling to which the agreement aspires. Moreover, the establishment of crisis-period voting would likely raise pressures for identical, or at least similar, noncrisis procedures in other areas of cooperation, fundamentally changing the character of the ASEAN+3, and potentially creating pressures for change within ASEAN itself.[86] This would not be an attractive prospect for the ASEAN states. Moreover, none of the plausible alternatives would solve the basic problems of crisis decision making—to avoid incentives that lead to moral hazard and to prevent Sino-Japanese rivalry from impeding crisis resolution.

A seemingly different possibility would be the establishment of an ASEAN+3-based regional organization with the expertise and autonomy to make decisions on bailouts, including perhaps even imposing conditionality.[87] (This would presumably have to be a new organization, since the Asian Development Bank operates under a U.S. veto and its members include a large number of other non–East Asian economies.) However, the preponderance of Japan and China in any such organization would make it impossible for them to disassociate themselves from a decision, no matter how articulated and technocratic that organization became. Instead, they should prefer to precommit to a joint position in order to reduce the temptation to undercut the other for short-term political benefit. For both, then, the political imperative is clearly to borrow credibility from the IMF or other third party.

These problems also apply to noncrisis-period surveillance, particularly if preconditionality is to be understood as a basic principle of CMI. Stricter

[84]These include simple majority, supermajority, weighted voting, or a combination of supermajority and weighted voting (as exists in the IMF and World Bank, for example). Voting rules could also be combined with the designation of specific veto rights. All of these procedural rules involve potentially divisive choices, since they assign power and privilege within the organization.

[85]Personal interview with former vice-minister Hiroshi Watanabe, September 16, 2007.

[86]Suzuki 2004 makes two points that are relevant to this discussion. First, it makes clear just how pervasive the consensus principle is throughout the ASEAN+3. Second, it demonstrates that partial consensus is in fact possible in the form of creating partial agreements—either ASEAN, or ASEAN+2, or just "+3." However, partial consensus does not apply to the Chiang Mai Initiative for two reasons: it is already established on an ASEAN5+3 basis, and the nature of emergency liquidity provision requires collective action.

[87]For an action plan created under an ADB study group, see Girardin 2004, 84–92.

and more institutionalized regional surveillance has been suggested as a means of reducing moral hazard by clarifying expectations of about regional help,[88] but here again basic problems come to the fore. For one thing, regional preconditionality would be infeasible for the same reasons the IMF's Contingent Credit Line was infeasible—removal of a state's pre-approval for emergency finance due to inappropriate policies would likely occasion a run on the currency.[89] Thus, the ASEAN+3 as a whole (with Japan at the center, presumably) would have to choose between instigating a crisis and accepting policy mismanagement that could eventually lead to a crisis. Operationally, stricter surveillance would be implemented by an "autonomous" regional organization, or it would depend on the willingness of individual members to enforce norms of good economic management. Institutionalization would not provide meaningful deniability to Japan and China for politically unpalatable decisions, but paradoxically it could reduce their actual control over their own funds—the very source of both their regional currency power and their ability to improve economic stability in the region. Indeed, practically speaking, the existence of the CMI swap lines and the lingering uncertainty over whether they would be disbursed in a crisis is more likely to make surveillance meaningful in terms of affecting the policies of potential crisis economies than the other way around.

The problem remains—probably irreducibly—that the United States and the IMF may not care sufficiently about East Asian problems to suit the CMI participants.[90] Although borrowing credibility from the IMF addresses the moral hazard problem, the IMF link does not guarantee that regional governments will see eye to eye with either the IMF or the United States regarding the proper actions to resolve a future crisis. The threat of a regional hedge, however, provides some leverage, and the ambiguity of that hedge may be particularly valuable.

The Chiang Mai Initiative and the Strategic Triangle

Moving beyond the issues of efficacy and institutional design, it must be remembered that the Chiang Mai Initiative operates within a political context and has political implications. To get the politics "right," it is essential

[88] This was a common theme in my interviews with Japanese policymakers in 2005 and 2006. See also the recommendations of the Kobe Research Project (IIMA 2002a), 12–16.

[89] ERPD is in principle not public, and decisions about preconditionality could also be designated as nonpublic information. It is hard not to imagine leaks, however.

[90] Katada 2001 argues that this is due to the constellation of transnational private sector financial interests, which make U.S. connections with Asia much less close than those of Japan.

to understand what opportunities and constraints CMI creates in the context of the strategic triangle among Japan, China, and the United States. By virtue of its unique position "between Asia and the West" and as the key source of ideas about regional liquidity provision,[91] Japan is the pivotal player and will receive the greatest (though not exclusive) focus in the rest of this chapter. In its overall strategic environment, Japan faces the challenges of the relative rise of China, alliance management with the United States, and the growing economic integration of East Asia.

The Chiang Mai Initiative as Regional Hedge

The Chiang Mai Initiative can be read as a regional hedge against overreliance on the IMF and United States to solve currency crises.[92] This is clear from the history that links CMI to the 1997 AMF proposal via the Manila Framework and the New Miyazawa Initiative. Certainly the ASEAN states have perceived it as a means of reducing dependence on the IMF and have accordingly sought to eliminate the IMF link and increase regional decision making. The concept of hedging is also a useful means of explaining Japanese actions. The Japanese government understood in 1997 that the process and conditionality involved in obtaining an IMF standby agreement were problematic for the crisis economies. But despite its role as second largest quota-holder in the IMF, Japan was not in a position to do anything to change either the pace of the negotiations or the terms of the agreements.

For Japan, the Chiang Mai Initiative also fits into longer-term attempts to insulate its domestic economy from currency vulnerability. After the Asian Financial Crisis, Japanese financial policymakers decided to look to regionally based insulation, reasoning that Japan's vulnerability to dollar politics could be reduced by increasing the use of the yen in international transactions.[93] While the primary focus of this strategy has been to try to increase the correlation between the yen and regional currencies, CMI has become an integral part of the effort to support greater regional currency cooperation.

Chiang Mai constitutes both a hedge and a lever for Japan. As a hedge, it reduces reliance on IMF conditionality and eliminates the need to secure funding for its regional economic partners from the United States in the event of an emergency. It also provides a lever for Japan and its partners vis-à-vis the IMF. While the IMF currently has the de facto capability to trigger release of CMI funds, the existence of a swap network that exceeds

[91] To borrow from the title of Wan 2001. See also Hayashi 2006.
[92] See also Katada 2004.
[93] Grimes 1999, 2003a, 2003b.

funds available from the IMF constitutes an implicit threat that CMI could be rapidly transformed from a complement into a regional substitute for the fund.[94] If a currency crisis were to recur in East Asia, this would likely have a powerful influence on the conditions that the IMF (and the United States as largest quota-holder) might choose to impose. Never again do the ASEAN+3 states want to experience conditions as intrusive as those imposed by the IMF during the Asian Financial Crisis, many of which were seen as an opportunistic ploy by the United States to push an unrelated political agenda at a time when the states had little choice but to agree.[95] The Chiang Mai Initiative also serves as the basis for a potential voting bloc within the IMF. Together, the leverage created by CMI as a form of collective action among the East Asian economies raises the possibility of advancing an East Asian agenda within the IMF that corresponds with Japan's own interests.[96]

Squaring Hedge with Commitment:
The U.S.-Japan Alliance

As in other aspects of East Asian economic regionalism, a basic strategic issue for Japan is how to square its de facto economic hedge against the United States with its continuing security dependence and political alignment.[97] The long-run maintenance of U.S. interest in East Asian stability and in keeping Japan from falling under the sway of Chinese hegemony is widely presumed to depend on the continuation of U.S. economic interests in the region.[98] Moreover, the region generally is heavily dependent on trade with the United States. Meanwhile, Japan's economic interests in

[94]Cohen's 1998b analysis of the attempt of the OECD to create a $25 billion financial-support fund in the mid-1970s suggests a parallel. The fund was proposed "strictly as a back-up to the IMF rather than as an alternative" (178). Nonetheless, "with $25 billion at its disposal, the FSF threatened to eclipse the activities of the IMF, whose loanable resources at the time were nearing exhaustion. The IMF suddenly faced the prospect of a formidable regional rival" (161).

[95]Wade 1998; Bello 1998; Stiglitz 2002.

[96]Such an agenda would presumably include the major elements of agreement among East Asian governments regarding the international financial architecture, including, inter alia, more proportionate quotas, recognition of the legitimacy of capital controls as a macroeconomic policy tool, greater respect for currency-basket systems and other forms of managed float, and more symmetric responsibility for payments imbalances. I am not arguing that these are necessarily bad ideas from the standpoint of global welfare, stability, or fairness, but they do tend to go against the general goals of the U.S. government within the IMF. That means conflict at some level.

[97]Many analysts (see, e.g., Green 2001, 2002) agreed that Japan's security dependence (and U.S. focus on Japan as an essential ally) waned considerably after the end of the cold war, and indeed that period coincided with some of the most contentious episodes in the bilateral relationship. The rapid rise of China has been a major force in refocusing both sides on political and military cooperation. Samuels 2007.

[98]See, for example, Armitage and Nye 2007.

a variety of nonmonetary economic areas have increasingly converged with the United States and other developed economies—within East Asia, that means free trade, openness to investment and other financial activities, protection of intellectual property, and nondiscrimination against multinational corporations, among others.[99] This means that U.S. structural power in the economic realm, albeit not necessarily its role in shaping IMF policies, has become generally beneficial from a Japanese point of view.

Thus Japan has a strong incentive to keep the United States engaged in East Asia even as it seeks to hedge its dependence and to build its own independent power base in the region. In the context of the Chiang Mai Initiative, where it is indeed a leader and where some of its interests differ considerably from those of the United States, it must work both to exclude the United States from interfering with decision making and institutional development and to keep the swap network from becoming a flashpoint in bilateral relations. Fortunately for Japan, the IMF link goes a long way toward reconciling its interest as a creditor in avoiding blame and preventing moral hazard, on the one hand, with U.S. concerns about undermining the IMF, on the other. In this case, the regional hedge does not get directly in the way of the bilateral commitment. However, it does provide a low-key form of leverage that threatens to kick in if Japanese interests are not heeded in regional bailouts or discussion of the international financial architecture.

China and Japan

How does CMI fit into the path that Japan must wend between its U.S. ally and Chinese regional partner? Looked at purely from a functional point of view, the China-Japan relationship adds no additional complication to the story presented above. As I have argued, the interests of the two dominant regional economic powers converge in their desire to ensure rapid and massive liquidity provision in a crisis, prevent moral hazard, and avoid the political costs of establishing credibility in achieving the first two ends.

However, CMI also creates a potential battleground for broader issues in the strategic triangle. It is conceivable that CMI could become a wedge issue for China in a larger-scale assault on Japanese regional leadership. At the least, it could be a useful lever with which to exert political pressure. Given the strongly stated preferences of the ASEAN participants for making CMI fund disbursement more automatic and less linked to the IMF, either Japan or China could gain political benefit in the region by supporting elimination of the IMF link. (This would have to be a political calculation, since significant dangers of moral hazard, and thus potential economic costs for

[99]See, for example, MOFA 2006, especially 167–69.

creditors, would ensue.) If either made such a move, it would put the other in the position of either hurting its economic interests by agreeing or hurting its political interests by refusing. In principle, the expectation that the other state would veto the change might make it appear that there would be political gains at no economic cost (in other words, first-mover advantage) to making such a proposal, thus creating an incentive to do so quickly. But potential dangers of such a tactic would include uncertainty about the other state's response, the possibility that a serious proposal could add to organizational momentum to force the change at a later date, and the possibility of being considered disingenuous or cynical by Southeast Asian governments. To make such a proposal in the first place, a state would have to be willing to take a chance on actually eliminating the link.[100]

Although in principle Japan could embark on such a gambit, practically speaking it could be used only by China. If Japan put forward a new proposal for an Asian monetary fund, it would be costly, not only in a potential economic sense, but also in an actual political sense, since it would be an implicit attack on U.S. interests. Given Japan's desire to keep the United States engaged in East Asia both economically and politically, that would be a dangerous move. Moreover, as the richest CMI participant, Japan would find itself expected to bear the brunt of the shift in substance. But if China were to initiate the process, it would not have to worry about jeopardizing an alliance with the United States or (probably) increasing its own burden in the event of a crisis. In other words, while China would incur low political costs by initiating a shift to an Asian monetary fund or going along with a Japanese initiative, Japan would incur significant costs.

If China were willing to risk eliminating the IMF link for political gain, Japan would have to choose between injuring its economic interests and its relationship with the United States, while shoring up its relationships with ASEAN states by agreeing, or defending its economic interests and its relationship with the United States, while injuring its relations with ASEAN states by refusing. Only if the other CMI participants saw China's move as a cynical ploy to gain power in the region might they be forgiving of a decision by Japan to defend its interests and its alliance with the United States by vetoing elimination of the IMF link.

Thus, the strategic triangle significantly complicates Japanese calculations regarding the Chiang Mai Initiative. While CMI provides economic functionality and some useful hedges and levers, on the one hand, and reassurance, on the other, vis-à-vis the IMF and United States, it also creates a strategic vulnerability to Chinese action.

---

[100]Schelling 1966, 92–99, remains the classic statement of how things can get out of hand in such situations.

Effects of the Chiang Mai Initiative on Follower States

For the ASEAN4 states, the debate over the Chiang Mai Initiative understandably hits close to home. They are, after all, the economies that the initiative is designed to protect against the threat of currency crisis. Given the power asymmetries within ASEAN+3, as well as the asymmetries inherent in the relationship between crisis borrowers and lenders, they are not the central players in institutional design. Nonetheless, they are essential as veto players, and their interests are significantly affected by both the politics and economics of financial regionalism.

Economically, the potential borrower countries want to ensure ready access to liquidity with minimal conditions, and they want regional arrangements to constrain the IMF rather than the other way around. Although they would prefer to reduce or eliminate the IMF link, they are not in a position to do more than to encourage Japan and China to do so. The current CMI configuration does provide benefits from their point of view, both in terms of expanding the pool of funds that could be used for a bailout and in providing pressure on the IMF not to impose excessively harsh conditions. At the same time, their extraordinarily high current levels of foreign exchange reserves partly reflect their unwillingness to trust either the IMF or their ASEAN+3 partners to help in an emergency.

Politically, the Chiang Mai Initiative contributes to broader efforts to lock China and Japan into cooperative regional management. Both the ASEAN states and South Korea have benefited strategically from a situation in which the United States, Japan, and China are trying to maintain their favor rather than being subject to the hegemony of one major power or the conflicts of two. Thus, they must be sensitive to the concerns of the United States even as they seek to reduce their reliance on the IMF. In this sense, the subtle regional hedge that the CMI currently constitutes is very much in their interests. They should also be very cautious about providing space for a cleavage between Japan and China in the CMI context, both because of the potential effects on the roles of Japan and the United States in the region and because it could disrupt access to funds in the event of a crisis.

Opportunities for Japanese Leadership

Despite the vulnerabilities for Japan created by asymmetric incentives with China, CMI also offers valuable opportunities for Japanese regional leadership. Indeed, in perhaps no other regional endeavor is Japan as well situated to lead regional efforts that will stabilize its economic, and potentially political, environment.

The basis of Japan's opportunity is its enormous situational power, in terms of money, expertise, and access.[101] If handled carefully, this situational power can be used not only to ensure effective regional emergency liquidity provision but also to leverage improvements in its other interest areas.

The first element of Japan's situational power is money. While China surpassed it in 2006 as the world's largest holder of official foreign exchange reserves, Japan still held $988 billion as of March 31, 2008. In any event, the yen's status as an international reserve currency means that Japan's ability to provide hard currency to its neighbors is essentially unlimited. More important, Japan is a rich country. With a GDP of over $4 trillion on an exchange rate basis, the government can continue to make significant increases in contingent commitments to its neighbors with minimal need for domestic political justification.[102] Nowhere was this point made more clear than in the New Miyazawa Initiative, which rapidly transformed Japanese aid policy in terms of both size and recipients for several years with no negative domestic political impact.

Japan also is unique among the ASEAN+3 for its expertise in the international monetary system. It has nearly half a century of experience in participating in financial cooperation at the pinnacle of the international financial architecture.[103] Most salient to CMI, Japan was an original participant in the 1962 General Arrangements to Borrow and the 1998 New Arrangements to Borrow, which were created to supplement IMF lending in the face of a large-scale crisis. With regard to surveillance, Japan was also an original participant in G5 and G7 financial ministers' meetings; indeed, the vice minister of finance for international affairs at the time of the announcement of the Chiang Mai Initiative, Haruhiko Kuroda (now governor of the ADB, where he continues to promote regional economic and financial efforts), was involved as a junior official in preparing for the first G7 efforts at multilateral surveillance in 1986–87.[104] And with the exception of the 2001 Argentine crisis, Japan has played a major role in all of the most prominent international bailouts of the last thirty years, from the 1978 dollar rescue plan to the Latin American debt crisis in the 1980s to the 1995 Mexican peso crisis to the Asian Financial Crisis in 1997–98.

---

[101] Grimes 2005.

[102] Of course, official aid to other countries can be deeply politically unpopular in Japan. See, for example, Komori 2002, chap. 4. But for many relevant actions—including the contingent commitments represented by the Chiang Mai Initiative—there has been no public complaint at all of which I am aware. And the New Miyazawa Initiative certainly demonstrated the Japanese government's ability to make funding decisions quickly.

[103] Volcker and Gyohten 1992.

[104] Ironically, Haruhiko Kuroda's view at that time of G7 surveillance and economic policy coordination was rather unimpressed, as seen in a very clever article he wrote for *International Economy* (Kuroda 1989).

Finally, Japan plays a role in the global financial architecture that has no parallel among the East Asian countries. Japan alone can act as middleman between the global financial institutions and regional financial efforts, particularly in the Chiang Mai Initiative. It is better able both to gauge the reaction of the IMF management and board of directors to CMI developments and to shape that reaction through its role on the board and the networks formed through years of short-term postings of MOF officials to the fund. These bridges can be used to affect both IMF decisions and CMI decision making and surveillance.

To what extent can these apparent strengths be translated into gains? To date, Japan has indeed been the main proposer of all the liquidity provision efforts in East Asia since 1997, in terms not only of overall institutional design but also on the technical level of how to structure and manage swap agreements. And, of course, Japan's role as largest funder gives it implicit veto power over any proposals that arise.

These advantages have had clear effects so far. As demonstrated, the Chiang Mai Initiative in its current version does a good job of meeting Japan's economic interests in promoting regional stability at minimal cost. Japan's leading role in CMI and its predecessors may also have contributed to the willingness of regional partners to consider its other financial proposals. This is important for the strategic thinkers in and around the Ministry of Finance who see the four streams of financial regionalism as a "package deal" rather than as an à la carte menu from which to choose bits and pieces, as some ASEAN+3 policymakers apparently prefer to see it.

CMI and other regional financial projects expand Japan's structural power in the region, improving its ability to advance other issues. Generally speaking, clear leadership in the financial aspects of ASEAN+3 cooperation maintains Japan's credibility as a leader and attractiveness as a potential partner for regional states looking to hedge against the rise of China.

Will the Status Quo Last? Challenges to Delegated Decision Making

As I have argued, the basic structure of the Chiang Mai Initiative addresses the primary concerns of likely creditor states better than any available alternatives, at least from the perspectives of power and interests. It offers the credible promise of large-scale provision of foreign exchange, while maintaining a credible threat of strict conditionality via the IMF link. Moreover, it does so without requiring the dominant states to establish credible reputations with both markets and potential crisis country governments that under some circumstances they might refuse aid to an economy in need.

It is thus a functional solution for the leading states despite their disagreement with the IMF's response to the Asian Financial Crisis.

Nonetheless, it has been widely predicted that CMI will evolve into a more ambitious set of regional monetary arrangements—indeed, that is explicit in the 2005 "roadmap" and the 2007 Kyoto agreement, as well as writings of a variety of current and former Japanese officials and outside observers. Moreover, that appears to be the preference of several of the less dominant CMI participants, including potential future crisis economies. But while my analysis leaves considerable room for purely *functional* enhancements of CMI (i.e., ones that will make it more effective in a crisis, such as the decision in 2005 to predesignate "coordinating countries" to aggregate and manage CMI swaps in the event of an actual crisis), I am far more skeptical about the possibility of meaningful changes in the decision-making structure. This analysis is in sharp contrast to the claims of scholars and professionals who see the Chiang Mai Initiative as one component of a much broader drive toward some sort of East Asian economic community.[105]

These writers argue that the Chiang Mai Initiative is a step along a path of substantive change toward something like an Asian monetary fund. The supposed endpoint includes true reserve pooling, regional crisis decision making, and elimination of the IMF's role.[106] Even where writers are pessimistic about the prospects for something like this occurring, they foresee the prospect of political events *derailing* the process, as opposed to my portrayal of the current configuration as stable in its own right.

Some aspects of CMI can indeed still be enhanced, including its size, transparency, procedures, and perhaps even membership.[107] Multilateralization of the current network of BSAs is also a likely functional enhancement, and it is indeed in the works. But a fundamental change in character would mean a shift away from the IMF link (a form of delegated decision making) toward a regional decision-making structure. The major question, then, is what would motivate regional states to make such a change. The answer must lie in changes in the political environment or participants' interests.

To avoid spinning an endless web of hypotheticals, my analysis starts from two simple principles. First, I assume that substantive changes will require the active support of both Japan and China, in addition to a significant subset of other ASEAN+3 governments. Second, while smaller economies

---

[105]Lee 2006; Kuroda 2005; Kondō 2003; Kishimoto 1999; Sohn 2007.

[106]Some authors add the longer-range goal of a single currency. Kondō 2003; Kuroda 2005; Ōnishi 2005.

[107]Given the logic of the regional hedge and the preferences of both Japan and China to maintain regional leadership, membership would presumably continue to exclude the United States and instead be limited to less powerful potential creditors such as Australia and New Zealand.

may be willing to go along with large-scale changes that add only marginally to their utility, neither Japan nor China will initiate or accept changes that are not significant improvements to their overall political and economic interests.

Thus, we must answer the question of what plausible shifts in the political economic environment would be substantial enough to change Japan's and China's basic incentives with regard to emergency liquidity provision. I argue that we should look first to changes in the strategic situation and second to significant changes in economic costs and benefits to each major player. This contrasts with the constructivist—and to a lesser degree the neoliberal—approaches.

The Role of Crisis

The one point on which all interpretations agree—albeit following different logics and leading under some circumstances to differing predictions—is the potential for a future currency crisis to lead to fundamental change in how CMI works, just as the Asian Financial Crisis changed regional states' approaches to crisis management. If, in the event of a currency crisis, the IMF link were to work as planned and IMF conditionality were seen as appropriate, the crisis would add no additional pressures for change. Failure, however, would likely spawn significant change.

A failure of CMI to provide funds in a timely way despite approval from the IMF would most likely destroy the initiative, as that would demonstrate its inadequacy in providing funds as promised and would require substantial intervention from outside the region to save the ASEAN+3 from its own inability to manage the problem. This would injure its claims to competency (the greatest concern from the neoliberal perspective) and demonstrate the fault lines within the region (of greatest concern from constructivist and realist perspectives). In point of fact, however, I do not consider this a likely event, given the simplicity of the CMI mechanism and the strong interests of the +3 states in regional financial stability.[108]

The more likely scenario would be for some or all of the ASEAN+3 states to determine that IMF conditions were misdirected and harmful. If this were the interpretation of all the CMI participants, analysis from any perspective would expect a strengthening of regional decision making and a de-linking from the IMF: for constructivists, it would increase the chasm

---

[108] The only likely scenario for refusal of agreed-upon funds would be if the crisis were threatening potential creditor states as well. The secret preconditions built into the BSAs could in theory kick in as well, but it hardly seems conceivable that creditor states would strictly adhere to these in the event of a real crisis. More likely, they would just be supportive of stricter IMF conditions in such a case.

between regional identity and structural power at the global level; realists would anticipate that the ASEAN+3 would employ de-linking as an ultimatum to achieve more appropriate conditionality, on which it would need to follow through; neoliberals would expect that the failure of the existing decision-making mechanism would make alternatives more attractive. With true regionalization of decision making as an alternative already implicit and readily available in the very existence of regional liquidity arrangements, that would become the default option.

Most interesting would be if there were serious divisions *within* the ASEAN+3 about crisis resolution. It is hard to imagine a strengthening of regional decision making under such circumstances, but the different approaches do suggest varying predictions as to which states would choose which side. In terms of economic interests, the primary dividing line is between likely creditors and likely borrowers. Thus, the neoliberal approach would seem to suggest that China and Japan would side with the IMF against the ASEAN4. (Singapore and South Korea are more equivocal cases; their preferences would depend on the specific circumstances.) For realists, the most likely split would be between China and Japan. Even if their economic interests were identical, China might well side with the ASEAN states in order to isolate Japan. (This prospect could also force Japan into solidarity with its CMI partners, even if internal analysis agreed with the IMF.) The constructivist approach does not really offer a clear prediction, since it would most likely depend on the intervening political process. To the extent that the East Asian regional identity is about an anti–Washington Consensus view of the role of the state in domestic economies, the most liberally oriented states would be the more likely to accept the IMF judgment and thus the continued hegemony of global institutions and standards.

Alliance Politics

Under what circumstances might CMI be transformed in the absence of a crisis? From the perspective of power politics, the key questions would be whether and how the strategic situation is changing. This is essentially a question of how Japan weighs its dislike of U.S. structural economic power against its need for the U.S.-Japan alliance. As long as the United States sees a functionally autonomous East Asian institution of crisis-liquidity provision as detracting from the authority of the IMF and U.S. structural power, any decision by the ASEAN+3 to move in that direction would have a negative impact on the overall U.S.-Japan relationship. Japanese policymakers are aware of this fact, and thus would only be expected to make such a move if they believed that the U.S.-Japan alliance was of decreasing relevance to Japan's own security.

For realists, the only reasons this would happen would be if the credibility of the U.S. commitment were seen to waver or if China (perhaps in alliance with other Asian states) were to become so powerful that Japan made the strategic decision to bandwagon with it rather than try to balance it. Neither of these appears likely over the next ten to fifteen years, although it is always conceivable that some crisis could change the U.S. commitment. Therefore, I predict that CMI will not be made into a truly autonomous regional organization absent a serious crisis. However, Japan will continue to find the current configuration, most probably with incremental improvements, to be an attractive hedge.

Constructivist approaches suggest alternative scenarios that would be based on changed understandings on the part of U.S. and/or Japanese policymakers. First, there is no fundamental reason to expect, from either a constructivist or neoliberal perspective, that the U.S. government must understand the creation of an effective regional alternative to the IMF (if one could be designed) as an attack on its structural power. If U.S. policymakers were to understand financial regionalism not as an "us vs. them" act or if they were to reinterpret the national interest so as not to emphasize global financial standards, there would be no particular reason to expect a weakening of the U.S.-Japan alliance to result from de-linking from the IMF.

Based on existing constructivist accounts of East Asian financial regionalism, a more likely story would be the development of trust between Japan, China, and their ASEAN+3 partners based on the strengthening of a regional identity, common regional purpose, or changed perception of the intentions of China.[109] With the incentive to balance against China reduced, Japan would worry less about impacts of its regional activities on the U.S.-Japan relationship. Presumably, one of the ways in which this would happen would be if the processes of ASEAN+3 cooperation were to improve personal trust among policymakers, as several authors have argued.[110] This contrasts sharply with my own realist expectations, and I see its probability as essentially nil.

A neoliberal interpretation of what it would take for Japan to be willing to take a chance on weakening its alliance with the United States rests on different grounds. First, as a precondition, the redesign of CMI would have

---

[109]The first of these is implicit in the CMI "roadmap" and is made more explicit in the work of writers such as Kondō 2000, 2003; Kuroda 2005; and Sakakibara 2005. The second is argued in Higgott 1998; Bello 1998; Lee 2006. The third is argued by Kang 2003a, 2003b, 2003–04, albeit not with a direct reference to financial issues. See also Johnston 2003b; Rolfe 2003.

[110]Kuroda 2005; Kawai 2005; Kawai and Takagi 2005; Zhang 2005. In this, they recall the "socialization" stream of constructivism, such as Johnston 2003.

to mitigate the risk of moral hazard while also being effective in managing crises. Beyond that, Japanese policymakers would need to be convinced either that regional economic integration or that the web of Chinese institutional obligations would ensure that a rising China would not be in a position to significantly threaten Japan's political or economic interests.[111] Moreover, any potential economic losses created by upsetting the U.S.-Japan relationship would need to be outweighed by the benefits in terms of increasing regional economic integration.

While there are some overlaps, the crucial difference between the realist and neoliberal interpretations is on the question of whether economic institutions can sufficiently constrain the political actions of a rising power over the long term. My prediction is that they cannot, that Japanese policymakers will not be willing to take the bet that they can, and that therefore friendly Chinese actions will not be enough to change Japanese calculations. Even if institutional arrangements could be designed to adequately address the problem of moral hazard in CMI—which I have argued is not feasible—only a reduction in the credibility of the U.S. commitment to protect Japan should be sufficient to change Japan's acceptance of the role of the IMF, however reluctant it might be. This would presumably occur through a chain of events exogenous to East Asian financial regionalism.

Alternative Narratives: Economic and Functional Considerations

There are other ways of looking at the question, of course. From a neoliberal point of view, the key to eliminating the IMF link is to create viable regional decision-making alternatives. Japanese policy economists such as Takatoshi Itō and Masahiro Kawai argue that moral hazard and enforcement issues can be managed through a combination of clear decision rules and enhanced surveillance. I have already argued at length in this chapter that problems of credibility of enforcement in a small regional organization make that highly unlikely, especially given the lack of clear political consensus between Japan and China.

If my analysis is correct, then the only way that a fundamental change in crisis decision making is rational would be if the IMF link were perceived to be even worse than a regional alternative. In other words, regional states

---

[111]This is a popular point of view among Japanese elites, as seen in Keidanren 2001. Essentially, the argument is a "specific assets" one—that the benefits to continued cooperation (Chinese prosperity and positive relations with neighbors on all or most sides) would be so great that their loss would override the benefits to China of exerting unilateral power. On specific assets, see Oye 1986; Axelrod and Keohane 1986; Koremenos, Lipson, and Snidal 2001.

might rationally choose heightened moral hazard over inadequate response to a crisis. Such a choice would only be forced on the ASEAN+3 states in the event of an actual crisis.

An additional functional pathway is conceivable, although it does not really fit into the simple categorization of realist, neoliberal, or constructivist. Already, the funds available through CMI swap lines exceed IMF quotas for all of the ASEAN+3 economies except Japan—indeed, for the ASEAN states, by several times. As the size of the CMI network expands, the differential will likely become even larger, and it may become politically difficult to justify the IMF tail wagging the CMI dog—as a political matter, it might be very attractive to domestic opposition parties to attack a sitting government for allowing the IMF discretion over the disbursal of regional funds.[112] This would presumably be most likely in ASEAN countries or Korea, which have had recent negative experiences of IMF crisis management, which have effective opposition parties (unlike China), and where CMI-committed funds are potentially a significant proportion of reserves (unlike Japan or China). This appears to be a major concern of the U.S. Treasury.

While it is possible for international organizations to become political actors in their own right, that seems less likely in this case, given that neither CMI nor ASEAN+3 yet have any autonomy of their own in terms of personnel, funding, or even rules.[113] The key issue from the point of view of power-based analysis is that in the end such a decision would require Japanese and Chinese support, which is unlikely in the absence of other major changes. Moreover, there does not appear to be any plausible domestic political economy story that would lead us to that decision.[114]

Alternative Narratives: Constructivist Considerations

I end this chapter by considering the remaining counterargument to my assessment—that is to say, constructivist notions of regionalist sentiment. One version of this is to see East Asian regional economic cooperation as analogous to the development of the European Union. Bit by bit, in this interpretation, economic integration and institution building can support a

[112]This point recalls the OECD's financial support fund proposal. Cohen 1998b.

[113]In this sense, they differ greatly from the IMF, the nature of whose autonomy is addressed in Barnett and Finnemore 2004, chap. 3.

[114]For example, the International Bureau of the Japanese Ministry of Finance is increasingly focused on regional cooperation, which might lead its officials to focus on "improving" regional cooperation of all sorts—including CMI—to justify the bureau's role and to secure their own advancement within the ministry. But even a powerful ministry would need to gain much broader political approval for any major change. Given the potential costs to Japan of something like a reconstituted AMF, it is hard to imagine that it would supercede strategic considerations.

regional process of rapprochement.[115] Some evidence for this is to be found in developments in ASEAN over the last two decades or so, where cooperative economic projects of minor practical import, supported by a political consensus among the leading states and an increasing sense of a Southeast Asian identity among their populations, proved to be building blocks for more ambitious schemes such as the ASEAN free trade area and the ASEAN investment area. Changing understandings of regional identity are seen to have fundamentally shifted political calculations within ASEAN.[116] Increasing sentiments of an East Asian identity within the ASEAN+3 countries might make this appear possible.[117]

However, from a realist point of view, it is extremely unlikely. For one thing, even ASEAN's regional solidarity has led to only minimally binding cooperation. Also, unlike ASEAN, which has no dominant power and has a collective incentive to navigate among the shoals of interested outside powers like the United States, China, and Japan, ASEAN+3 contains two potentially hegemonic actors with differing preferences regarding the outside power of the United States. To put it bluntly, for Japan, adoption of an East Asian "regional" identity means acceptance of Chinese hegemony in the long run. While that may happen in time if China's long-term peaceful rise makes reliance on the U.S.-Japan alliance to balance China untenable, it is hard to see it as a serious medium-term choice.[118] Even some advocates of the importance of regional identity argue that national interests are unlikely to bedefined primarily by that identity. As Takashi Terada puts it, "When it comes to a more rule-governed form of regional cooperation, however, strong leadership and clear awareness of potential interests...are more significant."[119]

Also in question is the content of regional identity. A pan-Asian cultural identity may well be developing, but it is hardly obvious—at least to me—how that might translate into official political and economic cooperation.[120] The more promising argument would appear to be based on an East Asian

---

[115]Kishimoto 1999; Kondō 2003; Terada 2003; Kuroda 2005; Lee 2006. See also Haas 1964; Breslin and Higgott 2000.

[116]Acharya 2000; Stubbs 2004.

[117]This argument has been made by Kurlantzick 2006, for example.

[118]If Kang (2003a, 2003b, 2003–04) is correct about the historical limits on Chinese hegemony and the possibility of a peaceful transition to "hierarchy" in East Asia, this may prove to be less of a problem for Japan than I (and many Japanese analysts) assume.

[119]Terada 2004, 66.

[120]For differing views on the regional spread of popular culture, see Kurlantzick 2006; Leheny 2006; Shiraishi 2006. All see a meaningful diffusion (with Shiraishi focusing on formation of middle classes), but Leheny argues that it is unlikely to have direct effects on regional cooperation.

consensus against the hyperliberalism advocated by the United States.[121] This is a cogent point, although it is not clear how or why we should expect regional opinions regarding economic management to evolve over time. If it is correct, then Chiang Mai should become quite separate from the global financial architecture over time. At this point, all we can say is that this prediction is different from mine. Only time will tell which is more accurate.

[121] Higgott 1998; Breslin and Higgott 2000; Lee 2006.

4

Currency Management and Contestation

The most ambitious aspect of financial regionalism is currency cooperation. Given the almost total lack of coordination to date, it is tempting at
first blush simply to dismiss the whole discussion, with its aspiration of a
common currency and regional central bank, as nothing more than regionalist rhetoric. But there is actually a great deal to the debate that deserves
our attention. Currency cooperation comes in many forms short of currency union (although the development of a regional currency is indeed
part of the ASEAN+3 rhetoric); globally, in fact, voluntary currency union is
quite rare, but less ambitious schemes are common.[1] The goal of all forms
of currency cooperation is to reduce intragroup currency volatility, usually
by formal agreements on currency bands, macroeconomic policy coordination, or both. The main themes in East Asian currency cooperation are the
development of a regional basket of currencies and enhancement of Chiang
Mai macroeconomic surveillance. Regional currency cooperation is not just
about dreams of an Asian community or even a technocratic exercise for
imaginative economists and policymakers; rather, the debate concerns real
economic and political issues at both global and regional levels.

Political and Economic Stakes in Regional
Currency Cooperation

The regional currency cooperation debate is fundamentally about how
to protect economies from currency volatility and the effects of global

[1] Kenen and Meade 2008.

imbalances. In part, it constitutes an expansion of a longer-term Japanese effort to insulate its economy from the U.S. power to deflect payment adjustments onto its trading partners. It is also an effort to be prepared to better manage the inevitable adjustment of current global payments imbalances, which many ASEAN+3 policymakers agree are unsustainable. The East Asian economies have been caught in the center of the storm both because of their dependence on U.S. markets and the dollar and because of the unforeseen effects of policy choices to which they committed years ago but which are now threatening domestic and global financial stability.

So far East Asian states have mostly attempted to deal with these issues individually. But, as the question of sustainability has become more unavoidable and the need for adjustment more imminent, they are also increasingly aware that collective action may be called for to prevent a hard landing both for themselves and for the global economy. Unfortunately for them, the economic and political difficulties of collective action in this situation are immense, as are the uncertainties about what may be accomplished by it. Efforts at serious coordination of regional currencies are almost certainly bound to fail in the medium term, but they may still prove to be effective in reducing negative side effects of adjustment.

If effective regional currency cooperation does prove possible, it could have profound effects on the global role of the dollar and on the structural power of the United States. Regional insulation policies are meant to blunt U.S. power to deflect and to delay adjustment, but the (remote) possibility of success raises the question of what a global financial system without a single dominant leader might look like. In the language of monetary power, regional currency cooperation threatens systemic disruption in the face of U.S. misuse of structural power. The question is whether that threat will create enough leverage to persuade the United States to adjust its policies. If not, it will take us one more step toward a multicurrency world in which no single power has the ability or incentive to set rules or to act decisively to stop a crisis. The realist tradition suggests that we should be very nervous about such a world, even if we do not sympathize with the U.S. policies that have helped to bring us to this point.

Currency Cooperation as Insulation

The desire to insulate regional economies from U.S. macroeconomic policy choices and from the intrusiveness of global financial institutions and standards lies at the heart of East Asian financial regionalism. The greatest support for de-linking in terms of currency management comes from Japan, which has struggled longer with the implications of U.S. monetary power than the others and which already floats the yen more or less freely.

After decades of seeking to manage the volatility of the yen-dollar exchange rate through domestic macroeconomic policy and direct negotiation with the United States, Japanese leaders had tired of the efforts by
the late 1990s. Thus, the biggest push for regional currency baskets has
been from Japan. At least until 2007, the greatest resistance in practical
terms came from China, with its de facto dollar peg. Interestingly, U.S.
currency policy regarding East Asia has focused not on whether there is
a challenge to the dollar's global role but on the question of undervaluation of East Asian currencies. The political confrontation over that issue
between the United States and China has been gaining momentum in
recent years.

Meanwhile, the unprecedented rise in reserves that has resulted from
uncoordinated soft dollar pegging has created a new incentive for East Asian
states to coordinate their policies to achieve insulation. If the value of the
dollar starts to crash, states will be tempted to sell off a significant part of
their dollar holdings. A credible regional plan for coordinated, incremental unwinding of dollar positions would reduce negative effects on both
regional and global levels by preventing a rush for the exits. The global
weakening of the dollar that accelerated in 2007 in the midst of weaker U.S.
growth and the emergence of the subprime crisis made the importance of
this issue all the more apparent.

The Global Role of the Dollar

Underlying global currency politics, there is one issue of structural power
that overshadows all others: the international role of the dollar. If the dollar represented an "exorbitant privilege" for the United States in the 1960s
world of fixed parities and the gold-dollar standard, that privilege has in
many ways actually expanded in the post–Bretton Woods world. This was
a surprising development—most contemporary observers shared the assumption that the end of the gold-dollar standard would mean a gradual
move toward a multicurrency world.[2] While this happened to some extent,
as seen for example in the gradual decline of the value of the dollar over
the course of the 1970s and greater inclusion of European currencies and
yen in official foreign exchange reserves around the world, the dollar has
retained its overwhelming roles as invoice currency, vehicle currency, and
store of value.

Indeed, even by the mid-1970s, international economic policymakers
had concluded that "the notion that the United States needs the ability
to create 'international money' to finance American political or military

[2]Bergsten 1975; Solomon 1977, chap. 18.

activities abroad is easily exaggerated."[3] Over time, it has become apparent that it is America's seemingly limitless ability to borrow from abroad—in its own currency, no less—that has ensured that the political system has not been forced to make truly difficult choices about how to fund government expenditures.[4] The fact that virtually all U.S. debt, to nonresidents as well as to residents, is denominated in dollars effectively eliminates depreciation concerns as a short-term or even medium-term constraint on macroeconomic policy. This is an exorbitant privilege indeed—even more so when we recall that many U.S. policies in the dollar's supposed heyday of the 1960s "were enacted or considered in order to solve the payments problem [and] conflicted with the larger goals of U.S. foreign policy."[5] Such an economic decision-making calculus is hard to imagine now.

Dollars are to be found everywhere in the world today. It is the very ubiquity of the dollar that makes it attractive to international investors and traders. Known in economics as "network effects," the pervasiveness of dollar assets and transactions lowers the transaction costs of using dollars relative to other currencies, making it hard for other currencies to supplant the role of the dollar in functions from invoicing of commodities to international lending to foreign exchange trading.[6]

For the dollar to be supplanted in global markets, other options would have to be superior in these respects (which would be difficult), as well as acting more effectively as a store of value (which may already be happening). More likely than global replacement of the dollar is regional shifts in currency usage, as we have already seen in and around Europe. The U.S. government can limit the erosion of the dollar's role by pursuing more responsible macroeconomic policies, while also maintaining a financial regulatory regime that ensures liquidity and low transaction costs. Whether the former is realistic in the absence of hard constraints is questionable;[7] unfortunately, once such constraints arise, the shift toward regionally distinct currency systems will be well on underway.[8]

---

[3] Solomon 1977, 332.

[4] Perhaps the most extraordinary demonstration of this was President George W. Bush's simultaneous pursuit of massive tax cuts and vastly increased military and homeland security spending in the wake of September 11, 2001, all while admonishing Americans not to disrupt their spending habits.

[5] Gavin 2003, 197 (quotation); Volcker and Gyohten 1992, 35–38.

[6] This point was made eloquently by Kindleberger 1972 even before the era of fixed rates had finally come to an end.

[7] This is not just an issue of government policy but also household and corporate behavior. Recall that the Clinton administration's elimination of the federal budget deficit was accompanied by a *worsening* of the current account deficit.

[8] There were indications by early 2008 (see, for example, "It's a Multi-Currency World We Live In," *FT*, December 26, 2007, 10) that the process was moving forward more quickly than expected, but the enormous structural role of the dollar made clear that the process would not be a sudden one.

The Asian Financial Crisis as a Formative Experience

As in other aspects of East Asian financial regionalism, the Asian Financial Crisis of 1997–98 was a formative experience for thinking about currency management. The crisis laid bare the dangers of combining nominal dollar pegs with capital liberalization and dependence on dollar-based finance. Monetary authorities in Thailand and elsewhere had found it economically and politically difficult to sterilize the massive inflows of short-term capital that this policy mix encouraged, leading to asset-price bubbles, appreciation of the real effective exchange rate, and deterioration of current account balances. While other factors were of course important in sparking and sustaining the crisis, its scale and contagiousness resulted from the formula of nominal dollar peg plus capital liberalization.[9]

Although the de facto dollar standard had constituted a loose, tacit sort of coordination, government responses to the AFC were anything but coordinated. Most East Asian governments allowed their currencies to float, at least temporarily, as it was impossible to defend them in the midst of sustained speculative attack. The exceptions were China and Hong Kong, which stuck tenaciously to their existing dollar pegs—in the case of Hong Kong, so tenaciously that the authorities not only raised interest rates and intervened heavily in currency markets but also invested public funds in the stock market and levied a substantial surcharge on large futures positions.[10] Chinese authorities, meanwhile, stressed at the time that they were avoiding devaluation as a contribution to international stability as appropriate to China's role as a "responsible great power."[11]

In the wake of the crisis, U.S. and Japanese authorities offered conflicting policy advice to East Asian policymakers. The U.S. Treasury, like the IMF, advocated the so-called two-corner solution—in which states could follow either a free float or a strict dollar peg (in the latter case, abandoning independent monetary policy), but in which managed floats would invite attacks.[12] The Japanese Ministry of Finance, on the other hand, argued strongly in favor of currency baskets (i.e., a weighted average of U.S. dollars, Japanese yen, and European currencies, or the euro beginning in 1999) as targets for managing

[9]Geithner 2007.

[10]"Hong Kong Exchange Acts to Curb Currency Raids: New Rules May Fuel Concern over Market Intervention," *FT*, August 31, 1998, 1.

[11]The effects on China ended up being far less severe than might have been predicted, largely because the trade of its competitors whose currencies had depreciated severely (such as Thailand, Malaysia, and Indonesia) was so disrupted as to minimize the impact of their relative depreciation against the RMB. But although the economic effects proved not to be too damaging, Hongying Wang (2003) has argued convincingly that political considerations related to the reversion of Hong Kong and Chinese WTO accession were the overriding reason for this stance.

[12]Geithner 2007, 3–4.

exchange rates.[13] Advice differed regarding capital account liberalization as well, with U.S. authorities calling for full liberalization and Japanese authorities arguing for the applicability in some cases of capital controls.

Despite contrary advice from the U.S. Treasury and the Japanese Ministry of Finance, East Asian currencies after the crisis showed a remarkable, if incomplete, reversion to various forms of dollar pegs (figure 4.1).[14] Even though that has not always been reflected in official rhetoric, standard econometric measurements have continued to show high correlations with the dollar even for those currencies that were formally floating.[15] In the economically stable market economies of East Asia, only the Japanese yen and the Singapore dollar showed much of a float between 1999 and 2004, and

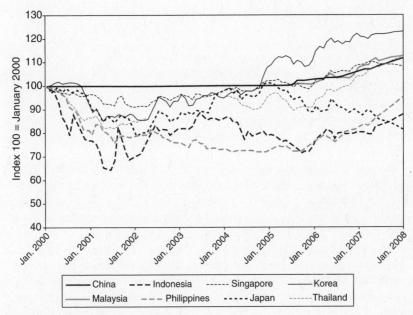

Figure 4.1. Nominal Dollar Exchange Rate, 2000–2007.
Source: U.S. Department of Agriculture.

[13]Foreign Exchange Commission 1999.

[14]Yoshino, Ishikawa, and Asonuma 2004; McKinnon and Schnabl 2003, 2004; Ogawa 2002; Kawai and Akiyama 2000; Kawai 2007.

[15]The standard method was introduced by Frankel and Wei 1994 and is known as the "the Swiss franc method." It involves comparing the values of the currencies to the Swiss franc. The Swiss franc is used purely as a numeraire to eliminate issues of collinearity and serial correlation. Other methods, including cluster analysis and the intellectually ambitious but much less influential two-stage regression model (Yoshino, Ishikawa, and Asonuma 2004), have been used as well, and show similar results. See also the articles cited in note 14.

even the yen was heavily managed compared to the euro. From about 2004, the Korean won began to diverge somewhat from the nominal dollar path, while the other currencies (except for Japan) increased more modestly starting in 2006. As of fall 2007, there remained some debate over the importance of the reductions in correlations with the dollar that have occurred. Duck-Koo Chung and Barry Eichengreen make this point nicely: "Not for the first time, different economists are able to discern support for…different positions in the same set of data. East Asian currency regimes, it would appear, are a bit like a Rorschach test: there is a tendency for economists to see in their evolution more or less what they expect."[16] But even though East Asia could no longer be interpreted as a pure dollar peg, the dollar remained by far the largest determinant of all the region's currencies as of fall 2007.

China and the Dollar

In the face of regionwide currency depreciation in 1997–98, one emerging market economy stood alone in East Asia as a vast island of currency stability. China, which had allowed the RMB to depreciate by over 30 percent only three and a half years earlier in January 1994, quickly made the decision to maintain its dollar value in the face of the crisis. This decision had several causes that are of interest, but the longer-term implications are more important for our purposes.

Regarding causes, the Chinese government stated repeatedly in 1997 and 1998 that it was maintaining the value of its currency as part of its role as a "responsible great power." Hongying Wang has argued convincingly that this stance was closely connected to China's accession negotiations to enter the WTO, which were the subject of intense scrutiny and concern in the United States.[17] But other political benefits also accrued to Beijing. China's stance was deeply reassuring to ASEAN and South Korea, which feared that RMB depreciation would lead to intensification of competition in goods markets and thus to further currency instability. Moreover, the formulation of "responsible great power" was an attractive one for China, for two reasons. First, it made a claim for China's status as an economic great power, a status that was confirmed by the reactions of the United States and other participants. Second, it drew an intentional contrast with the currency policies of the other East Asian economic great power—Japan, which allowed the yen to sink by about 30 percent against the dollar in 1998 and which U.S. policymakers were already painting as irresponsible.[18]

---

[16]Chung and Eichengreen 2007, 6.

[17]Wang 2003. See also McKinnon and Schnabl 2004, 246.

[18]Then U.S. Treasury secretary Robert Rubin states in his memoir that "Japan's weakness contrasted with China's role in contributing to stability." Rubin and Weisberg 2003, 226.

The purposefulness with which Chinese leaders wielded this new tool of power was impressive. Indeed, through much of 1998, they maintained a high degree of attention from U.S., Japanese, and regional audiences by employing a formulation that China would maintain the RMB-dollar rate only as long as other great powers (i.e., Japan) behaved responsibly. Many contemporary U.S. analyses excoriated Japan for its willingness to plunge China—and with it, the rest of East Asia and emerging markets around the world—into depreciation as a result of its selfish policies to maintain a weak yen.[19] In reality, Chinese exports were never hit as hard as some feared, at least partly because its major devaluation in 1994 meant that the RMB was not overvalued coming into the crisis. Moreover, the economic, political, and social instability that occurred in neighboring economies inevitably made foreign investors deeply nervous, whereas China stood out as an island of stability. When FDI to East Asian began recovering partway through 1998, it skewed heavily toward China.[20]

Ironically, although China acted as a regional bulwark of stability in 1997–98 by maintaining the dollar peg, by 2004 or so it had become apparent that that same policy was increasingly a threat to global stability. (In this role, of course, it was aided by the unprecedented dissaving of the American people and their government.) China's continuation of the dollar peg also complicated currency management for its neighbors and competitors, who feared the results of unilaterally allowing their currencies to float. They too pegged more or less rigidly against the dollar, making East Asia once again a de facto dollar area. To maintain their various hard and soft dollar pegs despite current account surpluses and substantial private capital inflows, East Asian states have engaged in massive accumulation of reserves. Massive global imbalances and the accumulation by East Asian central banks of vast dollar reserves create an additional rationale for East Asian economies to try to stabilize their currencies relative to each other.[21]

Dealing with the Dollar: To Peg or to De-link?

Taking advantage of the hegemony of the dollar, U.S. administrations going back to the early 1970s have relied at various times on "benign neglect" of the value of the dollar or even outright pressure on trading partners to encourage their currencies to appreciate. However, they have also experienced

[19] See, for example, "China Signals Desire for Stable Currency," Washington Post, June 27, 1998.

[20] UNCTAD *World Investment Report* database http://www.unctad.org/Templates/Page.asp ?intItemID=3277&lang=1.

[21] This point is made in Chung and Eichengreen 2007, 3.

serious pushback at times as states have sought to insulate their economies against spillover effects from U.S. economic policies. This has been most significant in Europe, where the breakdown in Bretton Woods–era fixed exchange rates was rapidly followed by a series of cooperative efforts starting with the "tunnel" and the "snake in the tunnel," then the Exchange Rate Mechanism, and eventually the introduction of the euro and the establishment of the European Central Bank.[22] In East Asia, resistance to U.S. dollar politics has more often existed at a national level, as governments have managed their currencies through a variety of means, including currency controls, exchange market intervention, and macroeconomic policies. Whereas the main European economies chose to de-link from the dollar and float together, currency management in East Asia has remained uncoordinated and heavily focused on the dollar.

U.S. dollar pegs are common in the world, but the reasons for them are varied.[23] In many cases, such as in Latin America, policymakers and scholars have seen dollar pegs as a means of providing credibility of macroeconomic management by acting as a nominal anchor.[24] For most East Asian states in recent decades, in contrast, the dollar peg has had less to do with monetary stability (except at certain moments, such as commodity price spikes or the immediate aftermath of the Asian Financial Crisis), than with concern over the viability of export-oriented growth policies.[25] Dollar orientation in East Asia has been fundamentally a policy of choice rather than of near necessity, especially for the major economies. This fact opens the door for regional cooperation.

Japan, the Yen, and the Drive for Regional Insulation

In looking at East Asian currency cooperation, we see that Japan occupies an interesting and ambiguous position as both a leader of the formal process and a nonparticipant in the de facto dollar area. It is unique in the region as a result of both the global role of the yen and the substantial penetration of East Asia by Japanese financial institutions. Alone among East Asian currencies, the yen stands on the global stage as one of the three major

---

[22]Frasher-Rae 2008. The "tunnel" and the "snake in the tunnel" were early versions of currency bands.

[23]See, e.g., Cohen 1998a, 2004; Kenen and Meade 2008.

[24]Schamis 2003; Grabel 2003. Cohen 2004 refers to this as "vertical regionalization" (39). Several of the articles reprinted in McKinnon 2005 make the case that East Asia too can benefit from using the dollar as a nominal anchor, although much of McKinnon's concern is over the possibility of Japanese and Chinese monetary authorities being forced into deflationary rather than inflationary policies if they allow their exchange rates to float.

[25]As we shall see, the argument in Dooley, Folkerts-Landau, and Garber 2003 depends on this assumption.

international currencies—on a different tier from the dollar or euro, certainly, but with a greater global role than any other world currency. Nonetheless, Japanese economic policy has been deeply affected by the dollar.[26]

Although dollar predominance has effectively been a fact of life for all participants in the global economy, that does not mean that all economies have benefited equally, or even on net, from it.[27] The Japanese government has often expressed concern at the extent to which its economy has been subject to vagaries of U.S. policy through U.S. government manipulation or neglect of the dollar exchange rate. Particularly from the mid-1980s to the mid-1990s, periodic upward pressures on the yen, often induced by U.S. administrations' "talking down the dollar," had profound effects on the Japanese economy and economic policy.[28] Policymakers and commentators at various points discussed promoting greater international use of the yen as a possible counter to those pressures, arguing that U.S. administrations would be forced to act less cavalierly if there was meaningful currency competition.[29] This argument was never really translated into policy because of the many economic and political costs, not to mention practical difficulties, of challenging the dollar.

Meanwhile, in East Asia, despite the importance of Japanese firms and financial institutions in regional economic integration, the yen has continued to play second fiddle to the U.S. dollar, even in the trade and financial activities of Japanese firms and financial institutions.[30] In principle, the impact of the nominal dollar-yen rate on the yen's real effective exchange rate should have declined over time, as the United States became a proportionately less important trading partner and as the (dollar-denominated) resource commodity proportion of Japanese imports also decreased. But East Asia's de facto dollar standard has meant that Japan has remained surprisingly subject to the dollar-yen rate.

[26]According to figures from BIS 2007, 7, the Japanese yen figured into over 20% of all foreign exchange trading between 1992 and 2004 (falling to 16.5% in 2007), and yen-denominated debt securities are widely recognized as an international store of value. Moreover, Japan has been involved in all the great currency realignment experiments of the postwar period, from the 1971 Smithsonian Agreement to the 1978 dollar rescue package to the 1983–84 yen-dollar talks to the 1985 Plaza Agreement and 1987 Louvre Accord to the 1995 ultra–high yen episode to the Asian Financial Crisis itself. Indeed, most of these cases can be understood largely, albeit not entirely, within the context of U.S.-Japan economic tussles. For general references, see Volcker and Gyohten 1992; McKinnon and Ohno 1997; Grimes 2001.

[27]Kuroda 2005, 26–27.

[28]Funabashi 1989; Destler and Henning 1989, chaps. 2–4; McKinnon and Ohno 1997; Cargill, Hutchison, and Ito 1997; Mieno 2000; Henning 2006.

[29]Hayami 1995; Oka 1996; Kikkawa 1998. For a full analysis of Japanese efforts to internationalize the yen after the Asian Financial Crisis, see Grimes 2003a, 2003b; Katada, forthcoming.

[30]Foreign Exchange Commission 1999, BIS statistics.

Recognizing this fact, and having spent decades focused on mostly in-effectual attempts to stabilize Japan's exchange rate environment by focus-ing on the yen-dollar rate,[31] Japanese policymakers shifted their efforts to East Asia following the Asian Financial Crisis.[32] The regional turn consisted of a set of policies designed to promote greater use of the yen as an invoice currency, a vehicle currency, and store of value in East Asia. The policies included encouragement of Japanese firms and financial institutions to in-voice their international transactions in yen rather than dollars, attempts to make Japanese financial markets more attractive to foreigners, and some rather clever aid programs. But the centerpiece of Japan's regional efforts was a campaign to promote use of currency baskets as the basis for East Asian governments to manage their currencies. Japanese policymakers en-visaged currency baskets composed of the world's leading currencies (dol-lar, euro, and yen) that would reflect the relative importance of the United States, European Union, and Japan in each East Asian economy's external transactions.[33] Given the prevalence in East Asia in the 1990s of pegging purely on the U.S. dollar, any such shift would increase the role of the yen in East Asian currency management, thus reducing the effective volatility of the yen.

Japanese policymakers saw internationalization of the yen not only as a means of insulation for the Japanese economy.[34] They also felt that the nominal dollar peg had been inappropriate for other East Asian econo-mies, arguing that if currencies had been managed against an appropriately balanced currency basket that included the yen and European currencies instead of just against the U.S. dollar, East Asian economies' real effective exchange rates would have been much less volatile and would not have invited the kind of current account deficits that contributed to the AFC. Thus, they articulated a case not just for internationalization of the yen as insulation for Japan, but as insulation for the *region*.[35] As it turned out, the campaign to internationalize the yen led to virtually no change in the international use of the yen and thus proved to be disappointing for its proponents. However, the rationale for regional insulation, as well as the conception of currency baskets as a means of achieving it, have taken on new life in the quest for regional currency coordination to improve macro-economic stability in East Asia.

---

[31] Funabashi 1989; Volcker and Gyohten 1992; Sakakibara 2005; Utsumi 1999; Foreign Ex-change Commission 1999; Komiya and Suda 1991; McKinnon and Ohno 1996.

[32] Grimes 2003a, 2003b; Katada, forthcoming.

[33] Foreign Exchange Commission 1999; Study Group for the Promotion of the Internation-alization of the Yen 2000.

[34] I develop this idea at length in Grimes 2003a, 2003b.

[35] Grimes 2003b, 177; Yoshino, Kaji, and Suzuki 2004; Yoshino, Kaji, and Asonuma 2005a.

Sustainability of Global Imbalances and the Growth of East Asian Reserves

Regional governments have good reason to worry about threats to macroeconomic stability. This concern links to one of the great anomalies of the modern international monetary system: the continuing predominance of the U.S. dollar more than thirty years after the end of the global fixed–exchange rate system, a period during which its nominal value has declined substantially against other major currencies. That dominance can be attributed to a variety of factors, including network effects, the openness of U.S. capital markets, the sheer economic power of the United States, and U.S. political preeminence. But while the dollar is ubiquitous, the sustainability of its global role has increasingly been called into question due to serious concern about the sustainability of U.S. current account deficits.[36] The fundamental global macroeconomic questions today are how sustainable the deficits are and whether and how adjustment can be managed.

The other side of the global imbalance story is to be found in massive East Asian (especially Chinese) current account surpluses. One of the defining characteristics of the global economy after the Asian Financial Crisis has been a pattern in which unprecedentedly large U.S. current account deficits are financed through dollar purchases by East Asian central banks (figure 4.2). Japan (with nearly $1 trillion in reserves, equivalent to over 20% of GDP) and China (with over $1.5 trillion, or nearly 50% of GDP) had accumulated by far the largest official reserves by the end of 2007, but a similar story can be told about South Korea, Taiwan, and the ASEAN5. Even the Philippines and Indonesia had foreign exchange reserves in excess of 10 percent of GDP, while South Korea, Thailand, Malaysia, and Singapore all had reserves in excess of 25 percent of GDP. For most, the post-AFC period saw an extraordinarily rapid run-up; as the most extreme case in point, Chinese reserves surpassed $200 billion only in 2001 and topped $1.5 trillion by the end of 2007.[37]

This situation has alarmed observers who are concerned about the sustainability of that pattern (and thus the likelihood of a crisis, or at least an abrupt transition), as well as the inappropriateness of developing countries financing the consumption of the world's richest country. The sustainability debate is framed by the fact that U.S. borrowing from abroad exceeds the money that is being made to pay it back and that the situation will get worse over time absent major changes.[38] With U.S. current account deficits

[36] Obstfeld and Rogoff 2004; Cline 2005; Chinn and Frankel 2005.
[37] IMF, *International Financial Statistics* data series.
[38] Obstfeld and Rogoff 2004; Cline 2005; Ahearne, Cline, Lee, Park, Pisani-Ferry, and Williamson 2007.

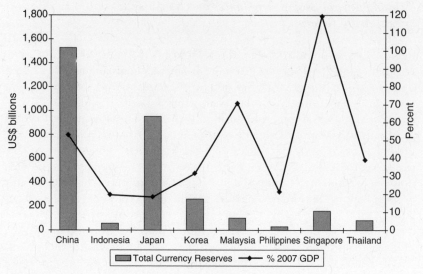

Figure 4.2. Foreign Exchange Reserves (end of 2007).
Source: Asian Bonds Online (reserves), CIA World Factbook (GDP).
Note: GDP figures are dollar-dominated GDP at current exchange rates (as of January 2008).

persistently exceeding 5 percent of GDP—a level typically seen as a serious warning sign for balance of payments crises—the United States has entered into uncharted waters. However, one brake on a sustainability crisis remains the fact that U.S. debts are denominated in dollars, which means that currency risk is being borne by foreigners. The dollar's key currency role makes this situation possible, but the possibility of a crisis also brings into question whether dollar hegemony will persist over the long run.[39] It also creates an incentive for major foreign holders of dollars to try to reduce their vulnerability.

In the United States, U.S. reliance on Chinese capital has raised national security concerns and led to emphatic finger-pointing between Democrats and Republicans. The fear is that U.S. economic prosperity has become dependent on an outside power, and one that is authoritarian and potentially a rival or even enemy to boot. Meanwhile, there is unease in East Asia as well, as populations and policymakers grapple with the implications of having such substantial national savings tied up in a currency whose value could fall precipitously in the event of an unwinding. Given the size of East Asian reserves and their dollar exposure, that could easily lead to a loss of

[39] Cohen 2007; Chinn and Frankel 2005.

wealth on the order of 5–10 percent of GDP for many countries.[40] Former U.S. Treasury secretary Lawrence Summers has characterized the situation of mutual vulnerability as "a kind of balance of financial terror."[41] And, as already noted, there is the larger context of dollar hegemony. If a substantial part of the economic basis of the dollar's key currency role erodes, the question will arise whether the political basis is sufficient to prevent an abrupt shift away from the dollar.

Foreign Exchange Accumulation: Insurance or Mercantilism?

By 2007 East Asian economies had, across the board, accumulated levels of foreign reserves that were unprecedented. This was true not only of the amazing absolute amounts held by China and Japan, but also of smaller economies in the region—for example, as of fall 2007 South Korea and Taiwan each held more than $250 billion and Singapore more than $140 billion. On a relative basis, most of the governments of the CMI economies held reserves equivalent to 25 percent or more of GDP.

How should we understand the extraordinary scale of this accumulation? Clearly, a certain proportion can be seen as a form of insurance against future financial crises. One of the lessons of the 1997 crisis was that countries with insufficient reserves to defend their currencies from speculative attack could experience devastating effects from movements of hot money across their borders. Thus, all of the more or less open economies of the region worked to build up their reserves to fend off disaster. This desire continued even after the establishment of the Chiang Mai Initiative. The beginning of the reserve buildup paralleled actions in several countries, most famously Malaysia, to tighten capital controls. (Like large-scale reserves, capital restrictions have the effect of buffering currencies from the effects of rapid movements of capital; both also have significant negative effects on the efficiency of capital allocation.) But we have seen substantial lowering of capital controls since 1998, leaving reserves as the primary defense against speculative attack.[42]

---

[40] Goldstein and Lardy 2005, 8–9.

[41] Summers 2004, (from Internet, no page numbers). It is interesting that Lawrence Summers, an economist, chose to invoke a national security metaphor, rather than the more generic game theory term "mutual hostages."

[42] There is some disagreement about how much capital controls have been lowered. Whereas the Chinn-Ito index (1970–2005 data available at http://web.pdx.edu/~ito/kaopen_2005 .xls, accessed February 26, 2007) shows little change between 2000 and 2004 for the East Asian economies, McCauley 2003 finds a return to 1997 levels of openness for Malaysia, the East Asian economy that had gone the furthest in reversing capital liberalization after the 1997 crisis. More recent policy shifts, including in the Philippines and Indonesia, tend

At the same time, the scale of reserves accumulated by many of the East Asian economies seems inexplicable if we look only to the insurance function of reserves. First, it is hard to imagine an economic crisis involving, say, South Korea that would require reserves of over $250 billion to address. Second, even states like South Korea and Thailand that have officially allowed their currencies to float—which presumably should reduce the potential of speculative attack—have continued to accumulate reserves.[43] Meanwhile, China, with its impressive array of capital controls, surely does not need over $1 trillion to prevent a currency attack. Finally, if seen as credible, the Chiang Mai Initiative should contribute significantly to the defense of regional currencies, and thus *reduce* the need for individual economies to maintain high levels of reserves for insurance purposes.

For all these reasons, analysts typically see mounting East Asian reserves as a clear sign of mercantilist efforts to maintain undervalued exchange rates. Indeed, that is the premise of the Bretton Woods II hypothesis, as we shall see.[44] Most likely, states have acted out of mixed motives, responding to domestic political pressures and bureaucratic politics in addition to concerns over competitiveness. The last of these may be particularly important for Korea and the ASEAN economies, which compete with massive, dollar-linked China in export markets and for foreign investment.

Bretton Woods II and the East Asian Dollar Standard

In contrast to the concerns I have described regarding sustainability of the current situation, a minority of economists has sought to demonstrate that the current status of global payments is neither unprecedented nor unsustainable. There are two evocatively named versions of this argument: Michael Dooley, David Folkerts-Landau, and Peter Garber's "revived Bretton Woods system" (or Bretton Woods II, as it is commonly known) and Ronald McKinnon's "East Asian dollar standard" hypothesis.[45]

Dooley and his coauthors argue that there is a clear economic logic to the accumulation of dollars by the developing and middle-income countries of East Asia:

> We are interested in a very asymmetric version of a fixed rate system in which, for some time period, periphery countries are willing to underwrite future

---

toward liberalization as well. Information on Southeast Asian capital controls can be found at http://www.aseansec.org/carh/index.html.

[43] Thailand's effort to impose inward capital controls on portfolio investments in December 2006 was premised specifically on the need to reduce upward pressure on the baht. "A Huge Blow to Thailand's Financial Credibility," *Nation,* December 22, 2006.

[44] Dooley, Folkerts-Landau, and Garber 2003.

[45] Dooley, Folkerts-Landau, and Garber 2003; McKinnon 2005.

deficits of the United States....We emphasize the idea that it has been a successful development strategy to subordinate the objective of maximizing the value of reserve assets in order to subsidize and build a domestic capital stock capable of competing in international markets.[46]

They claim that rapidly industrializing economies (the "periphery") are trading off low and potentially risky returns on U.S. dollar assets for the opportunity to achieve economies of scale in industrial production.[47] As long as the rewards of increased scale exceed the opportunity cost of holding dollar assets, this constitutes a rational strategy for the state in question. From a systemic perspective, the authors see it as sustainable because new industrializing peripheries will arise as old ones change their evaluation of the trade-off: "The Bretton Woods system does not evolve, it just occasionally reloads a periphery."[48] They suggest that if and when China and the other East Asian states change their behavior, India (and, one might suppose, Brazil and Russia) will be waiting in the wings to make this investment in rapid industrialization.

The Bretton Woods II hypothesis is clever, but it is not convincing.[49] First, while it initially appears to provide an explanation of why central banks and governments in East Asia might be willing to accumulate dollars while Europeans do not, there is no empirical evidence that policymakers are actually calculating the trade-offs that Dooley and his coauthors posit. Second, while its predictions are more or less consistent with China's currency management between 2002 and 2006, it does a poor job of explaining other East Asian states' behavior.[50] For example, Japan has accumulated almost as many dollar reserves as China, over half of them since 2000, and yet it is one of the world's most developed industrial economies—the Bretton Woods II hypothesis does not provide a satisfactory explanation for why this behavior might be rational. Meanwhile, other East Asian states appear to have accumulated their massive reserve positions originally with the intent of defending their currencies from attack, and more recently to prevent appreciation versus the RMB. It is not obviously in their interest to continue amassing reserves for those purposes. Other problems with the economic argument include the authors' blithe dismissal of the financial trade-offs of excessive reserve accumulation; as analysts have noted, they are overly

[46]Dooley, Folkerts-Landau, and Garber 2003 (from Internet, no page numbers).

[47]Subsequently, they developed an argument that this constitutes a "total return swap" between the U.S. and home economies. Dooley, Folkerts-Landau, and Garber 2004.

[48]Dooley, Folkerts-Landau, and Garber 2003, from Internet (no pages).

[49]The concerns detailed below are fairly widely held—see, for example, Goldstein and Lardy 2005; Cohen 2007.

[50]Goldstein and Lardy (2005) point out many problems even with its interpretations of Chinese policy, however.

optimistic about the ability to sterilize the accumulation and ignore the impact of capital controls on domestic financial-system development.[51] Prescriptively, Bretton Woods II appears to be a recipe for asset bubbles and capital misallocation in East Asia and complacency in the United States. Meanwhile, the presumption that peripheries will "reload" appears to have no logical basis at all, since it simply assumes that newly industrializing economies will follow an export-led, state-directed set of economic policies.

McKinnon also forecasts a preference for the continuation of the dominant role of the dollar, but follows a different economic logic.[52] He focuses on the benefits of dollar usage per se rather than on the importance of U.S. domestic demand. Essentially, he is arguing for the utility of a nominal anchor for domestic monetary management. For East Asian economies, only the dollar is a viable candidate, due to the dollar's extraordinary network effects and a lack of regional alternatives. Interestingly, he argues that a dollar peg system works best on a *regional* basis, constituting an opportunity for regional monetary convergence. Also, unlike Dooley and his coauthors, McKinnon expresses real concern about global payments imbalances and the buildup of dollar holdings by East Asian governments and central banks. He defines this buildup as a case of "conflicted virtue," with the virtue being the East Asian states' responsible domestic macroeconomic policies and the conflict being between their interests in domestic monetary stability, on the one hand, and desire to protect their economies from the potential international instability caused by U.S. profligacy, on the other. His preference would be to see convergence among all East Asian currencies (including the yen) around relatively fixed dollar values, combined with more responsibility on the part of the U.S. government and American consumers.

McKinnon's argument differs from the mainstream on two main points. First, he sees the greatest need for a nominal anchor as growing out of the deflationary effects of currency appreciation on East Asian economies, with Japan as a prime example.[53] But the argument that exchange rates drove Japan's stagnation in the 1990s ignores the many domestic policy mistakes made by Japanese macroeconomic authorities, as well as the central role of banks' nonperforming loans in perpetuating that stagnation.[54] It also goes against the usual monetarist expectation that monetary policy determines a country's price level. Second, he argues that adjustment of global imbalances does not call for appreciation of the East Asian currencies against the dollar,

[51] Goldstein and Lardy 2005, 6–9.

[52] McKinnon 2005 is a compilation of seven of his papers on the subject (including McKinnon and Schnabl 2004), in addition to a new introduction and conclusion. For an update, see McKinnon 2006.

[53] McKinnon and Ohno 1996 is an extended version of his argument about the role of the yen-dollar rate in forcing recession and liquidity traps on Japan.

[54] Mikitani and Posen 2000; Grimes 2001; Amyx 2004a.

whereas most analyses assume that a combination of fiscal and exchange rate adjustment will be necessary to address them.[55]

Finally, neither explanation adequately addresses the political aspects of international structure and power. The 1960s version of Bretton Woods relied on Japan and Germany—two of the closest allies of the United States—to be willing to hold onto excess dollars. Bretton Woods II, on the other hand, relies heavily on China, which is signally not a U.S. ally, in addition to Japan (which, of course, is).[56] Also, currency competition was not even in the air in the old Bretton Woods system, as both West Germany and Japan actively resisted the internationalization of their currencies.[57] In the early twenty-first century, the euro exists as a potential global rival to the dollar, Japan has made clear its preference for internationalizing the yen, and discussions of currency cooperation among the ASEAN+3 are premised on reducing reliance on the dollar. Meanwhile, within both the East Asian creditor countries and the United States, there are likely to be distributional effects related to exchange rates as well as popular resentment (resentment against the United States in the East Asian economies, and vice versa) that could easily change the political terms on either side of the Pacific. In sum, whatever is driving the current East Asian preference for hard or soft dollar pegs, it is likely to be much more politically and economically contingent than the Bretton Woods II and East Asian dollar standard hypotheses imply.[58]

The Next Crisis? Domestic Consequences of the East Asian Dollar Standard

As noted, post-AFC foreign exchange reserve accumulation in many of the ASEAN+3 economies (excepting Japan and China) was originally meant to provide ammunition for fending off currency attacks, but over time it appears to have come to reflect a strategic preference for suppressing currency appreciation. Despite the benefits of an undervalued currency for their export sectors, regional states must increasingly worry about whether the current situation is in fact destabilizing domestically and internationally.

---

[55] Obstfeld and Rogoff 2004; Cline 2005; Ahearne, Cline, Lee, Park, Pisani-Ferry, and Williamson 2007; Bergsten 2007.

[56] With its burgeoning reserves, Russia too has become a de facto player in this game, albeit with much less of an economic motive to keep the U.S. economy afloat. Perhaps reflecting this point, the Russian central bank has been quite upfront about its intention to diversify the currency composition of its reserves.

[57] An exception could be seen in France's periodic demands for conversion of its dollars into gold. See Kirshner 1995, chap. 5, on "systemic disruption."

[58] And as Volcker and Gyohten 1992 (chap. 3), Gavin 2003, and many others have noted, Bretton Woods was itself politically and economically precarious by the mid-1960s.

I have already noted the question of sustainability of U.S. current account deficits. But in many ways, the potential negative effects on the East Asian economies themselves are likely to be at least as serious for those economies as the effects of unwinding on the U.S. economy.

Three main problems for emerging economies are inherent in this sort of foreign exchange reserve accumulation. One, which is unlikely on its own to lead to a crisis, is that reserve accumulation is a misallocation of resources. Reserves are held in foreign currencies (typically the U.S. dollar), largely in short-term securities, such as Treasury bills, that yield low interest and are highly liquid. But rapidly developing economies by definition have substantial investment opportunities. Thus, governments are in a very real sense trading off improvements in the living standards of their own populations in order to fund the living standards of foreigners who are far more affluent.[59] To the extent that they are trying to stave off appreciation of the home currency, the trade-off is even worse, since likely future appreciation will further lower the local-currency returns of U.S. debt instruments. A second problem, which I explore more fully in chapter 5, is that by bypassing domestic means of financial intermediation, those markets are liable not to develop as fully as they should.

The third problem is the difficulties for domestic monetary policy of accommodating massive reserve accumulations.[60] Such accumulations constitute an equivalent increase in base money, forcing central banks to carry out substantial sterilization if they want to prevent domestic inflation from resulting. Even where price inflation can be avoided, the likely results over time are asset-price bubbles and negative effects on the quality of financial intermediation.

If these patterns persist over a sufficient period of time, they set regional economies up for financial crises. These would be different from the crisis of 1997, which began as an attack by outside speculators on currencies with insufficient reserve backing.[61] Rather, a crisis would likely begin domestically, as a burst bubble and/or crisis of financial institutions, possibly mimicking the onset of Japan's "great stagnation" of 1991–2004.[62] While spiraling depreciations of regional currencies against the dollar would be less likely than in 1997, that would be of little comfort to individuals, businesses, and banks that experienced devastating losses. Such crises could occur regardless of formal currency regime or the sustainability of U.S. deficits.

---

[59]Kikkawa's (otherwise deeply flawed) 1998 book has a wonderfully indignant postscript about this phenomenon that invokes Aesop's fable about the ant and the grasshopper.
[60]Goldstein and Lardy 2005; Mohanty and Turner 2006.
[61]Goldstein and Wong 2005.
[62]This is the name given by Hutchison and Westermann 2006.

The case of China is instructive in this regard. In the space of a few years, China went from unexceptional holdings of foreign exchange reserves to the world's largest, surpassing $1.5 trillion by the end of 2007. From June 2004 to June 2006, reserves doubled from $470 billion to $940 billion; as recently as 2000, China held less than $200 billion (which at the time seemed enormous). The bulk of this accumulation has been due to China's massive trade surpluses, but capital inflows have also contributed.[63]

The buildup of reserves, in combination with the strict dollar peg prior to July 2005 (and an only slightly looser dollar peg through 2007, despite the claim of transition to a currency-basket approach), has had two macroeconomic effects. First, it has put pressure on domestic monetary policy, with observers particularly concerned about asset-price inflation, including property bubbles.[64] Second, it has been self-reinforcing. With the relative weakness of the U.S. dollar, China's effective exchange rate stayed weak through 2006, leading to greater overall price competitiveness and supporting further growth of the trade surplus.[65] And widespread expectations of an eventual appreciation of the RMB led to a "one-way bet" on the currency. Although currency speculation per se is not allowed in China, foreign investors flooded the market with FDI (contributing to several urban real estate booms) in order to get in before the inevitable RMB rise would make investments more costly.[66]

One of the great challenges of Chinese macroeconomic policy by 2005 was how to end the "one-way bet" and dampen domestic price pressures, while simultaneously maintaining price competitiveness on international markets and not causing serious dislocation among producers of tradable goods and services. Most observers agreed that some change in the exchange rate would be needed, but this posed several problems for the Chinese authorities.[67]

Part of the genesis of China's problems was the simple fact of an administered exchange rate that had been held steady for over a decade. This meant that any change in the dollar rate would be taken as a major policy shift. In general, the transition from one administered rate to another calls into question the government's commitment to the exchange rate—not only because change is in principle no longer out of the question, but also because whatever level is chosen can be seen as arbitrary (especially if the transition process does not include a temporary float to determine market

[63] Goldstein and Lardy 2005, 7–8.
[64] See, for example, Richard McGregor, "Bubbly Asset Prices Hold a Nasty Surprise for China," *FT,* August 23, 2007, 38.
[65] BIS data series.
[66] PIFS 2006a.
[67] Goldstein and Lardy 2005, 2006; Ahearne, Cline, Lee, Park, Pisani-Ferry, and Williamson 2007; Bergsten 2007.

pricing). Both aspects are likely to inspire additional attempts by market participants to profit from future changes by taking long or short positions, thus reducing stability of expectations and reducing the ability of the government to maintain the rate.[68] This problem is not easily soluble by making incremental changes or instituting a crawling peg, since such a policy very clearly invites the likelihood of future shifts, thus whetting the appetite of investors looking for a one-way bet. From a domestic political perspective, China's central concern has been to avoid disrupting the growth of employment, much of which has depended on manufacturing for exports.[69] Any future economic effects that could be even remotely attributed to the exchange rate shift would create the potential of placing blame on the officials who carried it out, thus creating a strong incentive for procrastination and blame-shifting. Chinese officials also have had a strong desire not to be seen to be bending to the will of either financial markets or U.S. government pressure.

Currency Baskets

Japanese finance officials and policy academics from early in the decade had a ready answer for how to handle this issue: a currency-basket system. For example, a Japanese MOF memo presented to Chinese Ministry of Finance officials in late 2004 or early 2005 analyzes the pros and cons of a variety of currency regimes, but clearly comes down on the side of currency baskets.[70] Government officials at the time were forced to be quite circumspect about suggesting any shift in currency regime for China, and thus they typically presented such discussions in general terms rather than as a policy prescription.[71] Japanese policy academics were less constrained and by their own accounts were forthright but diffident in their communications with Chinese think tank researchers and at seminars attended by Chinese Ministry

[68] This indeed is part of McKinnon and Schnabl's (2004) justification for recommending that China maintain its dollar peg.

[69] This has been clearly recognized by the Chinese central bank. See, for example, Hu 2007. (The author is the deputy governor of the People's Bank of China and administrator of the State Administration of Foreign Exchange.)

[70] This is an undated, unpublished (but not classified) memo printed in Japanese and Chinese entitled "On the Asian Monetary System: Basket Systems and the Path to a Common Currency." Given the frequency of contacts at all levels between the two countries' ministries of finance, it seems likely that this was not a unique effort. A similar, but publicly available, example can be found in a discussion paper entitled "Exchange Rate Regimes for Emerging Market Economies," prepared jointly by the Japanese and French staff for the fourth ASEM finance ministers meeting in Copenhagen, July 5–6, 2002.

[71] Personal interviews.

of Finance or People's Bank of China (PBOC) officials.[72] These informal efforts reflected the considerable published work by Japanese economists on the impacts of currency baskets and their optimal design.[73]

The economic thrust of the argument for currency baskets remained the same (i.e., better reflecting economies' actual patterns of international economic transactions and reducing macroeconomic volatility), but currency baskets were also seen as solving some of the complications of a transition away from the strict dollar peg of 8.29 RMB to the dollar. By shifting to a currency basket with unannounced weights,[74] China would be able to alter the RMB-dollar exchange rate without creating a specific target for speculative attacks. It could also introduce flexibility without explicitly stating it: since basket weights would be unannounced, it would not be immediately obvious whether the RMB-dollar rate had changed because of a desire to appreciate, movements of nondollar currencies in the basket, or internal shifts in basket weights. According to some economists, it might also provide a rationale for diversifying foreign exchange reserves.[75]

On July 21, 2005, the PBOC announced the introduction of a basket-based currency regime that addressed those very problems, although it differed from the standard currency-basket system in important ways. The announcement was accompanied by a 2 percent appreciation against the dollar. It is worth quoting from the communiqué at length:

1. Starting from July 21, 2005, China will reform the exchange rate regime by moving into a managed floating exchange rate regime based on market supply and demand with reference to a basket of currencies. RMB will no longer be pegged to the U.S. dollar and the RMB exchange rate regime will be improved with greater flexibility.

---

[72]Personal interviews with several policy-oriented Japanese economists. For example, in May 2005, one stated to me with conviction that he had received clear signals that China would be shifting to a currency-basket system by the end of the summer. Events proved him to be correct, although he was subsequently disappointed by the low level of de facto flexibility and high level of dollar correlation that ensued.

[73]For example, Kawai and Takagi 2005; Yoshino, Kaji, and Asonuma 2005b; FEC 2000.

[74]When a currency-basket–based system was introduced in July 2005, both the currency composition and weighting were unannounced, but after several weeks, on August 10, the PBOC announced eleven currencies that were included in the basket—U.S. dollar, euro, yen, Korean won, Singapore dollar, UK pound, Russian ruble, Malaysian ringgit, Canadian dollar, Australian dollar, and Thai baht.

[75]Yoshino, Kaji, and Asonuma, 2005c. This opinion is not universally shared, as noted in Kenen and Meade 2008, 163. Generally speaking, reserves are understood to be meant for currency intervention, which means that the most liquid and easily traded units are the most appropriate. But if we are looking at excess reserves or otherwise have a reason to worry about stabilizing the value of the reserves in the home currency, such diversification might make sense.

2. The People's Bank of China will announce the closing price of a foreign currency such as the U.S. dollar traded against the RMB in the inter-bank foreign exchange market after the closing of the market on each working day, and will make it the central parity for the trading against the RMB on the following working day.
3. The daily trading price of the U.S. dollar against the RMB in the inter-bank foreign exchange market will continue to be allowed to float within a band of 0.3 percent around the central parity published by the People's Bank of China, while the trading prices of the non-U.S. dollar currencies against the RMB will be allowed to move within a certain band announced by the People's Bank of China.[76]

In principle, if the RMB were allowed to appreciate the maximum 0.3 percent against the dollar every trading day, a 20 percent appreciation could be achieved in three months. In fact, Chinese authorities were more cautious. Even eighteen months later, the RMB had appreciated less than 7 percent against the dollar (and slightly less in terms of its real effective exchange rate). There was a significant acceleration beginning in May 2007, apparently due to concerns about domestic inflation, but even by the end of the year its appreciation relative to its pre–currency basket level was only about 14 percent against the dollar (and slightly less than 9% in terms of real effective exchange rate).

It is also interesting to note that, while flexibility was explicitly built into the system in the forms of both a currency basket and the 0.3 percent band, the operational target remained the U.S. dollar. The currency basket is only the subject of PBOC "reference," leaving the currency regime simply a more flexible dollar peg with just enough ambiguity to create some uncertainty (and thus risks) for currency speculators. In retrospect, it was clear that the decision introduced a system that could effectively accommodate flexibility, but that actual flexibility would be a political choice made in the future, as policymakers gathered more experience. Whether the appreciation that began in mid-2007 was a sign that they had made that choice was unclear as of early 2008, but it did appear that abrupt change was not on the menu.

East Asian Reserves Management as a Domestic, Regional, and Global Issue

The vast accumulation of foreign exchange reserves in East Asia poses a variety of problems for regional states. As we have seen, the domestic implications

[76]"Public Announcement of the People's Bank of China on Reforming the RMB Exchange Rate Regime," July 11, 2005. http://www.pbc.gov.cn/english//detail.asp?col=6400&ID=542.

stem from the difficulty of sterilizing the increases in the monetary base, raising concerns about inflation and asset bubbles. Problems arise internationally as well, at both the regional and global levels.

Regionally, the current situation presents a collective-action problem. If (or when) authorities start unwinding their dollar positions, lack of coordination could lead to a very abrupt drop in the value of the dollar and uncoordinated appreciation of the various East Asian currencies. Authorities are likely to be concerned about the value of their reserves and the effects of large-scale currency shifts on their economies, so they should prefer some mechanism to prevent competitive sell-offs of reserves. Maintaining relative intraregional currency stability as the dollar falls in value is one means of doing so that would be more transparent (and thus more easily enforceable) than behind-the-scenes bargaining among central bankers.[77]

Globally, of course, the same point holds, and recent efforts to promote multilateral cooperation to eliminate payments imbalances seek to address it. If the dollar falls enough in value, states with large dollar reserves will be tempted to sell off their reserves before the plunge deepens; given that they will all have the same incentive, a dollar crash could occur in the absence of some sort of coordination. If that were to occur, U.S. access to foreign credit would tighten, interest rates would spiral, and demand would drop, with repercussions felt around the world.

What makes this story interesting is the involvement of a limited number of states rather than a profusion of private sector actors as the great holders of dollars. On the one hand, this would seem to create political leverage on the part of creditor states, whose actions could severely damage the U.S. economy. As usual, however, systemic disruption is most attractive as a threat, since the aftershocks would severely hurt the disrupter. States are more likely than private investors to be stable holders of dollars for several other reasons. First, it is much easier to solve the collective-action problem with a handful of states holding major reserves than among a multitude of private actors. Second, states do not have shareholders and are typically not holding onto dollars with the primary expectation of making profits on them. Third, governments like those of Japan, Taiwan, and South Korea (not to mention some major creditors outside East Asia, such as Saudi Arabia and Kuwait) that are dependent on the United States for their security cannot credibly threaten a large-scale sell-off, significantly reducing the stock of dollars in danger. Even China, rival though it is for influence in East Asia, would have no incentive to cause a dollar crash, as the economic effects on it would likely be as bad as those on the United States; moreover, regime survival would be threatened by domestic economic chaos.

[77] Chung and Eichengreen 2007.

The characterization by Lawrence Summers of the current situation as a "financial balance of terror" is therefore quite apt. Neither side benefits from hostile action, but miscalculation could lead to an unleashing of mutually assured economic destruction.[78] All players would benefit from reducing the raw materials for financial meltdown.

Even if systemic dangers are manageable, however, bilateral frictions are likely to continue. We have already seen a variety of attempts by the U.S. Congress to target China (and to a lesser extent Japan) with sanctions based on their manipulation of the value of their currencies.[79] But the need for governments to get better returns on their foreign exchange reserves will increasingly lead also to frictions over how those reserves are managed. One battlefield is likely to be the management of sovereign wealth funds, through which governments will increasingly become owners of foreign firms and other assets.[80]

Regional Currency Cooperation: Options and Prospects

Bringing these disparate threads together is the notion of regional currency cooperation. Meaningful currency cooperation is hard under the best of circumstances, as the last century and more of monetary history makes all too clear.[81] And, with the exception of its high and growing degree of economic integration, East Asia does not present the best of circumstances for currency cooperation. Even if we consider only the ASEAN5 plus China, Japan, and Korea, the differences in economic level and composition, financial openness, state capabilities, and currency regimes are immense; moreover, there is no clear leader that can provide the kinds of public goods needed to secure cooperation. Nonetheless, the ASEAN+3 states have officially endorsed the idea of currency cooperation (although Japan appears much more enthusiastic about it than its partners).

Options for Currency Cooperation

Before addressing the politics of currency cooperation, we need to clarify what cooperation actually means in the East Asian context. Several proposals for currency stabilization are in the air, all of which involve some sort

[78] Bowles and Wang, forthcoming.
[79] These included the Schumer-Graham, Hunter-Ryan, Grassley-Baucus, and Dodd-Shelby bills introduced between 2005 and 2007.
[80] The position of the U.S. government on sovereign wealth funds is clearly and intelligently laid out in Lowery 2007, and Kimmitt 2008.
[81] Volcker and Gyohten 1992; Webb 1995; Kenen and Meade 2008.

of currency-basket arrangement(s), whether as a goal or an intermediate step.[82]

The concentration on baskets as the basis of cooperation reflects a preference not only for stability but also for reducing dependence—after all, if intraregional currency stability is the goal, then the closest thing that East Asia has had to a stable currency system in the post–Bretton Woods period has been uncoordinated nominal dollar pegging. Despite the stability achieved in exchange rates in East Asia (notably excepting the yen) in the decade or so prior to 1997, an explicit return to dollar pegging throughout the region has already been definitively ruled out on economic and political grounds.[83] In any event, as I have already argued, the de facto dollar standard has become dangerous, and a key role of currency cooperation will be to manage an exit strategy.

Currency basket–based plans vary along three dimensions: which currencies make up the baskets, which economies participate, and whether there are rules of enforcement. In the yen internationalization efforts of the Japanese Ministry of Finance in the late 1990s, it was assumed that individual economies would manage their currencies on the basis of self-determined currency baskets that would include the global key currencies—that is, the yen, dollar, and euro.[84] Other plans envisage regionally constructed baskets, in which multiple economies base their currency management on a common set of currencies and weights.[85] Baskets can comprise either global key currencies or regional currencies, a distinction that has both economic and political implications. In addition, the policy coordination process itself is an important factor in how plans will actually work. For example, are there agreed-upon bands or reference ranges for currency movements? Are there obligations to intervene in cases of both overvaluation and undervaluation? How does rebasing occur?

While Japan's initial promotion of individual country exchange rate management based on currency baskets would have increased use of the yen and better contributed to the stability of East Asian economies' effective (trade-weighted) exchange rates, they could not be seen as a form of regional cooperation. That element was assumed to be plausible only in the future, through convergence.[86] A different approach, which is explicitly patterned

[82]The most recent efforts of the research sponsored by ASEAN+3 on the subject are detailed in IIMA 2007. See also Ito 2007; Chung and Eichengreen 2007, especially the introductory chapter.

[83]In contrast to the political facts on the ground, McKinnon 2004 calls for an "East Asian dollar standard."

[84]Foreign Exchange Commission 1999.

[85]Kwan 2001; Ito 2007; Ogawa and Shimizu 2007.

[86]For one approach, see Kwan 1997, 2001. These works are based on Kwan's 1996 dissertation, marking him as one of the earliest East Asian theorists of regional currency cooperation.

on Europe's experience with the European Currency Unit (ECU), focuses on the creation of a single regional basket based on regional currencies themselves.[87] This would allow for joint floating against the dollar and euro. Moreover, it would remove the yen from a position as an external reference point, which is symbolically (and thus politically) meaningful, but is also intended to have the effect of making Japan a full partner in the process of currency cooperation.

As of fall 2007, there were two main existing projects, both based on the designation of a single basket of regional currencies. In this approach, individual currencies are tracked against the value of a weighted average of regional currencies; those whose relative values diverge would be expected to take action to move back into line with their initial values. Japan's semi-official Research Institute of Economy, Trade, and Industry, for example, has promoted the Asian Monetary Unit (AMU) indicator project.[88] Unlike the old ECU, the AMU has no legal significance, and there have been no AMU-denominated securities issued. While the AMU has remained a purely academic exercise, in 2006 the ASEAN+3 asked the ADB to develop an official Asian Currency Unit that could be used both to track currency movements and to denominate regional financial instruments and transactions. This effort was announced with considerable fanfare by the ADB in January 2006; however, after months of internal disagreements, the ACU effort was transferred back to the ASEAN+3, where a research project was established in May 2006.[89] No concrete results had been announced as of early 2008.

[87] See, for example, Kawai 2005; Kawai and Takagi 2005; Ito and Park 2004; Ogawa 2005; and RIETI's AMU project, headed by Eiji Ogawa. http://www.rieti.go.jp/users/amu/en/index.html.

[88] The AMU is calculated as a weighted average, based on GDP (on a purchasing power parity basis in this case) and total trade shares. Interestingly, the use of PPP means that the weight of the Chinese RMB is significantly higher than that of the yen (35% vs. 28%). Given the RMB's rigid dollar peg prior to July 2005 (and de facto soft peg since then), this actually increases the apparent role of the dollar in regional exchange rates. The AMU is measured against a weighted average of dollar and euro. "We should quote the value of the AMU in terms of a weighted average of the U.S. dollar and the euro because both the United States and EU countries are important trading partners for East Asia. The weighted average of the U.S. dollar and the euro (hereafter, U.S.$-euro) is based on the East Asian countries' trade volumes with the United States and the euro area. The weights on the U.S. dollar and the euro are set at 65% and 35%, respectively." http://www.rieti.go.jp/users/amu/en/detail.html#01.

[89] Most observers and participants with whom I have discussed these issues (including former ADB officials) seem to agree that the ADB had to drop the effort due to lack of consensus among ADB member economies—by this, I do not mean only the United States, but also a number of other members whose currencies were not going to be included. One working-level Japanese participant stated to me that the real reason was that ASEAN+3 central banks (some of which have formal authority over exchange rate issues) objected to the idea of currency issues being driven by an organization in which they had no role. This appears to

One problem facing these efforts is that there is no apparent private sector demand for a synthetic regional currency. If there were, someone would be making money off it, either by making use of an existing model like the AMU or by making a market in a privately designed unit of account.[90] The fact is that private sector financial institutions can diversify their regional currency risks more effectively and with lower transaction costs through existing market measures than through use of a basket currency.

Neither of the current proposals for currency baskets actually calls for the standard institutional measures that one would expect, such as defined reference ranges for currency movement, requirements for intervention as the edges of ranges are approached, or macroeconomic policy coordination. Instead, the idea is that a voluntary regional currency basket will be a stepping-stone to a longer-run vision of more and more ambitious economic coordination that could eventually lead to a single Asian currency.[91] The reasoning, which seeks to build on the experiences of the European countries, is that the exercise of maintaining rough stability against other regional currencies will lead over time to a convergence in macroeconomic policies.[92] As more and more states realize the benefits of such benchmarking in terms of reduced currency volatility and (presumably) more stable domestic macroeconomic policies, they will have an incentive to participate and to involve themselves ever more deeply in policy coordination.

Politics and Prospects for Regional Cooperation

What really is going on here? Economists associated with the projects argue that they are using market-based measures to demonstrate the usefulness of cooperation and that the voluntary approach allows states to enter into cooperation when they are ready.

This is rather hard to take seriously, however. The point can be made most effectively in comparative terms.[93] Looking at the development of the European Monetary Union, there were three ways in which public goods

---

be a minority interpretation, although central bank concerns may have contributed to the ADB's decision.

[90] Kimura 2006 calls for a two-stage process that begins with a "private-sector ACU," then moves forward with using it as a unit of exchange between governments and central banks. Eichengreen 2006b calls for essentially the opposite, suggesting that if governments and central banks start accepting an ACU as a settlement currency, that will help to induce a preference for currency stability around the benchmark.

[91] Kawai 2005; Kawai and Takagi 2005; Kuroda 2005, chap. 4.

[92] The incrementalist premise of these efforts is seen clearly in the various proposals in Chung and Eichengreen 2007. See also Letiche 2000; Murase 2000; ADB 2004; Girardin 2004; Ito and Park 2004; Kimura 2006.

[93] Rhee 2004 makes this case nicely.

were credibly provided to make participation in currency cooperation attractive. First, Germany, with its highly independent Bundesbank, was already providing a credible nominal anchor to its regional partners, as shown by the de facto DM area in the Benelux countries. Second, the European Community had already developed considerable institutional abilities over time, and these legal tools and linkages to other forms of cooperation could be adapted to the task of creating a framework of joint responsibility for currency intervention and later for macroeconomic coordination. Third, the actual rules of the European Exchange Rate Mechanism required unlimited currency intervention when the edges of the bands were approached, with Germany taking the de facto role of lender of last resort.

In East Asia, only Japan is even theoretically capable of providing such public goods, and it has not done so.[94] It does not even provide an equivalent of the minimal level of public goods that the United States has for countries that have dollarized in Latin America and elsewhere.[95] Nor does the ACU/AMU approach promise either liquidity or lender-of-last-resort function.

China, meanwhile, has apparently amassed the de facto power to make its rivals try to avoid allowing their currencies to appreciate relative to the RMB, even at considerable cost to their own macroeconomic policy management. But it is a developing country with a soft-dollar peg and strict exchange controls. It is in no position to provide ongoing liquidity or to be a market for distressed goods, and it has been cautious about even providing emergency liquidity, of which it has vast amounts.

Thus Japan is not willing to make currency cooperation attractive, while China has neither the means nor the interest to do so.[96] If we ask ourselves the question of what sorts of institutional arrangements would be needed to support currency cooperation, the inadequacy of either Japan or China (much less the two in concert) to provide the necessary leadership becomes crashingly apparent.

Hurdles for East Asian Currency Cooperation

One issue concerns the coordination process itself. Other than the purely passive approach embodied in the AMU and ACU efforts, any form of meaningful currency cooperation would require the establishment of bands (or at least reference ranges) within which participating currencies should be managed. This would require agreement among participants, perhaps with separate guidelines for various sets of economies. There would have to be some level of consensus as to when and how to rebase exchange rates,

---

[94] Rhee 2004.
[95] Steil and Litan 2006, chap. 6.
[96] Katada, forthcoming, makes this point as well.

whether to target nominal or real rates (the latter presumably requiring provision for crawling pegs), how to address differential rates of inflation, and how to accommodate differential rates of growth, among other practical difficulties.[97]

The coordination process would also call for an enhanced process of multilateral surveillance among regional economies. The ERPD process provides at least a rudimentary framework for this.[98] Effective surveillance is difficult, however, especially if there is no effective means of enforcement, such as the IMF's ability to threaten the withdrawal of support. If a regional organization is unable to make such a threat in a crisis, how is it to have any meaningful effect in less dire circumstances? Participants would be left only with peer pressure; the G7 process is but one good practical example of how ineffective that can be without brawn to back it up.[99]

Even if these procedural difficulties were to be adequately addressed, there would likely still be a need for participants to commit to supporting the level of other participants' currencies relative to the index. In the G7's 1987 Louvre Accord, this problem was (ultimately unsuccessfully) addressed by mandating intervention when one or another currency began to move beyond the reference range. In Europe, the former Exchange Rate Mechanism also mandated intervention when currencies pushed the limits of the bands, but backed up the commitment with a reserve pooling arrangement.[100] In East Asia, whereas the Chiang Mai Initiative—or a possible future Asian monetary fund—could serve as the basis for true reserve pooling (as was agreed on in principle in Kyoto in 2007),[101] it is not obvious that the political will would exist at any foreseeable time to use such funds for ongoing currency management, as opposed to crisis management.

Finally, even the purpose of coordination would be open to contestation. The EMU only became possible, even within the cooperative and highly institutionalized context of the EU, once France and Italy had accepted the German position that monetary policy should be focused entirely on price stability. In contrast, there is at present no consensus about optimal

---

[97]Rapid growth relative to other economies should lead to an appreciation in a given country's exchange rate, due to the "Belassa-Samuelson effect."

[98]But as noted in Kenen and Meade 2008, the ERPD framework is minimal compared to what would be needed (156–59).

[99]From an economic perspective this may not be a negative point. Following Goldstein 2002, Rose (2006) argues that there is an emerging global currency standard of domestic inflation targeting paired with more or less freely floating rates. Rose suggests that it is much more stable than one based on fixed rates, or even a managed floating system in which authorities target the exchange rate as an important variable of monetary policy. If that is the case, then the benefits of formal regional currency cooperation in East Asia would be negligible, except for dealing with crises or orderly reduction of foreign exchange reserves.

[100]Funabashi 1989, 204–7; Webb 1995, 211–16.

[101]See also Olarn 2004; Ito and Park 2004.

macroeconomic management in East Asia, and indeed the basic interests of Japan and China differ. At the risk of oversimplification, Japan's overall economic goal in regional exchange rate cooperation is to stabilize its external economic environment and to pressure the United States not to shift the burden of balance of payments adjustments onto its trading partners, whereas China's is to support its own rapid industrialization and economic growth, while accommodating its growing underclass of internal migrant labor. Japan's interests call for a continuation of the goals of the yen internationalization project—in other words, increased weight of the yen in regional currency management; expanded use of the yen throughout the region as a vehicle currency, store of value, and unit of invoicing; and the establishment of settlement systems that support the role of the yen and of Japanese financial markets in the region. For China, it implies the need to keep dollar prices of its exports stable and the RMB slightly undervalued relative to its regional competitors. From an economic perspective, for the time being, China has no intrinsic interest in de-dollarization, apart from the need to prevent overheating in its own economy and perhaps to diversify its vast holdings of foreign exchange.[102]

A More Modest Agenda

So what then is the point of discussing currency coordination in the ASEAN+3? It seems to me that a much more minimalist agenda is in order, and may even be feasible. The single most important thing, both economically and politically, that regional currency cooperation has the potential to achieve is to provide a regional basis of support for the global process of reducing imbalances. It is generally agreed that under either hard-landing or soft-landing scenarios, East Asian economies (especially China and Japan) will need to experience significant reduction in their net savings and appreciation of their currencies, while the United States undergoes the opposite.[103] Regional efforts could provide a means of monitoring the actions of the governments and the effects on the economies, as well as a bargaining venue to reassure the Chinese and Japanese governments that they will not be acting alone.

As for the regional impact of cooperation, one important element will be to provide a venue for discussion of how to deal with unwinding of foreign

---

[102]There is at least anecdotal evidence that diversification is beginning. One such report is "China Plans a Policy Switch on Massive Foreign Reserves," *FT,* January 22, 2007. But if Dooley, Folkerts-Landau, and Garber (2003) are correct, Chinese economic policymakers may have relatively little interest even in safeguarding the value of the country's reserves. The rise of sovereign wealth funds, meanwhile, could help to reduce the opportunity costs of holding reserves, but they are likely to increase tensions with other countries, especially the United States.

[103]Cline 2005; Ahearne, Cline, Lee, Park, Pisani-Ferry, and Williamson 2007; Bergsten 2007.

exchange reserves (especially dollar positions). ASEAN+3 governments can also enhance the ERPD process. Although it is too much to expect that consideration for the preferences of regional partners will affect the policy choices of major economies like China, greater transparency regarding currency policies can provide important informational inputs into macroeconomic and exchange rate policymaking, especially given the importance of exchange rate pass-through in the smaller economies. China over the next several years is likely to go through a process of increasing the flexibility of its exchange rate and liberalizing capital inflows and outflows.[104] This is bound to have major effects on its regional partners, and regional discussions can clarify their options and perhaps deter beggar-thy-neighbor policies.

Longer term, as China becomes more of a regional leader, it may become willing to provide public goods or accept free riding from its partners. Until then, perhaps the most important thing for all the economies of East Asia is to choose the right exchange rate regime for themselves—not a single regional basket, but perhaps a single regional approach. As of early 2008, Korea and Thailand had adopted a system of managed floating with inflation targeting.[105] This may become the eventual regional (perhaps even global) standard.[106]

As in all regional political issues, there is also an issue of timing. Given the unique position of Japan as the economy with the only globally important currency in East Asia and experience with multilateral surveillance, it is currently in the best position to be a leader in the design of currency cooperation. Meanwhile, as a direct economic competitor to its ASEAN+3 counterparts (other than Japan), China's actions have significant impact, so it is inevitably a major player, whether coordination is to be by agreement or just tacit. And, as in other aspects of multilateral action, China has time on its side. Why should its leaders choose to get locked in to an institutional framework that might be difficult to change given that (a) it is not yet clear what type of framework would most benefit the Chinese economy, and (b) China's ability to dictate the terms of the framework will improve over time in tandem with its economic growth?

Asia's Currency Future

Ironically, as things stand as of early 2008, and regardless of whether some level of regional currency cooperation can be established, the U.S. dollar

---

[104] Hu 2007.

[105] IMF 2006 classifies South Korea as "independently floating," but studies continue to show a high correlation of the won to the dollar and a lower correlation to the yen. It is also difficult to think of any currency as floating when reserves have increased so rapidly in the last several years.

[106] Goldstein 2002; Rose 2006.

looks set to remain the main vehicle currency within the region, for simple liquidity reasons. The most liquid exchange markets for currencies in East Asia (as indeed, throughout most of the world) trade against the dollar. It is still cheaper to trade Korean won or Malaysian ringgit for dollars and then dollars for Japanese yen than to try to settle directly. The costs would be even higher for trades between non-yen Asian currencies. To establish regional settlements mechanisms that bypassed the dollar would be technically difficult as well as costly.[107] At least in the short run, they would suffer from large bid-ask spreads; if netting were used as an alternative to real-time gross settlement, risks of nonrepayment would also increase.[108] If it is in fact possible to increase trading liquidity enough among regional currencies to make bypassing the dollar cost-effective in settlements, it would presumably be through the development of local-currency financial markets on a large scale within the region. I address efforts to promote such markets more fully in chapter 5, but for now it should suffice to say that this would be a long-term prospect.

Economic incentives may also persist to keep the dollar as an invoice currency. Given that global commodities are priced in dollars (again benefiting from network effects), that a significant share of East Asia's final products are shipped to North America, and that North American–based competitors invoice in dollars, many firms are likely to focus on dollar-based pricing regardless of whether an ACU is in place. This would parallel what Japanese officials discovered in the yen internationalization efforts of the late 1990s, which foundered partly because it turned out that Japanese firms preferred to maintain their focus on dollar pricing.[109] Thus, it is possible that the only key currency function that the dollar would lose in the face of regional competition would be as store of value.

This does not bode well for regional economic stability. In the absence of an effective global process to address payments imbalances, domestic macroeconomic management will continue to be difficult. If there is such a process, regional states are bound to have to make major economic changes in order to facilitate orderly adjustment of global imbalances. If the global adjustment process proves to be disorderly, prospects may be even worse, especially if ASEAN+3 states compete among themselves to minimize the fallout. With effective regional currency coordination difficult, states will be wise to try to reduce their exposure on an individual basis. Ideally, this would

---

[107] Nonetheless, some analysts like Shinohara (1999, 200) continue to call for the establishment of regional settlement systems. Discussions of regional options are part and parcel of the ASEAN+3 agenda on currency cooperation and bond market development, but there appears to be no economic traction for any of them as yet.

[108] Such settlement risk is also known as Herstatt risk, after a German bank that went bankrupt in 1974, leaving its creditors in the money market in the lurch.

[109] Keizai Dōyūkai 2000.

probably look like "managed floating plus,"[110] with retention of substantially smaller (but still substantial) and more diversified foreign exchange reserves than we currently see. The best hope for economic stability is that at least some of the necessary changes are likely to be attractive to the governments of China and Japan, as reflected in the action plans they submitted as part of the IMF's Multilateral Consultation on Global Imbalances.[111]

The Strategic Triangle and the Political Economy of Exchange Rates

Given the immense difficulties of achieving effective currency cooperation in East Asia, as well as the uncertain benefits, a reader might reasonably ask what the point might be of this discussion, let alone of the efforts themselves. I argue that at the heart of these efforts lies a series of political challenges to the existing regional and global economic order, as well as efforts on all sides to create a template for the future regional financial architecture. The theme of currency cooperation also helps to tie together the other strands of financial regionalism into a single, coherent package. This point is particularly important for Japan, for which the first decade of the twenty-first century may be a final (albeit limited) opportunity to establish regional arrangements that will benefit it politically and economically in the face of the changing global and regional power structure.[112]

Regional Currency Cooperation and the Global Role of the Dollar

In August 2007 a sensational article in the UK *Daily Telegraph* claimed that "the Chinese government has begun a concerted campaign of economic threats against the United States, hinting that it may liquidate its vast holding of U.S. Treasury bonds if Washington imposes trade sanctions to force a yuan revaluation."[113] Although the evidence and logic presented in the article were dubious at best, markets reacted nervously, necessitating strong rebuttals from the PBOC and other official Chinese sources.[114] The event

---

[110] Goldstein 2002.

[111] IMF 2007.

[112] See also Katada, forthcoming.

[113] "China Threatens to Trigger U.S. Dollar Crash," *Daily Telegraph,* August 8, 2007, 1.

[114] The PBOC's response of August 13, posted on its website, was entitled "PBC Official Interview with Xinhua News Agency on Western Media Report of 'China Threatening to Sell Dollar'." http://www.pbc.gov.cn/english//detail.asp?col=6400&ID=894, accessed August 27, 2007. Chris Nelson, a Washington-based analyst of trade politics, reported on August 9 that a Chinese source had contacted him to state that China "has neither the goal nor the

quickly blew over, but it clearly fed off of a profound sense of unease with the immense and growing stockpile of dollars in foreign hands.

Although the notion of a massive retaliatory sell-off of China's dollar reserves is unlikely on any number of levels, the possibility that policy decisions by ASEAN+3 governments could have a profound influence on the global role of the dollar over the longer term is not. This would not likely take the form of a unified Asian currency taking over the role of the dollar as key currency; if any currency were to have a shot at that, it would be the euro.[115] More likely, the rise of intraregional exchange rate management, settlement systems, and financial integration would erode dollar predominance to the point where the United States would lose some or all of the "exorbitant privilege" afforded it by the dollar. Practically speaking, this could mean a situation with no global currency leader at all. While some writers have argued that this would be good for preventing global imbalances, it could also make crisis management more difficult or even spark competitive efforts to create currency areas.[116]

If Dooley and McKinnon are right about the trade-offs being made by East Asian central banks and governments, then even a substantial shift toward cooperation in the way that those policymakers approach intraregional exchange rates and financial integration should make little or no difference in their aggregate willingness to accumulate dollars. After all, they are already pursuing a rational second-best policy in which the value of reserves is of minimal concern. (McKinnon does make clear, however, that this "conflicted virtue" presents serious problems for regional economies and that stability will call for U.S. action to stem its international borrowing.)[117]

But what if there is in reality no Bretton Woods II? What if the behavior of East Asian central banks has instead reflected short- or medium-term factors such as flight to quality, bureaucratic policymaking, and underdeveloped local-currency financial markets? In other words, what if we are actually in the world where most analysts assume we are, in which sustainability depends on returns on U.S. dollar investments?[118] Then it is indeed possible that substantial withdrawal of funds from U.S. assets will occur as better alternatives arise. With the development of better alternatives a key goal of East Asian financial regionalism (see chapter 5), pressure will increase on

---

intention" to sell off dollars, intimating that this line came directly from Premier Wen Jiabao. (*Nelson Report*, August 9, 2007, and personal communication.)

[115] Chinn and Frankel 2005.

[116] Advocates include Utsumi 1999, Kwan 2001, and Kuroda 2005. Cohen 2007 raises the specter of a leaderless system, calling to mind the earlier arguments of Kindleberger 1981 and 1986.

[117] McKinnon 2005, 245–49.

[118] See, for example, Cline 2005; Kuroda 2005, 123–28; Ahearne, Cline, Lee, Park, Pisani-Ferry, and Williamson 2007; Bergsten 2007.

U.S. macroeconomic authorities to maintain the attractiveness of the U.S. economy for international investors. Improvement of economic growth and investment opportunities in Europe would add to these pressures. And while it is still hard at this point to imagine what a world would look like where basic commodities and the main world financial benchmarks were not all invoiced in dollars, the world of currency competition that has been predicted for so long could conceivably come into view.

The Dollar and Global Leadership

A world of currency competition among the U.S. dollar, euro, and East Asian currency (or currencies) would have profound effects on the "exorbitant privileges" of the U.S. government and residents. It would create pressures to reduce—and in the long run, reverse—the persistent U.S. current account deficits that have been a part of the global economic landscape for so long. This would require substantial belt-tightening by both government and households; in the absence of high productivity growth, it would mean a reduction of U.S. living standards.[119] This would, needless to say, have large-scale domestic political effects in the United States. Although some of them would be unpredictable, one likely outcome would be measures of financial protectionism, aimed especially at China.[120] Given the fact that the United States and China have together accounted for over a third of world growth since 2000, the prospects of weakening economic ties would be serious for everyone.

Whatever else occurs, belt-tightening policies on the part of the United States could be enough to retain the global role of the dollar. This would be a "Goldilocks" solution in some ways—discipline for the United States, but without disrupting the global financial system. We have seen several cases in the past where this has occurred, including the 1978 dollar rescue package, the 1985 Plaza Agreement, and the 1987 Louvre Accord. However, the fundamental point that the United States is able to fund all its external liabilities in dollars has in each case allowed it to resume its profligate ways once the crisis has passed.

---

[119]Cohen 2006.

[120]Between 2005 and 2007 at least four bills were introduced in Congress that targeted currency manipulation. The first generation (Hunter-Ryan and Schumer-Graham) targeted China directly. The Grassley-Baucus and Dodd-Shelby bills, introduced in 2007, sought to conform to U.S. commitments in the IMF and WTO, and thus did not include language specifying China. As of early 2008, none seemed likely to be passed into law, but there were plenty of other opportunities for obstructing Chinese investment in the United States, as seen in the 2005 attempt by China National Offshore Oil Corporation to take over Unocal, as well as statements of outrage at the use of dollar reserves to take an equity stake in the private equity fund Blackstone in 2007.

We also need to consider relations among Japan, China, and the United States, as well as the political economy of the ASEAN+3 more broadly. One way of looking at the issue is by asking the question of what will be the source for global demand growth, if not the United States. Even if we reject the predictions of the Bretton Woods II writers, it is hard to dispute the basic point that U.S. domestic demand has been propping up East Asian—and thus, global—growth. In 2006, the IMF initiated a process of global negotiations over how to unwind these imbalances smoothly, which in practice would require massive increases in Japanese and Chinese domestic demand to offset the necessary U.S. declines.[121] It remained to be seen as of early 2008 whether this could be accomplished in a way that would allow for a smooth period of adjustment, but it is worth noting that we have been here before—in the 1960s, when SDRs were first proposed and created; in the London and Bonn summits of 1977–78, when the "locomotive theory" was first adopted by the G5 economies; and in the Plaza–Louvre period of 1985–88, when the locomotive theory was revived in concept if not in name. Although the global economy coped surprisingly well with those periods of challenge, it did so without the benefit of coordinated locomotive plans actually working, except temporarily and at the margins. If the U.S. dollar were really to be knocked off its pedestal, that would require much more effective and active global governance. This should make us nervous, given the history of macroeconomic coordination among major economies.

Any way that we look at the issue, political implications are unavoidable. The IMF's Multilateral Consultation on Global Imbalances process, begun in 2006, seems to give considerable responsibility to China (and to a lesser extent, Japan) to remake the global landscape.[122] Practically speaking, however, this process appeared likely to run into the typical problems of macroeconomic policy coordination among major states, which is that few are willing to shift policies based on the preferences of other states. The June 2007 IMF staff report on the consultations (the most recent statement as of early 2008) stated hopefully that "taken together, these policy plans include substantive steps that should significantly reduce imbalances over the medium term."[123] Looking over the actual country-policy plans, however, it was hard to find any evidence that the IMF process was having much effect; rather, they constituted reiterations of existing policy statements of each participant.[124] The best hope for the stability of the world economy, then,

---

[121] IMF 2007.

[122] IMF 2007. See also Obstfeld and Rogoff 2004, Ahearne, Cline, Lee, Park, Pisani-Ferry, and Williamson 2007.

[123] IMF 2007, 3.

[124] At least in my reading, the U.S. and Japanese plans are particularly banal and disconnected from likely domestic politics.

was that each participating government would find it in its own individual interest (and ability) to carry through with its own plans.

If the process does not work and the dollar eventually loses its position as global key currency, surplus countries will likely be left with considerable sway over deficit countries' economic policies. Economically, this is what the Japanese quest for insulation has had as a goal: "The emergence of international currencies that compete with the dollar may help impose discipline on the economic policy of the United States by rendering the international environment less forgiving of its mistakes."[125] Politically, one wonders about the ability of the United States under such circumstances to maintain its role of global hegemon and its ability to remain a dominant actor in East Asia. While the economic effects of a leaderless currency system—or at least a chastened dollar—may appear at the moment to be attractive to most if not all of the East Asian governments, the political implications of currency cooperation impact them in more varied ways.

Japan and the Politics of Currency Cooperation

Japan has had substantial and ongoing concerns about the economic effects of overreliance on the dollar combined with political dependence on the United States. Thus Japanese policymakers may well be tempted to restructure aspects of that overall dependence by making use of leverage created by regional currency cooperation. But if the time comes that the U.S. federal government and households are going through a period of significant economic retrenchment, it will not be a simple task to restructure Japanese dependence on the dollar while continuing to rely on the U.S.-Japan alliance to ensure its independence vis-à-vis China. China is likely to have greater freedom of action than Japan in this aspect of financial regionalism.

The Japanese quest for insulation from U.S. macroeconomic policies has been a long and frustrating one. Although instances of direct pressure in the form of "talking down the dollar" essentially ended in 1995, the Japanese government has continued to receive plenty of overt guidance and unsolicited advice from the United States regarding its currency policies in the years since.[126] Thus, it has sought to reduce its exposure to U.S. policy shifts while increasing its exposure to East Asia, where it has more power. Ironically, those efforts have been essentially ignored by the U.S. government (except in regard to specific proposals such as the AMF), suggesting

[125] Kwan 2001, 7.
[126] Congressional efforts in 2007 to include Japan in legislation targeted at the undervaluation of the Chinese RMB might arguably be seen as a new instance. (The most egregious of these was the *Hunter-Ryan Currency Manipulation Bill,* HR 782.)

that they have not been taken very seriously. Japan's regional currency co-operation efforts have been similarly ignored, although the U.S. Treasury has in general terms continued to advocate the two-corner solution and to warn of the instability of intermediate regimes.

This means that the impact of regional currency cooperation on U.S.-Japan relations has been and probably will be minimal at most. The only foreseeable ways in which that might change are if regional cooperation were to contribute to a loss of dollar hegemony or if the East Asian states acted as a bloc to force macroeconomic adjustment on the United States. Both are unlikely, so Japan can act in this sphere without fear of direct political consequences to the U.S.-Japan relationship.

However, unless it is willing or credibly able to provide the basic public goods of a currency area, Japan's regional currency ambitions will be confined to advocacy and persuasion.[127] This is partly an issue of choice, which would call for more in-depth analysis of Japanese decision making than is feasible here. But mostly, Japan is probably not in a position to provide them. Not only would the costs be high in terms of acting as a lender of last resort and market for distressed goods in the event of a crisis but Japan's leadership would presumably be challenged by China. As a realist, I see no reason to expect that advocacy and persuasion alone would be sufficient even if the ideas themselves were compelling. Japan would do better to seek to exert regional influence in less expensive and uncertain ways, such as through preferential trade agreements, aid, or technical assistance.

U.S.-China Relations

U.S.-China economic relations in general are heavily burdened with politics, and it is not surprising that currency issues are characterized by distrust and rivalry. In the United States, it has been the mercantilist aspects that have gotten the most attention, with fears of loss of jobs on the micro front and dependence on the largesse of an authoritarian, potentially hostile state on the macro front.[128] In China, most striking is the reluctance to eliminate the soft-dollar peg and liberalize capital restrictions, the combination of which is essential to China's economy over the long run, but which threatens loss of control and significant labor adjustment in the short run.

Looking through the prism of global imbalances, exchange rate rigidity, and Chinese reserve accumulation, we are immediately reminded of Lawrence Summers's characterization of the bilateral relationship as a financial balance of terror. But the U.S.-China economic relationship differs from

[127] Katada, forthcoming.
[128] Scheve and Slaughter 2007, 35, claims that there were twenty-seven proposals of "anti-Chinese trade legislation" introduced in the 109th Congress (2005–06).

the cold war nuclear balance of terror in being simultaneously deeply symbiotic and, most likely, unsustainable on its present course. Thus, there are strong incentives for both sides to try to act cooperatively, but there are also many opportunities for conflict and for leverage.[129]

The most likely form of conflict in the medium term would not be a decision by the Chinese government to sell off its U.S. Treasury bonds (the closest available analogy to a nuclear first strike), although by 2007 it appeared to be diversifying the currency composition of new reserve accumulation. Rather, the need for China to better manage its reserves automatically creates a situation where the Chinese government will be acquiring more and more real assets in the United States, including control over corporations. Indeed, in the spring of 2007, the government announced its intention to devote a portion of its foreign exchange reserves to profit-seeking investments in the form of a sovereign wealth fund; on September 30, the state-owned China Investment Corporation opened its doors and over the next few months made minority investments in several foreign private equity firms and other financial institutions. Such funds naturally lead to questions about transparency and political management; given the nondemocratic and opaque nature of Chinese policymaking, it seemed likely that concerns about the fund's operations would arise in the United States and other investment destinations.[130] Chinese corporations too will be increasingly taking large or controlling shares in U.S. and other foreign corporations. Given past U.S. experiences with large-scale Japanese acquisitions in the late 1980s and outrage about Chinese purchases and attempted purchases that had arisen by 2008, it is easy to imagine greater and greater tensions about acquisitions on both sides of the Pacific. The worst-case scenario would be a tit-for-tat battle of investment restrictions that could lead to a major disruption of trade and exchange rates. But the simple fact is that as long as the United States is running current account deficits of over 5 percent of GDP, it will need those inflows. This will likely give China considerable leverage to insist on equal access to U.S. markets.

There is little that East Asian regional currency cooperation can do to change any of these dynamics in the short to medium term. Longer term, however, it is possible that regional cooperation could have meaningful effects. If China were eventually able to achieve leadership in formal cooperation (not just effectively deterring its neighbors from allowing their currencies to appreciate in response to market forces), it would better be able to handle a large drop in the value of the dollar and thus be less constrained to prop it up. The United States, on the other hand, would be even

---

[129]Bowles and Wang, forthcoming.

[130]"$200b Investment Company Starts Operation," *China Daily*, October 1, 2007. Lawrence Summers, "Sovereign Funds Shake the Logic of Capitalism," *FT*, July 30, 2007, 11.

worse affected by such a drop, since other states and private investors will not be as constrained to hold dollars. This would fundamentally change the financial balance of terror even if China never gets around to unwinding its dollar reserves.

I have argued at several points so far in this book that time is on China's side versus Japan in terms of shaping regional cooperation. In the case of currency cooperation, time is on its side versus the United States as well. In the short to medium term, regional cooperation could have the effect of easing global payments adjustments and preventing a hard landing for the U.S. and world economies. In the longer run, however, we see its potential to support a potential challenge to the dollar that could discipline U.S. macroeconomic power. What we cannot foresee at all, however, is whether that is likely to happen before or after China acquires the ability and interest to provide public goods for the world financial system.

Contrasting Interpretations

Before closing this chapter, it should be useful to compare my interpretation with alternatives. In this case, the main alternative is the neoliberal approach, which has appeared throughout the chapter in the guise of rule-based efforts at regional and global cooperation. (I am not aware of any systematic constructivist analyses of East Asian currency cooperation, and it does not seem appropriate to create one just for the purpose of arguing against it.)[131]

The major distinction between the realist and the neoliberal approaches to the study of regional cooperation is that the neoliberal approach is much less skeptical of the possibilities for regional and global cooperation in the absence of a single leader. This means, for example, that the political rivalry between Japan and China should not be an insurmountable barrier to effective regional currency coordination and that market-based approaches stand a chance of working. It is also both much more willing to contemplate the likelihood of an end to the hegemony of the dollar (by focusing primarily on economic reasons for use or nonuse of specific currencies) and more sanguine about the ability of the international system to handle such an eventuality through effective rule-based coordination.

Neither approach expects cooperation to be easy, but the degree differs substantially. From a realist point of view, no serious challenge to the dollar is possible without successful regional currency cooperation in East Asia. Given the differences in economic and political interests of Japan and

---

[131]This does not mean that constructivist analysis of East Asian currency cooperation is impossible, or even implausible. Constructivists have had a great deal to say about European efforts, for example. Presumably, two elements that would appear in applying the approach to East Asia would be notions of regional trust or commitment and contestation of ideas about legitimacy of various types of currency and macroeconomic policy management.

China, that will likely have to await definitive Chinese ascendancy, which is clearly not a near-term prospect. The global transition is also likely to be difficult and the resulting situation unstable, with the possibility of unmanageable global crises or establishment of regional currency blocs ever present. While this is a rather pessimistic view of the future, there are some grounds for optimism if the development of regional and global leverage forces responsibility on the dollar while the inertia of network effects overrides other economies' desire to escape its hegemony.

5

Bond Market Initiatives

The final component of East Asian financial regionalism is to be found in efforts to promote bond market development. The political story in this chapter is significantly complicated by the role of private sector actors. Even more than in liquidity provision and currency policies, bond market development requires governments to cater to private sector actors whose collective decisions will determine the success or failure of the whole venture. Moreover, the strong and conflicting interests of various domestic and transnational financial actors in the outcomes means that the domestic politics of bond market promotion is much harder to isolate than with large-scale macroeconomic issues. We should, therefore, expect a conventional neoliberal political economy approach to explain a significant amount of what is going on. Nonetheless, the shadow of power politics still looms large even in this area of cooperation, both in terms of its political rationale and its potential impact on the ASEAN+3 and U.S. economies.

As in other components of East Asian financial and other economic regionalism, a major part of the background of the ASEAN+3 bond market initiatives is to be found in the 1997–98 Asian Financial Crisis. The crisis cast a new and damning light on a well-known aspect of East Asian countries' economic development: the weakness of their financial markets. Other than in Singapore, bank-based financial intermediation was the norm among ASEAN+3 economies.[1] Even in Japan, legacies of a postwar bank-based system remained apparent, and Japan's own domestic financial crisis in 1997

---

[1] See, e.g., Lejot, Arner, and Liu 2006, 80, table 3.9.

and 1998 made clear that banking-sector dominance was not synonymous with financial stability.[2]

A great deal of attention was paid during the Asian Financial Crisis to the apparently reckless and corrupt lending practices of regional financial institutions, from Thailand's underregulated nonbank real-estate financing corporations to the insolvencies and elite plundering of Indonesian banks to the allegedly cronyistic investment practices of Malaysian state-controlled trusts to the willingness of Korean banks to allow corporate leverage ratios in the double digits to Japan's problems with nonperforming and endlessly rolled-over loans.[3] Much of this scrutiny was indeed well deserved. But equity and bond markets functioned even less efficiently than the banking sector due to lack of financial-market depth and liquidity, and thus they were unable to act as a substitute means of financial intermediation.

So while many observers and commentators were still focused on the "crony capitalism" aspects of East Asian banking, a number of economists turned their gaze to the role played by the lack of alternative financial options for savers and borrowers. They saw financial-market underdevelopment not only as encouraging inefficiencies but also as creating vulnerabilities that became particularly acute due to the pervasive effects of financial globalization.[4] These analysts and policymakers saw the development of deep and liquid bond markets as an imperative to help prevent new crises from arising. Some also began to see bond market development as an essential building block for an effective East Asian community and a means of reducing dependence on the United States. In Japan this resonated with the reappearance of arguments for internationalization of the yen in the late 1990s.

Political Stakes in Bond Market Initiatives

To understand the choices being made, we need to understand the political stakes. Bond market promotion efforts are both permeated by international politics and have potentially significant implications for relations among Japan, China, and the United States. Political angles include insulation from fluctuations of the dollar, competition over standard-setting and market venues, benefits for domestic economic actors, and institutional design.

[2] Horiuchi 1998, 1999; Amyx 2004a.

[3] Haggard 2000; Kim 2000; Amyx 2004a.

[4] Kaminsky and Reinhart 1999; Foreign Exchange Commission 1999. Equity markets were also seen as important, but bond markets have been the focus of reformers. This reflects both the concerns over double mismatch and the fact that bond markets are the basis for interest rate benchmarking as well as hedging and other risk management techniques.

There is also considerable ambiguity about the relationship between regionalization and globalization, which complicates the playing board for everyone.

A key goal of regional bond market initiatives has been to reduce dependence on dollar-based finance and thus vulnerability to swings in the values of local currencies against the dollar. This is clearly an attractive economic goal, especially given the experience of the Asian Financial Crisis. But it also has important political implications. In this case, stability is to be improved by partial disengagement from the dollar; over time, and in combination with efforts in Europe and perhaps eventually other regions, such disengagement has the potential to reduce the structural power of the United States, including both the "power to delay" and the "power to deflect."[5]

Ironically, however, the effort to reduce exposure to the dollar via bond market development inevitably opens the door to greater exposure to the decisions and preferences of global market players.[6] In order to create viable local-currency bond markets, governments will have to significantly reduce their intervention in financial decision making, let go of their ability to enforce stability in credit markets, and allow substantial participation by outside economic actors who may not share their political or economic preferences. In other words, the attempt to insulate economies from dollar pressures by developing local-currency bond markets trades one type of vulnerability for another. Whether the overall level of vulnerability is reduced or expanded depends crucially on country-specific factors.

There are multiple economic goals in play at the micro level as well. The standard political economy question applies here: Who wins and who loses? One of the striking aspects of both of the major East Asian bond market initiatives is that they are predicated on moving toward "global standards." Whatever else global financial standards may be, they represent the values of global financial institutions and investors (largely based in the United States and Europe) more generally. In the East Asian context, the economic actors best positioned to gain from improved access to and functioning of bond markets are U.S., European, and (to a lesser extent) Japanese financial institutions, while local banks will lose their privileged positions if bond markets develop as envisioned.[7] At this level, the preferences of Japan, the United States, and "global capital" are nearly identical—indeed, bond

---

[5]Cohen 2006.

[6]The logic of "internationalization as insulation" is developed in Grimes 2003a and 2003b.

[7]Hong Kong–based financial institutions are probably more regionally competitive than Japanese ones, but they are backed by a less-powerful government. Once Japan had finally emerged from its domestic financial problems around 2005, Japanese financial institutions became increasingly focused on reducing their excessive reliance on Japan-based businesses by looking to East Asian markets. PIFS 2006b, 11–12.

market promotion is the one aspect of financial regionalism in East Asia about which the U.S. Treasury and IMF have expressed no concerns at all. Meanwhile, significant domestic coalitions of various sizes and composition in favor of market liberalization and development could be found in a number of other East Asian economies, including not only Singapore, Korea, Malaysia, and China but also Hong Kong and Taiwan, which were outside the ASEAN+3 process.[8]

In addition to developing market opportunities, Japanese financial institutions and officials see the bond market initiatives as a means of locking China into a commitment to a liberal financial regime before it is in a position to throw its weight around. In this sense, bond market initiatives are a time-bound contest between Japan and China. At the same time, however, Chinese authorities understand the practical benefits of improving the efficiency of financial intermediation both domestically and across their borders.[9] Indeed, it is the positive-sum game aspects of financial-sector development that create both uncertainty about likely relative benefits and an appetite among all the players to join the contest. And even if the bond market efforts do not actually lead to fully free, fair, and open financial markets in the region, it is very much to the benefit of Japanese financial institutions to ensure that they are involved from the ground up as opportunities for profit develop.

Another time-bound contest is in play as well, which may well determine the future geography of financial-market activities in East Asia. That is the implicit competition among financial exchanges. Whereas talk of regional bond market development sounds at first blush to be about harmony, efficiency, and mutual gains, the reality is that if truly regional markets do develop, they will most likely be centered on one or two specific market centers. Just as London has profited greatly by becoming the major financial-market center for Europe, there are riches to be made in becoming the next financial-market center for East Asia.[10] The question is, which center(s) will succeed—Tokyo, Hong Kong, Singapore, or Shanghai? For Japan and China (and of course even more so for Singapore), this is an important question indeed.[11]

Looking at the bond market promotion efforts themselves, politics surfaces clearly in terms of institutional design. Two aspects in particular stand

[8]The Taiwan example, which has been relatively neglected in English-language sources, is discussed in Noble 1997.

[9]See, for example, PIFS 2007a, 15–18; Hu 2007.

[10]See Committee on Capital Markets Regulation 2006, Section I, regarding competition among market centers. Grimes 2008 makes a case for why Japan should seek to make its financial markets into regional centers.

[11]For a window into discussions among Japanese financial professionals and regulators, see PIFS 2006b, 2–7. Also PIFS 2007b.

out. The first is the exclusion of the United States, despite the relevance of U.S. expertise and the implicit regional acceptance of global financial standards. The second is the self-paced nature of the cooperative efforts. I argue that this reflects the differing costs and benefits that participating governments see in moving forward with the liberal bond market agenda, combined with the lack of ability of Japan to lead except through offering (small-scale) incentives. Unlike in the Chiang Mai Initiative, which offers valuable protection to potentially vulnerable economies in the form of Japanese and Chinese foreign exchange reserves, there is no obvious way for the leading players to push their bond market agendas onto hesitant partners. In sum, the design of the initiatives is predicated on an "arm's length" relationship with the United States as well as a minimalist surveillance system that does not include any attempt at enforcement or even meaningful commitments.

Finally, it must be noted that the relationship between globalization and regionalization of financial markets is blurry to say the least. Is it possible to promote regional finance without having it be overtaken by financial globalization? If that does occur, are the benefits of local-currency markets lost? Or are the enhanced benefits in terms of efficiency, stability, and the possibility of decoupling from the "East Asian dollar standard" worth the effort even if some level of regional autonomy or initiative or political control over markets is sacrificed? These questions tie in as well with both the ambiguities about the U.S. role and interests and the trade-off between insulation from the dollar and vulnerability to global finance.

Identifying Power and Interests

These are the general political parameters, but to gain some analytical coherence, we need to look at the origins and limits of states' power and interests in advancing their various agendas. To do this, I will run through the insights and predictions of the main analytical approaches—realist, neoliberal, and constructivist—as they pertain to attempts to develop regional bond markets.

Given the many functional issues and the importance of private sector financial institutions and investors, I begin by examining the expectations and implications of the neoliberal approach.[12] In this approach, states' interests are driven by the aggregation of societal interests regarding changes

---

[12]As exemplified by, for example, Grossman and Helpman 1995; Frieden and Rogowski 1996; Garrett and Lange 1996; and Milner 1997 regarding states' interest formation, and Keohane 1984; Aggarwal 1998a; and Koremenos, Lipson, and Snidal 2001, regarding institutional design.

in market parameters. Institutional design concentrates on creating gains for all participants, although severe competition and bargaining may ensue regarding apportionment of those gains. Transnational coalitions of interest can expand opportunities for cooperation where collective action is needed to provide public goods, and cooperation is likely to depend on the ability of participating states (or their domestic support bases) to capture gains of cooperation.

Applying this framework to East Asian regional bond market initiatives yields several interesting insights and predictions. The first is that the willingness of ASEAN+3 states to participate in initiatives should be related fundamentally to domestic political economy questions: Who will benefit (or lose) through these efforts? By how much? How well are their interests represented within the government policymaking apparatus?

Second, those states that benefit the most should push the hardest for regional market promotion and be the most willing to provide necessary public goods to achieve it. If the truly regional (or privately capturable) gains of regional efforts are limited, then public goods will be underprovided, regional bond market development will be stunted, and states will act individually to maximize their own interests.[13] Thus, key questions are the degree to which gains are truly regional (or capturable) and whether a coalition can be assembled to provide the necessary backing. In the East Asian case, this translates into whether gains will be captured by regionally based financial institutions or global ones, and whether the benefits to Japanese financial institutions will move the Japanese state (the only viable candidate for solo provider of public goods) to provide sufficient initial liquidity to get the ball rolling.

The final neoliberal expectation regards the setting of market standards. If market participants do not see profits in local-currency bond markets relative to their other options, they will not participate. Those options include more than just direct lending in the domestic market, since both domestic and foreign financial institutions and investors operating in East Asia can participate in bond markets elsewhere. This means that in order to have a reasonable shot at vibrant local bond markets (except perhaps in China, at least for the moment), regulators will need to approach, if not meet, global standards of regulation, openness, disclosure, and transparency. Thus, regional efforts should emphasize global standards for participants, at least as a longer-term goal.

The realist political economy approach accepts that gains in prosperity will be attractive to states, but it does not have a standard means of

---

[13] In other words, to the extent that bond market development in, say, Malaysia has positive externalities in the form of benefits to market development in, say, Thailand and vice versa, development in both markets will be stunted in the absence of cooperation.

determining in advance what the national interest of a state should be in areas such as financial-market development and trade, where long-run consequences are unpredictable in terms of effects on national economic strength and vulnerability. The ultimate goal, of course, is wealth creation (not only absolute, but also relative to states with which it is competing for power) without increasing national vulnerability to potential competitors for power and security. If states follow policies that advantage specific interests at home and do not pay attention to relative power and vulnerability, realism expects that they will be punished by losing at least some degree of autonomy of action. However, this can only be known in retrospect, so the best we can do is to look at the apparent overall economic benefits to various states in predicting their preferences for regional cooperation. The decisions by governments as to their own economic interests are as good a proxy as any, especially for economically advanced democracies such as Japan and the United States.

Thus, in some ways, the realist approach parallels the neoliberal one. Those states that benefit the most from a given initiative are most likely to provide material support for it. (For example, we should expect that Japan will be most generous in providing funds to promote regional markets.) Both approaches also expect that states will compete to establish standards that fit their purposes better than those of competitors. It is not clear that they predict very different policies in terms of insulating against vulnerability, since presumably any new vulnerability in political terms would have to be created via an economic vulnerability. From a realist point of view, it probably would not even make sense for Japan or the United States to try to withhold help in developing China's financial markets, even if the expectation were that it would contribute to a relative rise China's wealth and influence—after all, China has access to other means of developing its markets, and not participating would inflict damage on the position of the United States or Japan without hurting China (and made worse because it would reduce credibility vis-à-vis ASEAN and South Korea).

The major differences in prediction have to do with the importance the realist paradigm attaches to currency and market insulation, particularly for Japan, which sits uneasily on the divide between regional economic interests and global political interests. As noted in chapter 1, we expect that the U.S. government (which must not only represent the commercial interests of U.S. financial institutions but also continue to access foreign funding for its current account deficits) will have a relatively greater interest in capital liberalization than in market development, while Japan and its ASEAN+3 partners will be more concerned with market development. Also, we should not expect regional governments to welcome U.S. participation in designing, monitoring, and making decisions about regional efforts, regardless of their content. As the state with the greatest resources at its disposal, Japan should seek to use influence to push a system that is aligned with its own national interest and try to head off attempts not only by the United States to impose the pace and sequencing of change but also by regional rivals to weaken its own preferred rules.

The constructivist approach offers markedly different interpretations and expectations. Here, I consider two separate but generally compatible versions: the familiar regionalist argument about identity and a broader one that sees globalized finance and financial regulation as based on a specific ideological construct that can be quite destabilizing.[14]

The regional identity argument works from an understanding that East Asian economies have practiced "a form of capitalism that is quite distinct from either Western European or North American capitalism...rooted in business networks and...characterized by strong state-business links...based more on social obligation and social trust than on the rule of law."[15] Thus, they see a need to insulate themselves from global finance by maintaining restrictions on markets, while also emphasizing relational financial arrangements rather than arm's length ones. As seen in analyses of the AMF and the Chiang Mai Initiative, this regional identity provides justification for regional cooperation to weaken the influence of the United States, IMF, and global financial institutions.

The second stream sees financial globalization as a hegemonic discourse. According to this line of argument, the logic of financial liberalization tends to privilege global capital (that is, financial institutions, not necessarily savers) and the dominance of the United States. Advocates of liberalization present their logic as scientific fact, based on a research paradigm that respects only quantitative studies based on liberal assumptions and aimed exclusively at "efficiency" over other potential values. Ironically, so the argument goes, the resulting system is actually much less stable than the more regulated systems it replaced, requiring public sector actors such as the IMF or the U.S. Federal Reserve to contrive at various points to bail out troubled economies or financial institutions in order to keep the whole system afloat.

Applying these constructivist interpretations to East Asian regional cooperation on financial regulation leads us to expect that such cooperation should be focused on insulating participating economies from U.S. influence and the disruptions of financial globalization. We should expect to

[14]On the regional identity side, representative writers include Higgott 1998; Stubbs 2002, 2005 (chap. 7); Beeson 2006; Lee 2006; and Rodan, Hewison, and Robison 2006. With regard to the ideational or ideological aspects of finance, see Wade and Veneroso 1998; Blyth 2003; Grabel 2003; Best 2005; and Woods 2006, among others. Of course, there is considerable overlap between the two streams.

[15]Stubbs 2005, 211.

see a preference for self-paced financial reform that excludes the United States and privileges relational finance over global standards, arm's length markets, and financial openness.

Although some aspects of constructivist arguments are congruent with actual experience (such as the exclusion of the United States and support for self-paced processes), on the important factors (preference for relational finance, suspicion of global standards and financial institutions) there does not seem to be a plausible constructivist story to be found in regional bond market cooperation efforts. Thus, the constructivist approaches do not offer a very useful way of looking at the actual situation, which instead appears to be driven by the opportunities for profit and prosperity to be found in local, regional, and global markets. With these themes in mind, I turn now to analyzing the initiatives on their own terms.

Bond Markets and Financial Vulnerability

To make political sense of the bond initiatives, we need first to look at economic justifications and obstacles. Advocates of bond market promotion in East Asia argue that better developed local and regional bond markets will reduce economies' vulnerability to sudden financial shifts and thereby contribute to regional economic stability.[16] This may sound on its face like an unlikely argument, but in fact there is a strong (if not open-and-shut) case to be made for the importance of bond market development, based on four main factors: elimination of the "double mismatch" problem, improvement of financial intermediation and efficiency of price formation, enhancement of opportunities for both borrowers and savers, and promotion of regional economic integration.

Double Mismatch

A basic issue for the ASEAN+3 economies is that their trade, and often their international financial obligations, are denominated in currencies that are not their own. This is true to a surprising degree even for Japan.[17] The developing and middle-income economies of the region, in particular, accumulated foreign currency–denominated (mostly U.S. dollar) debts in the years leading to the Asian Financial Crisis. Such a situation creates significant vulnerabilities for small economies with thinly traded currencies. Complicating matters, liberalization of capital controls in the 1980s and 1990s in most

---

[16]Ito 2004; Kawai 2005.
[17]BIS statistics; FEC 1999; Grimes 2003a, 2003b.

of the East Asian capitalist economies significantly increased those vulnerabilities. It is typically difficult for developing and middle-income economies
to obtain capital internationally by financing themselves with local-currency
bonds: economists have termed this apparent trap "original sin."[18]

One of the major concerns of East Asian financial regionalism is to address exchange-market vulnerability created by a "double mismatch." Indeed, ASEAN+3 governments have taken this to be an important lesson of
the Asian Financial Crisis. In the aggregate, savers in East Asian economies
invested a significant part of their savings in foreign currency–denominated
(primarily dollar) assets. They then borrowed the money back in short-term
dollar-denominated loans and bonds, and applied the funds to longer-term
domestic investments whose returns were in the local currency. The lack
of development of local financial markets made hedging costly or impossible, and the implicit guarantee of dollar pegs in any event appeared to make
it unnecessary. The result was that assets and liabilities were mismatched
with respect to both maturity and currency, thus making countries highly
vulnerable to movements in the value of the dollar.[19] In the 1997 crisis, the
free fall of local currencies versus the dollar made repayment of debt impossible, and in turn it fed back into further declines in currency values in
a self-reinforcing downward spiral.

It has been argued that if capital markets had provided more opportunities for domestic long-term financial intermediation in the local currency
within the East Asian emerging markets, the crisis may not have occurred,
or at least would not have been as severe.[20] Capital market development is
an important part of the effort to address the problems of currency mismatch and original sin. If better investment opportunities existed at home,
according to this analysis, there would be less need to export savings overseas
and then borrow it back to finance domestic needs in the form of foreign
currency–denominated debt.[21]

A related issue is capital controls. Considerable capital liberalization preceded and set the stage for the Asian Financial Crisis, as small financial markets such as Thailand's were unable to handle massive movements of money
across their borders.[22] Japanese policymakers entered the debate soon after

[18] Eichengreen and Hausmann 2005. Goldstein and Turner (2004) reject the notion of
"original sin," arguing that currency mismatches result from weaknesses of domestic financial and macroeconomic policies rather than defects of international financial markets.
However, they agree that currency mismatches can create serious vulnerabilities.

[19] See Goldstein and Turner 2004, chap. 2, regarding the dangers of currency mismatches.

[20] This claim is debatable, as Park and Park (2004) point out. However, there is a clear
consensus among those economists and policymakers involved in ABMI that lack of local-
currency bond markets contributed to the crisis. See also McCauley 2003.

[21] Ito and Park 2004; IIMA 2002. While I concentrate here on currency mismatch, maturity
mismatch was also a major problem.

[22] Kaminsky and Reinhart 1999.

the crisis with statements supportive of the reimposition of capital controls.[23] They argued that several of the crisis economies had lowered barriers to short-term capital movement before the necessary institutions, rules, and practices had been put into effect. Interestingly, advocacy of capital controls has become less pronounced as regional efforts have increasingly focused on local-currency bond market development, since capital controls can either prevent or make more costly foreign participation in local markets and thus reduce potential liquidity. Instead, policymakers now emphasize the importance of an incremental and well-planned liberalization.[24]

Efficiency of Financial Intermediation

The expansion of bond markets has also been seen as an important element in improving financial intermediation within the hitherto bank-based economies of East Asia. Bond markets can function as both substitute for and complement to the banking sector.[25] On the one hand, competition from bond markets can be a spur to banks to improve their efficiency; on the other hand, bond markets can provide useful information on risk and pricing of lending that can contribute to banks' risk management and decision making.

If bond markets become a viable alternative for potential borrowers to raise funds, they can improve financial efficiency in several ways. As a competitive threat to banks, they could induce banks to improve their practices and offer more varied and attractive financing options.[26] Bond markets can also provide opportunities to banks in the form of new financial instruments to hedge their own liabilities and expand fee-based services. Both of these changes, if managed well, could present attractive money-making opportunities to banks, reduce their risk exposure, and expand savings opportunities for firms and households.

Deep and liquid bond markets can also help to establish a robust yield curve by revealing information about societal preferences for supply and demand of credit. The key is the existence of a deep and liquid market in default risk-free bonds across a variety of maturities. In practical terms, this means heavy trading in government bonds that stretch continuously from short term to long term.[27] By observing the resulting yield curve, banks

---

[23]Sakakibara 1999. Kirshner 2007, 199, quotes several statements by top Japanese finance officials.

[24]Aramaki 2006; Hayashi 2006, 66–70.

[25]Eichengreen 2006a, 1–2, states this particularly well.

[26]There is no guarantee that efficiency will be served, of course. When disintermediation began to occur in Japan in the 1980s, banks managed the change poorly, lending excessively to fairly dodgy borrowers. For some examples, see Taniguchi 1993, Amyx 2004a.

[27]Ghosh 2006, chap. 5, provides an excellent discussion of how government policies can contribute to the creation of robust yield curves.

and other lenders can accurately price loans based on their assessment of potential borrowers' default risk.

This task is complicated by the need for accurate assessment of firms' default risk, which is especially difficult in the financial systems of developing countries. Both relational banking and rapid structural change in an economy make it more difficult to obtain such information on an economywide basis. The key is the accumulation and analysis of data on corporate characteristics and their correlation with full or partial defaults.[28] In this regard, the Asian Bond Markets Initiative calls for the establishment of competent bond-ratings agencies and data collection as part of its overall program for bond market development.

Diversity of Financing Options and Financial Products

Robust bond markets can benefit both lenders and borrowers by expanding the range of financial products available in terms of both extension of maturities and maturity matching.

Perhaps most important is the development of a market for long-term lending. One of the typical distortions of bank lending in developing economies is the prevalence of short-term lending even for longer-term uses. The existence of a market in long-term government bonds can help to reduce this distortion by creating a yield curve that can give more useful pricing information to banks or potential bond purchasers and allows for banks to match the maturities of their assets and liabilities. Maturity matching is the basis of financial risk management, and hedging more generally. Thus it can help to expand the reach of bond markets and can contribute to the willingness of investors to enter equity markets as well.

Financial efficiency is generally enhanced by expanded access to financial products. Assuming clear rules and good information—admittedly a big assumption—this means more efficient use of capital. It also weakens bases of relational banking (for better and for worse), which may make this course politically unattractive. Political processes can also produce partial liberalizations or incomplete regulatory changes that encourage dangerous practices.

Regional Integration

A final general justification for promotion of local-currency bond markets has to do with its potential impact on regional integration. The more obvious aspect of this justification is in the promotion of bond markets that

---

[28] I am grateful to Naoyuki Yoshino for alerting me to this point.

would actually operate on a regional basis, but there is also an argument (albeit more limited) to be made for the role of development of local-currency bond markets *within* countries.

The role of an integrated regional market in encouraging broader regional integration appears fairly obvious: if East Asian economic actors are involved in lending and borrowing internationally through the region, this is not only in itself an example of economic integration but also likely to support increased amounts of direct investment (by financial institutions, at the very least) and transnational joint ventures of various sorts. It could also create a demand for a regional synthetic currency like an ACU, and perhaps for regional payment and settlement systems.

It is important to bear in mind here that any regional markets that do arise are likely to be centered on a limited number of financial-market centers, regardless of how many governments are issuing local-currency or regional-currency bonds and regardless of how many dispersed regional investors in such securities there might be.[29] A basic reality of contemporary financial globalization is the tendency toward consolidation of markets. This trend has been enabled by improved access due to liberalization and communications technologies, but it is fundamentally driven by transaction costs. Financial markets are a classic scale industry, in which fixed costs are high and marginal costs are low—therefore, the more transactions made, the less expensive they become. Investors also value liquidity in and of itself, and thus they gravitate to markets that have more trades and smaller spreads.

In any event, the goal of regional bond markets is at the moment more aspirational than practical. Thus it is necessary to look at the impacts of local bond market development on regional and global integration. Bond market development can be supportive of other aspects of business, insofar as a foreign firm may be more willing to locate or expand its business in a country where it has low-cost access to local-currency credit through the bond market.[30]

However, it is important to note that this point is relevant for *any* corporation doing business in the region, not just East Asian ones. Indeed, given the size and credibility of many U.S. and European firms investing and trading with East Asia, not to mention the scale and expertise of Western financial institutions investing on a global basis, such firms may well be able to make better use of local bond markets than smaller East Asian firms and financial institutions.[31] So, while effective local bond markets

---

[29] Scott 2007.

[30] I am indebted to Martin Schulz for making this point to me.

[31] The Thomson "league tables" (a ranking of top underwriters for various securities) make clear that, except for local-currency debt, which is a small proportion of the total, U.S. and

should be supportive of greater *international* integration, it is less obvious why they should support regional integration per se. (There is, however, limited evidence of a preference among East Asian investors for investing regionally.)[32] Moreover, the participation of globally competitive financial institutions and expansion of sophisticated financial instruments raises the likelihood that local financial institutions will find themselves on the receiving end of much more risk than they or their regulators are prepared to handle.[33] This introduces the question of whether regional bond market efforts compete with global forces or just contribute to financial globalization. It certainly appears that it would be difficult to confine benefits to regional players or to guarantee that vulnerability to movements in global capital will be minimized.

East Asian Bond Markets: Conditions and Concerns

We can gain a general picture of the status and development to date of regional bond markets by considering a few key objective indicators, including size, composition, and turnover. Each indicator speaks to one or more of the functions discussed above. Size, measured as bonds outstanding, gives a rough picture of the importance of bond market financing as a source of funds in the economy. The composition of bonds outstanding gives a clearer picture of the role of bonds in government versus corporate financing, and of the availability of bonds of varying maturities. Finally, turnover is an important indicator of liquidity. Liquidity is important to actual or potential bondholders who prefer certainty in the price at which they can sell off their positions at any given time; it is also key to judging the quality of information revealed through pricing and yield curves.

Local bond markets in East Asia are generally not very highly developed, although they have been growing rapidly (figures 5.1 and 5.2).[34] Much of the increase in size after the Asian Financial Crisis came from an increase in government deficits that resulted either from revenue declines or public assumption of distressed assets. For the most part, government bonds predominate, even in Japan. In some economies, such as Korea, the need to liquidate assets of failed financial institutions after the Asian Financial Crisis led to significant increases in asset-backed securities issuance

---

EU-based financial institutions dominate in all areas of East Asian securities issuance. Thomson Financial 2007.

[32]McCauley and Park 2006, 36–41; Bae, Yun, and Bailey 2006, 105.

[33]There were some fears of this in August 2007, as the U.S. subprime mortgage markets began to melt down. As of early 2008, it appeared that Asian financial institutions had been much more wary of securities backed by such mortgages than their European counterparts.

[34]All figures on East Asian bond markets, unless otherwise noted, come from Asian Bonds Online, http://asianbondsonline.adb.org/regional/regional.php.

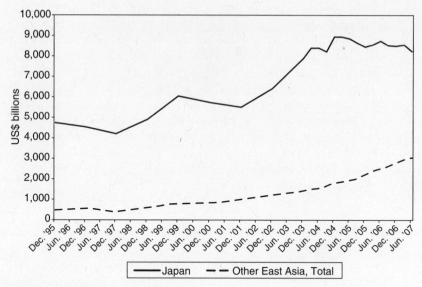

Figure 5.1. Local-Currency Bond Markets, December 1995–June 2007.
Source: Asian Bonds Online (BIS data).

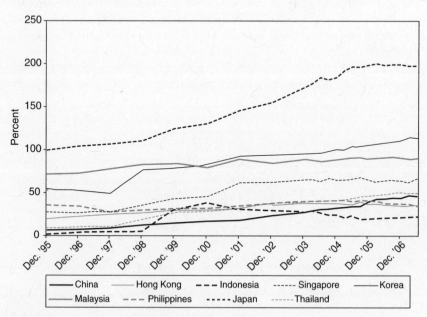

Figure 5.2. Local-Currency Bond Markets as Proportion of GDP, December 1995–June 2007.
Source: Asian Bonds Online (BIS data).

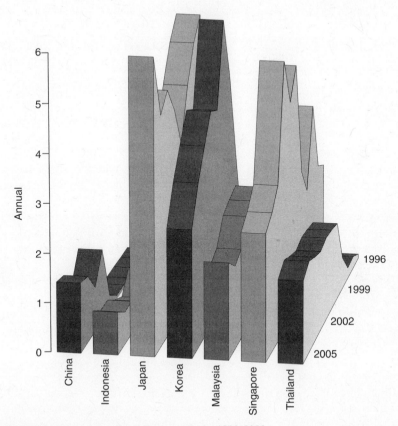

Figure 5.3. Government Bond Turnover Ratio, 1996–2006.
Source: Asian Bonds Online.

by quasi-governmental agencies as well.[35] Most strikingly, however, the turn-over ratios for bonds are extraordinarily low (figure 5.3). While the annual turnover ratio of U.S. treasury bonds is over thirty times, the highest ratio among the East Asian financial markets other than Hong Kong was slightly less than six in 2006 (Japan).[36] As for corporate bonds, they essentially do not turn over in most East Asian economies—here, the only ratio in 2006 that approached the U.S. level of 1.07 was China's 0.86. Low turnover ratios reflect a buy-and-hold strategy by institutional investors (often public pension funds, other quasi governmentals, or central banks) and other financial institutions.

[35]Tran and Roldos 2004, 137–39; Lee and Rhee 2007.
[36]The U.S. figure is for 2006, calculated from Securities Industry and Financial Markets Association (SIFMA) data on Treasury bonds.

Meanwhile, all the main ASEAN+3 governments allow some level of foreign ownership of local-currency bonds—even China, which since 2002 has allowed a limited number of established foreign financial institutions to become "qualified foreign institutional investors," a status that allows for ownership of local-currency bonds and equities.[37] Nonetheless, foreign bondholdings are a small percentage in all the economies except Indonesia and the Philippines.[38]

All in all, bond markets remain only a supplement to bank lending in most of the ASEAN+3 economies. The major shift has been in the expansion of government bonds, but most of these markets suffer from low liquidity and limited maturities of issue. Outside of Japan and Hong Kong, volatility along the yield curve is fairly high. Thus, emerging East Asian bond markets—even relatively advanced ones, like those in Korea and Malaysia—have a considerable way to go before they provide enough information to support efficient price formation. Meanwhile, regulations, liquidity issues, and transaction costs have made bond issuance unattractive as a financing method even for blue-chip firms in most East Asian economies. Bond markets are not a viable means of financing for small and medium-sized enterprises anywhere—even in Korea or Japan, where policies have encouraged it in the form of asset-backed securities, sometimes with public sector guarantees, and even though ABMI has put forward improved SME financing as one of its goals.[39]

Infrastructural issues remain as well. Legal infrastructure includes rules (including those on bond issuance, disclosure and accounting, and the consequences of default), penalties for illegal practices, and the quality and honesty of supervision, as well as the overall competence and quality of a given country's court system.[40] Market infrastructure such as settlement systems, the information dissemination system, and quality and coverage of ratings agencies also remains a major concern.[41]

---

[37]A translation of "Provisional Measures on Administration of Domestic Securities Investments of Qualified Foreign Institutional Investors" is available at http://www.csrc.gov.cn/n575458/n4001948/n4002030/4064521.html. The law tightly restricts the activities of and repatriation of funds by qualified foreign institutional investors. For example, Takeuchi 2005 notes that they are not allowed to trade bonds in the interbank market, which is where most bonds are traded in China (9).

[38]According to Asian Bonds Online data, both had nonresident ownership of over 25% in 2005, the most recent year reported. Among other East Asian economies, only Singapore and Hong Kong surpass the level of 10% by a significant margin. It should be noted that the meaning of "nonresident" can be fluid in weakly regulated financial systems.

[39]The reason that SME financing has been a specific goal of ABMI is unclear. But it is clearly attractive to the financial institutions that would earn fees on structuring and issuing such debt, as well as to institutional investors that would consider the resulting securities attractive. See, for example, IIMA 2005.

[40]Eichengreen and Luengnaruemitchai 2006; Ghosh 2006, chap. 3.

[41]Takeuchi 2005, 7–25; Ghosh 2006, 37–43.

Nurturing Bond Markets: Regional Initiatives

East Asian nations have begun to address the infrastructural and liquidity problems, both individually and collectively. The two main regional initiatives meant to address deficiencies in East Asian bond markets are the ASEAN+3's Asian Bond Markets Initiative and the Asian Bond Fund, sponsored by the Executives' Meeting of East Asia-Pacific Central Banks. The Asian Development Bank has played an increasingly supportive, albeit still subordinate, role in the East Asian initiatives. Strikingly, despite the strong interest of the United States and U.S. financial institutions in promoting financial-market development, APEC has had a truly minimal role.[42] And while IMF technical assistance was important in financial liberalization in East Asian countries dating back to the early 1990s, the IMF is now a marginal player at best. The exclusion of these two global backers of financial liberalization and market development is all the more striking because the rhetoric, practical actions, and policy prescriptions of ABMI and ABF are so fully consonant with their preferences.[43] Especially given the option of utilizing APEC as an organizational umbrella, it is evident that the exclusion of the United States is a conscious choice; this is consistent with the overall regionalist agenda of hedging against the United States and avoiding excessive U.S. intervention in East Asian economic affairs.

The Asian Bond Markets Initiative

The Asian Bond Markets Initiative is putatively meant to help create regional bond markets, but it can be better understood as two distinct but related projects: development of domestic bond markets, and attempts to create regional markets in the more distant future. The most immediate and practical effects of ABMI are at the level of promoting the development of local-currency bond markets within East Asian economies.

The problems of developing domestic bond markets relate to both liquidity and infrastructural issues. While ABMI seeks to address both aspects, it is much more feasible for government policymakers and regulators to address the infrastructural issues. The ABMI process has been most active in identifying and seeking to remove various impediments to development

---

[42] At this point, the only APEC initiative is the Policy Dialogue on Savings and Capital Market Development, which is engaged in trying to create a "Voluntary Action Plan for Supporting Freer and More Stable Capital Flows." The Asian Cooperation Dialogue, created by Thailand's former prime minister, Thaksin Shinawatra, also proposed an Asian Bond Market Development initiative, but that appears to be entirely rhetorical at this point, with the last meeting (as of fall 2007) having been held in March 2006.

[43] Grimes 2006.

of domestic bond markets in East Asia, such as lengthy approval processes for bond issuance, unclear default rules, lack of hedging instruments, difficulties in issuing asset-backed securities, problems of disclosure, and weak local ratings agencies, among others.[44]

Process

While ABMI's objectives are ambitious, its structure is minimal. Essentially, it is made up of a set of working groups and a steering committee (known as the "focal group").[45] There were six original working groups:

1. Creating New Securitized Debt Instruments (Chair: Thailand)
2. Credit Guarantee and Investment Mechanisms (Cochairs: Korea, China)
3. Foreign Exchange Transactions and Settlement Issues (Chair: Malaysia)
4. Issuance of Bonds Denominated in Local Currencies by Multilateral Development Banks, Foreign Government Agencies, and Asian Multinational Corporations (Chair: China)
5. Rating System and Information Dissemination (Cochairs: Singapore, Japan)
6. Technical Assistance Coordination (Cochairs: Indonesia, Philippines, Malaysia)

Following the ASEAN+3 finance ministers' meeting in Istanbul in May 2005, Working Group 4 (WG 4) was eliminated and the functions of WG 6 were transferred to a "coordination group" under the umbrella of the focal group. A few of the specific agenda items of the other working groups were also changed. The titles and tasks of the working groups give some indication of ABMI priorities. The designation of chairmanships also reflects the particular interests or expertise of states—for example, the South Korean government has been active in promoting credit guarantee methods at both the local and regional levels and is also cochair of WG 2.[46]

To understand how ABMI works at an institutional level, it is essential to look beyond structure to process.[47] What do participants actually do? Working

[44]MOF mimeo "Ajia saiken shijō ikusei inishiatibu" (Asian Bond Markets Initiative), June 2005; Takeuchi 2005.

[45]MOF mimeo, "Asian Bond Markets Initiative," June 2005. A summary can also be found online at http://asianbondsonline.adb.org/regional/asean_plus_three_asian_bond_market _initiatives/overview.php.

[46]For example, ADB 2003 shows that studies for establishing a regional guarantee mechanism were mostly funded by Korea. See also Oh and Park 2006, 232–39. The Phase 2 study that began in December 2006 was jointly funded by China and the ADB (ABMI 2006, 15–16). Why this has been a priority of the Korean and Chinese governments is not clear.

[47]This description is based on interviews with several former participants from the Japanese Ministry of Finance and Bank of Japan.

groups meet approximately bimonthly, as does the focal group. Country representatives to the focal group are midlevel bureaucrats (in Japan, the main representative is the director of the research division of MOF's International Bureau). Working groups can involve officials from several ministries or agencies—again using the Japanese example, officials from the Bank of Japan and Financial Services Agency supplement MOF participation on some working groups. Between meetings, working group participants carry out research and discussion at home and stay in e-mail and phone contact with their counterparts on relevant issues (while also carrying out their primary responsibilities within their own organizations). Working groups trade information and put together proposals for the focal group to consider.[48] Some of these proposals are then agreed upon as ASEAN+3 initiatives or guidelines and left to individual governments to enact.

Importantly, ABMI has no independent means of implementing the various proposals it generates. All actual implementation is left to participating states to carry out voluntarily and at their own preferred pace. Initiatives can be roughly divided into guidelines, on the one hand, and liquidity support, demonstration projects, and technical assistance, on the other.

The role of ASEAN+3 in all this is twofold. Most of what ABMI does is to create guidelines and share information on improving local-currency bond markets. To promote implementation of these guidelines, since 2005 ABMI has incorporated what might be considered a rudimentary surveillance process, known as "self-assessment," which is carried out in the focal group and higher-level meetings. Self-assessments are relatively brief documents produced semiannually that list accomplishments since the last meeting in addition to major short- and medium-term goals.[49] By informal agreement, discussion of any given country's bond market progress is kept to the topics presented by its government. Thus, self-assessment explicitly leaves both agenda and pace to each participating government. Although there appears to be some sort of peer pressure to move forward over time, both the lack of explicit goal-setting and the relatively junior level of the officials involved support the impression that pace is mainly set by domestic political processes outside of the ABMI process.

[48]Most of these proposals are available at Asian Bonds Online.

[49]These documents are not publicly released, although I was given access to one set of self-assessments in the summer of 2005. The contents were not particularly remarkable. My understanding was that the reason they were not released was so that participants could avoid publicly committing themselves to specific measures. The November 2006 deputies' meeting notes suggest future self-assessments may be released publicly: "Members are also considering developing a summary report on domestic bond market development in the region based on formatted individual self-assessment reports" (ABMI 2006, 5). As one indication of how premature it would be to think of this exercise as meaningful surveillance, even as of November 2006, several governments still had not submitted their first official self-assessments (32–33).

The other category of ABMI initiatives involves liquidity support, demonstration projects, and technical-assistance projects. Each of these requires an outlay of funds or personnel, but ASEAN+3 itself has no budget or staff to carry them out. So implementation of projects inevitably falls to participating governments and multilateral organizations. Liquidity support projects include local-currency bond issues by multilateral agencies (to date, these include the Asian Development Bank, International Finance Corporation, and World Bank) and ABMI governments or quasi-governmental entities, as well as bond guarantees by quasi governmentals. In each case, the government or agency in question decides on its own whether the action is a suitable one. The same is true of technical-assistance projects, many of which are actually bilateral. Japanese MOF officials have been particularly enthusiastic about providing technical assistance and funding policy-relevant research under the auspices of ABMI.[50] Finally, there are occasional regional demonstration projects that require cooperation between the participating governments—in such cases, participation is voluntary and roles are negotiated.

All in all, ABMI provides for extremely limited means of enforcement and promotion. Its main roles are as a forum for discussion of issues related to bond markets, a means of getting bond market issues on financial authorities' agendas, and a clearinghouse for information. In the end, it relies on exhortation and personal obligation to improve regional bond markets. Predictably, bond market development has in fact progressed at the pace dictated by domestic decisions about national and financial institutions' interests.

Infrastructure

As noted, there is a whole series of infrastructural issues that continue to retard East Asian bond markets.[51] Some can be broadly categorized as legal, others as informational, and still others as related to market structure. All have the effect of increasing transaction costs, uncertainty, or both. For example, most of the ASEAN+3 financial regulators require central approval for bond issues, which adds considerably to the time and expense involved in actually issuing a bond.[52] Personnel limitations in the regulatory agencies charged with such approvals also guarantee that the total number and value of bond issues will also be limited. Broader legal concerns exist as well, often including the ambiguity of bankruptcy laws and inefficiencies or corruption in regulatory agencies and courts more generally.

---

[50] In the November 2006 ABMI report, all the technical-assistance projects listed were carried out by consultancies attached to two Japanese financial institutions, Nomura and Daiwa. ABMI 2006, 27–31.

[51] A fairly comprehensive listing can be found in Lejot, Arner, and Liu 2006. See also IIMA 2005; Eichengreen and Luengnaruemitchai 2006; Takeuchi 2006; Ghosh 2006, chap. 3.

[52] Eschweiler 2006, 339–40.

As just one example of how financial regulations continue to make bond markets costly and inefficient, it is worth considering one of Japan's liquidity-support efforts under ABMI.[53] The government-owned Japan Bank for International Cooperation (JBIC) began early in the summer of 2004 to seek to issue local-currency bonds in Thailand and China, with the dual purpose of improving local-market liquidity and raising funds to cover the local-currency component of infrastructure projects to which JBIC lends. The Thai baht bond issue—a "plain vanilla bond" in the amount of 3 billion baht (about $75 million)—was not approved until September 2005, and the Chinese bond issue still had not been issued as of early 2008. From an efficiency perspective, it is hard to fathom why a government-owned financial institution with essentially no credit risk and with a stated plan to use the funds locally should have such trouble getting approval. Even as one-shot bond issues, however, the proposals became bogged down in seemingly endless negotiations with local regulators. The slowness of the process apparently reflected a combination of legal ambiguity and bureaucratic conservatism; regardless of the causes, the negotiations processes, especially with China, have not been encouraging to ABMI proponents. Indeed, JBIC appears to have abandoned plans to expand its local-currency bond issuance in Asia.

Other infrastructural problems often revolve around access to information. This is not just an issue of rules concerning disclosure, accounting, and insider trading rules, although those are crucially important.[54] There is also the question of whether market institutions have the scope and competence to effectively disseminate credible information. The lack of high-quality local ratings agencies that follow consistent methodologies significantly complicates the task of investors who are interested in purchasing corporate bonds. And the lack of a substantial set of data on defaults and corporate behavior makes ratings difficult in emerging bond markets. Finally, the efficiency of transactions depends also on technical facilities such as settlement systems, which can be costly to create and maintain, and involve significant economies of scale.

ABMI seeks to reduce these problems mainly through peer pressure, information exchange, and some technical assistance. For some issues, these means have a reasonable likelihood of success if a given government is receptive. For example, choice of settlement systems and procedures is largely a technical and budgetary issue for a given government or central

---

[53]Personal interviews with JBIC and MOF officials; JBIC, "Role and Recent Development: JBIC International Financial Operations" (briefing paper, July 2005); "JBIC Provides Thai Baht Two-Step Loan: First Asian Currency Loan under ABMI," JBIC press release, September 15, 2005. www.jbic.go.jp; "JBIC's Undertakings to Promote ABMI," http://www.jbic.go.jp/english/finance/abmi/jbicabmi/index.php, accessed September 3, 2007.

[54]Takeuchi 2006; Eschweiler 2006.

bank. To some extent, this is true also of how to review applications for bond issuance or underwriting. But other issues are harder. Ratings agencies, which have indeed been a major focus of ABMI discussions, can be encouraged and common standards can be drawn up, but in the end such agencies will only thrive if they are providing value and making money. (This is at least partly a question of the depth and liquidity of local-currency bond markets, leading to a chicken-and-egg problem.) Political concerns also intrude—for example, rules on defaults or insider trading are likely to require legislative action and are politically charged, to say the least. When it comes to the broadest issues, such as the rule of law, there seems to be no reason to believe that ABMI or any other soft regional process will be very effective.

Some governments (notably, South Korea and Malaysia) have made impressive strides in creating efficient and attractive bond market infrastructures, although it is difficult to link these improvements to the ABMI per se. Nonetheless, not only do significant obstacles remain, but many of those obstacles will be far more costly or politically sensitive to surmount than those that have already been met.

Liquidity

To improve the liquidity of bond markets in the region, the ASEAN+3 governments have also promoted local-currency bond issues by official actors (as in the JBIC case noted above) and various "credit enhancement" schemes. The most prominent liquidity promotion efforts in ASEAN+3 to date are to be found in "plain vanilla" local-currency bond issues by official actors. The Asian Development Bank and the International Finance Corporation have issued a number of local-currency bonds in the region, including in China, Hong Kong, Malaysia, Thailand, and the Philippines. The amounts have been mostly symbolic—the ADB issued a total of approximately $105 million in 2004, $267 million in 2005, $592 million in 2006, and $307 million in the first eight months of 2007.[55] In 2006 it made the dramatic announcement that it had launched a $10 billion Asian currency note program, which it claimed was "Asia's first multi-currency bond platform since the 1997 Asian financial crisis."[56] In reality, there is much less to it than that: it is simply an agreement with the financial authorities

---

[55] ABMI 2006, 12–13; ADB, "Multilateral Issuances by Supranationals," http://asianbonds online.adb.org/scripts/datatables.php?Graph_Title=Multilateral%20Issuances%20by %20Supranationals&SourceURL=multilateralgb&Graph_Desc=, accessed September 7, 2007. ABMI 2006 gives only annual dates for the bond issues, so I have converted them with yearly average exchange rates. (This makes little difference for 2005 and 2006 in any event, thanks to the "East Asian dollar standard.")

[56] "ADB Launches U.S. $10 Billion Asian Currency Note Programme," ADB news release, September 14, 2006.

of Malaysia, Thailand, Singapore, and Hong Kong that the ADB can issue up to a total of $10 billion in single-currency notes over the course of an unspecified number of years (including $455 million of the ADB's $592 million total Asian currency issues in 2006). The only thing that makes it a single platform is that the issues follow a "single unified framework with a common set of documents governed by English law." Ironically, even the ADB has tended to swap its local-currency proceeds immediately into U.S. dollars.[57] In principle, the point for ADB of doing Asian local-currency bonds is at least partly to raise counterpart funds for its lending activities, but the practice of swapping immediately into dollars calls this rationale into doubt.

The Japanese government has also made some efforts in this regard, primarily through JBIC; I have already noted JBIC's travails in Thailand and China. As another interesting example, it was widely expected in Tokyo financial circles in June 2005 that the government of Thailand would try to raise funds from Japanese investors by issuing a dual-currency bond (principal in baht, coupon payments in yen). At the last minute, the plan was dropped, apparently because the pricing was not attractive, and a "samurai bond" (that is, a yen-denominated bond issued by a non-Japanese entity) was issued instead.[58]

Credit enhancement is the other aspect of liquidity promotion efforts. Public sector credit enhancement primarily means issuing guarantees for private sector bonds in order to reduce the cost of financing for firms. For example, JBIC provided a secondary credit guarantee for a baht-denominated bond issue by the local affiliate of Isuzu Motors in Thailand in June 2004. (It has since provided secondary guarantees for a different Japanese corporate affiliate in Malaysia in 2006 and another one in Indonesia in 2006 and 2007.)[59] The Korean Development Bank has also provided several credit guarantees within Korea, in addition to its role in creating the Pan-Asia Bond, a complex one-shot cross-national asset-backed security.[60] The Korean government has also been supportive of a

---

[57] Personal interviews.

[58] In meetings and briefing materials in June 2005, Japanese MOF officials mentioned the dual-currency bond as an upcoming successful example of the ABMI process. Private sector financial professionals were also well informed about it—not surprisingly, since officials were hoping to convince them to buy and make markets in the bond. On the samurai bond issue, see "Thailand Business Briefs Column," *Bangkok Post,* June 21, 2005.

[59] "JBIC's Undertakings to Promote ABMI," http://www.jbic.go.jp/english/finance/abmi/jbicabmi/index.php, accessed September 3, 2007.

[60] To be more specific, the Pan-Asia Bond was a collateralized debt obligation that securitized the Japanese yen-denominated receivables of Korean SMEs, with primary credit guarantee by the Korean Development Bank and secondary guarantee by JBIC, sold by a Singapore-based special-purpose vehicle. (Details are provided in ABMI briefing materials.) If this sounds complicated, that is because it was. Although it worked in the sense that bonds were sold, it has not spawned any imitators.

regional guarantee agency that would presumably be located in the ADB.[61] There is some question whether credit guarantees are in general a good idea—Eichengreen argues that "such guarantees are not a step toward a market-based financial system. They simply reintroduce the same problems of moral hazard and implicit guarantees that plagued the market in bank credit in the first half of the 1990s."[62] Naoyuki Yoshino, a Japanese academic economist and member of the main Japanese MOF advisory council on the issue, has suggested that some of the problem could be ameliorated by making guarantees partial instead of total.[63] Studies are still ongoing, but there has been no concrete ABMI action to establish a regional guarantee agency.

ABMI also seeks to improve legal infrastructures to allow for more effective private sector credit enhancement, such as asset-backed securities.[64] However, while there have been some demonstration projects on both the regional and national levels, they remain few in number and minimal in impact.[65] The efforts to develop significant derivatives markets appear to go against constructivists' expectations that East Asian regional cooperation would be premised on a rejection of liberal financial markets, although the slowness of the progress suggests that the domestic politics of a number of economies are not yet willing to fully yield control over their financial sectors to market forces.

The Asian Bond Fund

The other major effort to promote regional bond markets is EMEAP's Asian Bond Fund, established in 2003.[66] In its first iteration (ABF1), the eleven member central banks invested a total of $1 billion in a BIS-managed fund composed of dollar-denominated sovereign debt in the emerging-market economies of EMEAP (i.e., not including Japan, Australia, or New Zealand). The intention was to encourage governments to issue benchmark bonds, stimulate private investment in them, and thus begin to establish market-based yield curves. Practically speaking, however, ABF1 was a small buy-and-hold closed-end fund, so it was not surprising that there was no

---

[61] ADB, "Technical Assistance," October 2003.

[62] Eichengreen 2004, 5, n. 7.

[63] See Yoshino's comments in Experts' Group on Asian Economic and Financial Issues 2005 (Internet version, no page numbers). See also Study Group for the Promotion of the Internationalization of the Yen 2005.

[64] For a study of Japanese financial institutions' preferences in this regard, see IIMA 2005.

[65] The only collateralized debt obligation issued under ABMI auspices was the 2004 Pan-Asia Bond described above.

[66] As noted earlier, the members include the central banks of Australia, China, Hong Kong, Indonesia, Japan, South Korea, Malaysia, New Zealand, the Philippines, Singapore, and Thailand.

noticeable effect on the liquidity of regional bond markets. In fact, it was doubly unsurprising, given that ABF1 invested only in dollar-denominated bonds, when the point of regional bond market promotion efforts was to encourage local-currency markets.

In contrast, ABF2 was formally established in early July 2005 with a mandate to invest in local-currency–denominated public sector bonds. The EMEAP central banks' investment of $2 billion is in the form of a closed-end fund, which is passively managed by professional managers, based on an index created by the prominent London-based International Index Company.[67] ABF2 has an unusual dual structure, with half the funds in a diversified regional fund (the Pan-Asia Bond Index Fund, or PAIF, managed in Hong Kong by State Street Global Advisors) and half allocated to another fund comprising a weighted average of eight single-country funds (each managed locally by a leading private financial institution).[68] The Pan-Asia and single-country funds are paralleled by open-end funds in which private investors can invest. The ABF2 effort is meant to enhance liquidity by making it easier and more attractive to purchase East Asian local-currency bonds. At least initially, officials saw Japanese financial institutions as well as Asian local institutional investors of all sorts as the target customers, but the participation of major Western financial institutions in the design and management of the funds was meant to be reassuring for U.S. and European investors as well.[69]

Another key goal is to establish benchmarks for regional bonds, in order to create robust yield curves and thus promote more efficient interest-rate formation for private sector bond issues. It is still too early to know whether

---

[67]International Index Company is a joint venture of ABN Amro, Barclays Capital, BNP Paribas, Deutsche Bank, Deutsche Börse, Dresdner Kleinwort, HSBC, JPMorgan, Morgan Stanley, and UBS.

[68]ABF2 funds are split between the regional fund PAIF and a Fund of Bond Funds (FoBF) comprising the eight country funds. The structure may appear to be unnecessarily complicated, with PAIF essentially replicating the FoBF. However, the hopes for private sector participation differ by type of fund. PAIF is meant to provide an overall Asian-currency index product denominated in U.S. dollars that will encourage investors to see the East Asian bond markets as a coherent unit. Since it is listed in Hong Kong, there are no restrictions on sales, purchases, or repatriation of proceeds. The country funds are denominated in local currencies and are meant to provide a low-cost vehicle for those who prefer to make their own allocations across economies. Potential investors are subject to applicable local laws. Investor differentiation among country funds could also be a spur for countries with less attractive bond funds to seek to improve them. As for central bank holdings, both PAIF and FoBF holdings are meant to be reallocated among country funds on a periodic basis, based not only on size of economy but also size of bond markets and a judgment of regulatory quality. Ma and Remolona 2005; "EMEAP Central Banks Announce the Launch of the Asian Bond Fund 2," EMEAP press statement, December 16, 2004; State Street Global Advisors, "Prospectus: ABF Pan Asia Bond Index Fund," June 28, 2005; personal interviews with MOF and BOJ officials.

[69]Personal interviews.

ABMI and ABF2 will be effective in achieving those goals—in the end, it will depend on private sector interest in assets denominated in East Asian currencies. There are some grounds for optimism on that score, but even more grounds for skepticism.[70]

What may be the most effective aspect of the ABF effort is that it has encouraged central bank cooperation regarding financial markets.[71] This is important because central banks are often the domestic financial regulators in their own countries. An example of how ABF negotiations contributed to improving market efficiency can be seen in China, where steps had to be taken to allow foreigners to purchase bonds in the interbank bond market (where the bulk of bond trading in China takes place) and then to be able to take their money out of the country up to a (publicly unspecified) limit. So, while the stated main agenda is to enhance liquidity, ABF has an indirect infrastructural promotion agenda that is complementary to ABMI.

As of fall 2007, the accomplishments of ABF2 were modest. The total amount of private investment in ABF2 parallel funds was in the neighborhood of only $3 billion—hardly enough to make an impact on markets.[72] Moreover, there had been little progress on a basic concern that had been recognized by the EMEAP Working Group on Financial Markets in 2006: not only had neither the country funds nor the regional fund seen major growth, but turnover in secondary markets remained low. Indeed, the working group identified the "buy-and-hold preference of Asian investors" as a major obstacle to increasing liquidity.[73] The greatest impact, albeit one that is hard to measure and is still incomplete, seems to have been on prompting regulatory improvements.

The Role of the Asian Development Bank

The Asian Development Bank until recently played only a minimal role in regional financial cooperation, including bond market initiatives. With

---

[70]The main reason for optimism about ABF2 is that major private sector financial institutions were willing to accept unusually low management fees for the private fund, apparently hoping that it would be a good chance to expand business. (Of course, they may also have been hoping for favorable treatment from regulators.) For a good summary of the arguments for why East Asian local-currency bond markets will or will not be successful, see Eichengreen 2004, 1–4.

[71]Ma and Remolona 2005; personal interview with BOJ official.

[72]I have calculated this based on the funds' own public reports, available on Asian Bonds Online, http://asianbondsonline.adb.org/regional/asean%203_asian_bond_markets_initiative/related_initiatives/emep_asian_bond_fund.php. It is hard to be more exact about the actual amounts, because the Korean and Indonesian private sector funds have not made their reports easily publicly available in English. Also, the fund reports are not updated on a uniform schedule. See also EMEAP 2006.

[73]EMEAP 2006, 21–24 (quotation, 33).

the appointment of Japan's former vice minister of finance for inter-national affairs, Haruhiko Kuroda, as president in early 2005, however, ADB became increasingly active in seeking to promote and support re-gional economic cooperation of all sorts, primarily through providing information and analysis to member governments and to the public at large. The primary locus for these activities has been the Office of Re-gional Economic Integration (OREI), which was significantly upgraded and expanded with the appointment of Masahiro Kawai to head it in Oc-tober 2005. Kawai had been an enthusiastic and sophisticated booster of regional integration in all its forms for a number of years and had developed a close working relationship with Kuroda when he worked as Kuroda's deputy at the Japanese Ministry of Finance for two years. Both had been major figures in the Japanese debate on financial regionalism well before their moves to Manila, and it remained an important goal for them.[74] Their appointments to leadership positions in the ADB (in which Japan is the largest shareholder) reflected Japan's interest in leading the ABMI process.

The ADB initiated three projects to support regional bond markets, in addition to the local-currency bond issues already noted.[75] The most impor-tant has been its project to disseminate information, beginning with Asian Bonds Online, which provides extensive data on ASEAN+3 bond markets. (This was created in 2004 explicitly as support for ABMI.) More recently, OREI has launched the Asia Regional Integration Center website, with links to a vast array of data and analysis on regional integration.[76] Secondly, OREI has sought to carry out economic research to support ASEAN+3's various endeavors. For example, it has put considerable effort into creating early warning indicators for regional financial crises.[77] It also sought to support East Asian financial regionalism by attempting (unsuccessfully) to create an Asian currency unit, as discussed in chapter 4. Finally, as of 2007, the ADB was still sponsoring ASEAN+3 technical studies of a regional guaran-tee mechanism; one possibility still under consideration was expanding the

[74]This can be seen in Kuroda's remarks at any number of venues since he went to the ADB—see for example his speech to the Governors' Seminar on a Roadmap for Asia's Economic Cooperation and Integration, at the first annual ADB meeting, in Istanbul, May 3, 2006. For an extensive sample of his speeches as president, see http://www.adb.org/Documents/Speeches/default.asp?spkr=75&name=President%20Haruhiko%20Kuroda&p=orgadbmg.

[75]ADB local-currency bond issues and borrowing are not confined to ASEAN+3 curren-cies. In August 2007, for example, the ADB even issued a five-year bond in Kazakhstan in the amount of 6 billion tenge. "ADB Issuing 6 Billion Kazakhstan Tenge Bonds," http://www.adb.org/Media/Articles/2007/12069-kazakhstan-bonds-issues/, accessed September 4, 2007.

[76]The Asia Regional Integration Center website is http://aric.adb.org/index.php. Asian Bonds Online can be accessed from it. Kawai left OREI to head the Asian Development Bank Institute in Tokyo in fall 2006.

[77]ADB 2005a, 2005b.

ADB's own existing credit guarantee programs to meet the specific goals of bond market development.[78]

Economic Prospects for Regional Bond Markets

Promoters of ABMI argue that the timing is excellent for local-currency bond market development in East Asia. Both global trends and local conditions can be invoked to make this case, and the excitement among market participants about Chinese markets in particular was palpable in 2007 and 2008.[79] At the same time, however, there are some formidable challenges facing local-currency markets, including issues of market structure, infrastructure, and cross-border transactions. Success in bond market development will be measured not only in the profit-making opportunities for global and local players but more importantly in whether those markets contribute to efficient price formation and capital allocation. For any of that to happen, there will need to be serious interest on the part of both issuers and investors.

For local investors, the main rationale would be that better rates and conditions are available through investing in bonds than through other savings and investment vehicles, such as bank accounts, equities, or real estate. As a general rule, well-functioning bond markets should provide higher returns than bank savings vehicles, less risk than equities, and greater liquidity than real estate.[80] Bonds could also offer investors the ability to match maturities of their assets and liabilities. Most of these benefits depend on adequate liquidity, however, leading to a chicken-and-egg issue. This is the reason why ABMI and ABF have included various efforts to promote increased participation by investors.

International investors have the same basic concerns as domestic ones. However, they have a far greater range of securities across the globe in which they have the capability to invest in order to maximize returns and minimize risk. An appetite for local-currency bonds of a variety of small or developing economies has developed in recent years, as global players have gained confidence in their ability to hedge away some of the risk. Bond market promoters in East Asia have emphasized several factors that should make local-currency East Asian bonds more attractive than those of other

---

[78]ABMI 2006, 15–16.

[79]See, for example, PIFS 2007a, 23–25.

[80]I should emphasize "well-functioning"—the subprime mortgage-backed securities problems that racked world finance beginning in August 2007 showed how lack of liquidity and imperfect understanding of derivative instruments and their underlying assets could create a dangerous market dynamic even in the world's most advanced financial systems.

economies.[81] These include strong fundamentals and conservative macroeconomic policies, superior returns relative to U.S. bonds over recent
years,[82] and (for non-Japan East Asian bonds) a low or negative correlation
with developed country returns.[83]

Local Market Limitations

Despite ASEAN+3 and EMEAP efforts, however, there are likely to be important limits to the development of large and liquid regional bond markets. These have to do with market size, infrastructure, credibility of legal
systems, and treatment of cross-national transactions. One way or another,
substantial foreign entry will be needed to expand liquidity in local-currency
markets.[84] But because of the small size of most domestic economies and
the lack of international usefulness of their currencies, it is likely that most
Asian markets will be of limited attractiveness to foreigners.[85] While it is
true that local-currency bonds from non-Asian developing countries such
as Mexico and South Africa have become popular with global institutional
investors, the risk premiums are high and the range of assets purchased is
limited. East Asia may have better attributes for attracting international investors, but the same basic dynamic will likely apply.

In general, foreign investors will be wary of investing in bonds denominated in a currency that is not itself attractive as a store of value. The sheer
size of the Chinese economy means that China will likely be an exception
to this point in the long run. (Already, foreign investors looking to China's
long term have shown their willingness to make major investments in a market that is currently limited and problematic.) In the absence of full capital
convertibility and well-developed markets in hedging instruments, however,
it is hard to imagine high liquidity in local-currency bond markets in most of
Asia. But capital liberalization is often seen as costly by developing-country
policymakers.[86] Budgetary costs stem from the need to improve regulatory
infrastructure. More important, the Asian Financial Crisis demonstrated

---

[81] Kawai 2005; Experts' Group on Asian Economic and Financial Issues 2005. Unpublished
briefing materials show that East Asian central bank officials have also made these arguments
directly to foreign investors in their "road shows" under the auspices of EMEAP.

[82] This depends very much on what one's starting date is—comparisons typically begin well
after the Asian Financial Crisis had done its worst. McKinnon and Schnabl (2004) argue that
the strong dollar returns reflect a risk premium that could be significantly reduced if governments chose to peg more explicitly to the dollar.

[83] State Street Global Advisors data, as cited in unpublished EMEAP briefing materials.
This is attractive for diversification and other risk management strategies that are typically
employed by major global financial institutions.

[84] Eichengreen 2006a, 4–7.

[85] On the relationship between market size and liquidity, see McCauley 2003, 92–94.

[86] See also Eichengreen 2004, 2006a.

the dangers of capital liberalization without proper sequencing and financial supervision, in the form of vulnerability to hot money flows and speculative attacks. It may be some time before the emerging economies of East Asia are prepared to fully liberalize capital flows again.[87] The dilemma also holds with regard to hedging instruments and derivative products, where the lessons of 1997–98 (as well as of the U.S. subprime mortgage crisis of 2007–8) give pause to many East Asian financial policymakers.

Costs of improving domestic bond market infrastructure are also high, and can be hard to justify as a high priority in developing or middle-income countries. These costs include the training and employment of a competent corps of regulators as well as development of sophisticated settlement systems. Developing means of rapid and accurate dissemination of market information is also costly and uncertain. On top of the government functions, there is the need for private sector development of ratings agencies, accumulation of market data, and analysis of default data. Moreover, those governments that have come to depend on imposing low-interest-rate debt on regulated financial institutions as a means of financing will incur additional costs by leaving the determination of treasury bond pricing to markets. Whether the benefits of reforms are worth these costs are fundamentally political decisions.

Specific goals, such as providing alternative financing mechanisms for SMEs or to support mortgage markets, will be even more difficult. To do that, the working groups of the ABMI have been promoting asset-backed securities, collateralized bond obligations, and a variety of other forms of internal and external credit enhancement, but the knowledge and legal bases are not fully in place anywhere other than Japan, Korea, and Singapore.[88] Even in Japan and Korea, however, securitized bonds were equivalent to less than 5 percent of GDP in 2006 (3.1% and 4.2%, respectively), as opposed to about 15 percent in the United States.[89] In any event, the meltdown in the U.S. subprime mortgage-backed securities market in 2007 has made it apparent that many of these asset-backed securitization schemes can introduce significant new risks into financial systems, particularly when

[87]There are exceptions, of course. According to Ma and Remolona 2005, Malaysia has "essentially restored the regime that was in place before it imposed capital controls during the Asian crisis" (88). There is plenty of evidence of continuing significant capital controls, however. For example, an index of formal capital openness developed by Menzie Chinn and Hiro Ito shows that ASEAN4 economies still had rather restrictive capital regimes through 2004. (Dataset available at http://web.pdx.edu/~ito/kaopen_2005.xls.) Detailed and up-to-date summaries of ASEAN economies' regulations on international capital flows can be found at http://www.aseansec.org/carh/index.htm.

[88]IIMA 2005. For a strong case for pushing the development of structured finance markets in East Asia, see Lejot, Arner, and Pretorius 2006; Park and Oh 2006.

[89]Statistics from Asian Bonds Online and U.S. Securities Industry and Financial Markets Association.

financial institutions or significant investors are not sophisticated at risk management.[90]

Meanwhile, market structures also limit liquidity in many East Asian economies. The prevalence of buy-and-hold strategies among institutional investors in most of the ASEAN+3 bond markets means that liquidity is low even when statistics of bonds outstanding seem impressive. Pension funds and insurance companies in particular tend to follow such strategies—this is especially apparent in economies such as China and Malaysia, where official or semiofficial actors such as social security funds, pension funds of state-owned enterprises, or state-controlled investment trusts are major financial-market actors. Unless the preferences of market and political actors change considerably or investors with significantly different preferences enter such bond markets, turnover and liquidity are likely to remain limited.

Finally, the development of the legal infrastructure of bond markets is important to international investors. Perhaps most obviously, they care very much about capital controls and withholding-tax rules.[91] But because they have the option of investing in other markets throughout the world, other aspects of the legal infrastructure, such as default rules, bankruptcy procedures, tort law, and so forth need to be competitive with already established local-currency bond markets in developing countries. More broadly, international investors must have some confidence in the credibility of the regulatory and legal systems of target markets, or they will require substantial risk premiums to invest there.[92] Other than Hong Kong and Singapore, none of the East Asian economies (including Japan) has the full confidence of global investors in this regard. Most East Asian governments have been slow to develop satisfactory rules because of the domestic political costs of doing so; it hardly makes sense to expect a government to change something as basic to the economic legal system as bankruptcy law just for the sake of promoting bond markets. Surveillance is in theory one way to deal with this, but as long as ASEAN+3 surveillance relies on moral suasion, consensus, and self-assessment, the only effective discipline for ABMI participants will come from markets. ABMI's loose and voluntaristic institutional design means that there are no sticks at all, and the carrots are small. Thus, unless the needs of the bond markets happen to coincide with a given

---

[90]One East Asian warning note in this regard was the revelation in August 2007 that the Bank of China was holding $10 billion in U.S. subprime mortgage-backed securities. Other East Asian financial institutions also held significant positions in collateralized debt obligations and other asset-backed securities, but to their benefit they had apparently entered those markets late and with greater caution than U.S. and European investors. "Bank of China in Subprime Provision," *FT*, August 24, 2007, 6; "Banks' Caution Cannot Prevent the Fear Factor," *FT*, August 18, 2007, 12.

[91]Takeuchi 2006, 253–54.

[92]Eichengreen and Luengnaruemitchai 2006; Ghosh 2006.

government's broad political objectives, it does not make sense to predict regulatory convergence to global best practices.

In summary, the current configuration of East Asian bond markets belies the ASEAN+3 hubbub about them. But it would be unwise to dismiss their potential altogether. As noted, the East Asian local-currency bond markets have several attractive aspects. Moreover, it is impossible to predict how developments in world bond markets and risk management may affect the region—in the mid-1990s, it would have been hard to imagine major global interest in the local-currency debt of Iceland and New Zealand, let alone Mexico and South Africa. Thus, some humility is in order in making any predictions. It is also possible that some of the ASEAN+3 economies will find lucrative market niches that respond to different incentives than bond markets operating on global standards—one potential example is Malaysia's play to become a power in Islamic banking and finance.

Beyond Local Markets? Efforts to Regionalize

Although I have focused on issues of local-currency bond market promotion *within* domestic markets, ABMI is ostensibly aimed at creating truly regional markets. Having regional markets trading in a local or regional currency would in theory address the problems of insufficient liquidity and of lack of economies of scale in small local markets.[93] This is indeed the stated long-term goal of ABMI and ABF.

At one level, the conception of regional financial markets appears to be a pipe dream rather than a meaningful goal. It is hard to imagine such markets thriving in the absence of open capital markets, more or less uniform regulations and ratings standards, and broad demand for East Asian currencies.[94] Moreover, the concept of deepening markets through the use of a synthetic regional currency (whether the ACU or some privately derived version) is much less convincing when we consider the inconvenient attributes of synthetic currencies. Their stability is highly dependent on the willingness and ability of individual governments to maintain macroeconomic stability; conversely, if one component currency were to drop dramatically against the basket, firms that earn most of their revenues in that currency would have the same difficulty in paying back in the basket currency as they would in any external currency. In other words, basket-denominated bonds would only be attractive if currency stability were achieved, which

---

[93]See, for example, Itō Takatoshi, "Ikinai kawase antei e zenshin" (Progress toward regional currency stability), *Nihon Keizai Shimbun,* July 29, 2005. See also the Asian Monetary Unit project of the Japanese government's Research Institute of Economy, Trade, and Industry, http://www.rieti.go.jp/users/amu/en/index.html.

[94]On harmonization, see Dalla 2003; Ghosh 2006, chap. 8.

is not a simple assumption to make. And even if currencies covaried considerably, it is not at all obvious that liquidity and currency risk conditions would be sufficiently favorable to make it cheaper for borrowers to issue their debt in the regional basket currency. Currency-basket bonds are difficult to handle and price and are not essential for diversification strategies; even the ECU did not prove to be an attractive currency for denominating private sector bonds.[95]

In any event, the concept of "regional" bond markets also provides rhetorical cover for de facto competition. The most practical means of unifying East Asian bond markets is not by integrating eight or thirteen or sixteen markets in a single network but rather by the development of one or two financial-market centers that centralize financial services on an offshore basis for the region as a whole.[96] This is the lesson of the eurocurrency markets of London as well as the development of New York as a hemispheric and global center of financial intermediation. While there are clear public goods created in the form of improved efficiency of financial intermediation, it is also likely that most of the local bond markets that are the target of the early phases of ABMI and ABF will wither if true regionalization of markets does occur. This expectation necessarily means competition among market centers with the potential to service regional needs, reminding us once again of the political dimensions of regional cooperation.

Political Economy of Regional Bond Market Initiatives

Potential effects of bond market initiatives are both economic and political. Economic effects include contributions to regional stability (or instability),[97] conformance with global financial standards and regimes, and competition among financial institutions and financial exchanges. ABMI and ABF efforts to improve infrastructure and liquidity can be understood through the prism of regional public goods provision. However, this begs the political questions of under what circumstances such public goods will be provided and what the alternatives are. From the point of view of political competition, I again look to the rivalry for regional influence among Japan, China, and the United States, with three issues paramount—contestation in standard-setting, competition over financial centers, and challenges to the hegemony of the dollar. I focus particularly on the interests and activities

[95] Eichengreen 2006b, 433. Kimura 2006 offers an opposing view of the utility of a synthetic currency for the private sector.
[96] Scott 2007.
[97] Blyth 2003; Best 2005.

of Japan, the closest thing there is to a regional leader in East Asian bond market promotion.

Financial Standards

One of the most striking aspects of East Asian bond market promotion efforts is the degree to which their stated aims and methods conform to "global standards" of openness and fairness.[98] Given the suspicion with which many ASEAN+3 governments have looked on financial markets in the past (particularly in the wake of the Asian Financial Crisis), this seems surprising. It is particularly difficult for constructivist scholars of East Asian regionalism to explain. Indeed, they appear to be silent on the issue.

Why have the East Asian economies embraced global financial standards? I argue that there are three reasons, all of which are compatible with neoliberal and realist political economy approaches, but none of which appear to make sense from the regional identity point of view.[99]

First, globalization and efficiency considerations have made it impractical to follow alternative financial-market standards and still achieve the benefits of bond market development. While governments may prefer greater control, international investors will not be willing to participate in bond markets that are not substantially free, fair, and open; and the further the markets are from those ideals, the higher the risk premium they will charge. This does, however, leave us with a domestic political question: Why have East Asian states decided to push bond market development instead of maintaining more controllable, bank-dominated systems, and how deep are their commitments to market-based finance?

The obvious answer is that the level of commitment depends on the efficiency of the alternatives and the representation of financial-industry interests in decision making. The domestic politics story helps to explain the voluntary nature of the process. Although globalization and efficiency concerns come into play at the level of incentives, the key point is that only a subset of the participating governments are actually using the ABMI and ABF processes to attempt to improve their bond markets, as well as those in which their investors and financial institutions have an interest. Japan, Singapore, and Hong Kong already had substantially free, fair, and open bond markets, while Malaysia and South Korea have seen substantial

---

[98] Grimes 2006 makes this point about ASEAN+3 financial regionalism in greater depth.

[99] As Blyth 2003 makes clear, there is a good constructivist argument to the effect that governments are forced by the global system to pursue "credibility," which in turn has been defined by global financial actors with the approval of U.S. and UK authorities as well as the IMF. See also Best 2005. Because of the structure of the global system, therefore, cooperative regional alternatives are not really viable. This says more about the global system than about regional cooperation, however, and so I do not address it directly here.

improvements over recent years. For these countries, the existence of institutional investors with major interests in the development of bond markets makes ABMI and ABF efforts far more attractive. For example, the resolution of the Asian Financial Crisis in both South Korea and Malaysia left official actors with burdens of debt (impaired or otherwise) that needed to be transferred back to the private sector; this could more effectively be handled through offerings of bonds than in any other way.[100] China and Thailand have taken more piecemeal approaches—all the more strikingly for Thailand, since it was from the beginning one of the most strident supporters of bond market initiatives.[101] For countries facing greater economic or political challenges, such as the Philippines, Indonesia, and Vietnam, bond market promotion efforts have not been a serious priority.

There follows a classic public goods story. Regional leaders are not willing or able to provide the necessary public goods or to make sufficient side payments to ensure compliance by followers. Thus, governments' choices about how ambitiously they will make the changes to support bond market development are primarily about the costs and benefits that they or their key constituents face. Access to global capital and efficiency of monetary policy are important values, but their importance varies across countries. Meanwhile, potential costs such as loss of control over exchange rates or interest rates, higher government debt service, and the need for court reforms vary as well. And there are also questions of priorities and opportunity costs—for example, when I asked two Philippine economic bureaucrats at a financial training session in Tokyo in the summer of 2005 about the status of ABMI implementation in their country, they laughed and said they were much more concerned about whether the president would survive impeachment and whether they would ever get their already delayed national budget passed. For Korea and Malaysia, on the other hand, benefits outweighed costs—both were able to leverage the bond market liquidity brought on by the aftermath of the AFC (due to budget deficits and government takeovers of distressed assets) and the existence of significant institutional investors such as pension funds and life insurers to jumpstart their bond markets. Malaysia has, moreover, sought to capitalize on increasing worldwide interest in Islamic banking and financial markets.

Japan's Quest for Regional Advantage

The third element of the rationale for following global standards has to do with relative benefits; in this case, it is the interests of leading economies in standard-setting. The key player in ABMI, ABF, and ADB bond

---

[100] For a succinct summary of this argument, see Hanson 2005, 18–20.

[101] Nominally, it still is, as "prime mover" in the moribund ACD Asian Bond Market Development project.

market promotion efforts has been Japan, which is the country in the region with both the largest, deepest, and most liquid bond market and the largest (if not necessarily the most nimble) internationally active financial institutions.[102] The Japanese government has been more willing to put public funds into ABMI efforts than others, and it also dominates the ADB, which has recently been seeking to support these efforts.[103] These observations shift the question away from why East Asian governments are pushing global standards to why the *Japanese* government is.

The simplest way to answer this is to say that it is in the economic and political interest of Japan to do so. At one level, there are profits to be made for Japanese investors, financial institutions, and exchanges. More broadly, there are political as well as general economic benefits to be gained by setting standards that support free markets for financial transactions in East Asia—in other words, regional structural power.

Japan has been a surplus-savings economy for the last forty years. In the past, the Japanese government intentionally funneled high savings into corporate investment via the banking system as part of a developmentalist agenda.[104] Even after Japan started posting huge current account surpluses in the 1980s, returns on (mostly U.S. dollar) foreign lending and portfolio investment were of secondary interest to Japanese financial institutions seeking market share, and those financial institutions relied on a basis of access to low-cost capital at home. Meanwhile, Japanese savers faced limited opportunities to earn strong returns on savings. The combination of the "lost decade" of the 1990s, where domestic returns were poor and many financial institutions found that their previous business model was unsustainable, and a rapidly aging society has forced a shift in focus to making higher returns on investment and expanding investment opportunities for households.

Japanese financial institutions have increasingly been offering foreign investment vehicles for these savers. From Inter-American Development Bank bond funds to Australian and New Zealand dollar bonds (*uridashi*) and savings accounts, foreign currency investing has gradually moved into the mainstream among Japan's famously risk-averse savers.[105] Economic bureaucrats have also begun to see this trend as a positive way to deal with the

[102]According to *The Banker*'s 2007 annual survey, the three biggest Chinese banks are larger than the three biggest Japanese banks by market capitalization but not by assets. Assets seems a more appropriate measure in this case.

[103]In this regard, the appointment of Haruhiko Kuroda as governor in 2005 was no accident. Kuroda was a close advisor of then prime minister Koizumi and a leading proponent of financial regionalism. See, for example, Clift 2006.

[104]Hoshi and Kashyap 2001.

[105]Nishi and Vergus 2006; Katz 2007a. Katz cautions, however, that such investments remain a relatively small proportion of most savers' portfolios.

need to ensure sufficient retirement savings for a rapidly aging population. The prospect of having robust bond markets in rapidly growing, responsibly managed economies with currencies at least partially linked to the yen is clearly a very appealing one from the point of view of both financial institutions and public policy. Thus, Japanese policymakers' promotion of free, fair, and open local-currency bond markets in East Asia fits well, not only with the interests they represent, but also with the strategic preference for a regional hedge against the dollar.[106]

Financial Interests and National Interest

Japanese financial institutions also seek opportunities to participate in regional bond markets in a variety of roles. (In this regard, it should be noted that Nomura Securities and its various subsidiaries have been involved in all the major pilot projects discussed so far, having been one of the five "authorized participants" in the ABF Pan-Asia Bond Index Fund as well as the underwriter in both the Pan-Asian Bond issue and Japan Bank for International Cooperation issues under ABMI. ABMI's technical assistance projects have so far been carried out by the consultancy arms of Nomura and Daiwa Securities.) While Japanese financial institutions have taken something of a battering in their global operations and reputations, they remain important presences in East Asian markets, where they service many of the financial needs of Japanese firms involved in manufacturing, services, and trading. Bond market development allows them to build on their servicing of this semicaptive market while also enjoying some financial backing of the Japanese government in ABMI projects. Meanwhile, they are seeking an early mover advantage relative to their global rivals in becoming primary dealers or otherwise participating in local bond markets.[107]

Regionalization of Bond Markets, Redux

Regionalization of markets sounds like, and to some extent is, a question of regional public goods provision. But there is also a significant element of competition over where regional markets will be based and what rules they will follow. Issues like standard-setting and provision for liquidity and infrastructure have a significant regional public goods component, even though costs and benefits vary by economy. Potential for conflict is more obvious in competition among financial exchanges. Financial exchanges are of great

---

[106] Grimes 2003a. See also Nishi and Vergus 2006 for statistics and analysis of trends in yen-denominated (samurai and euroyen) bonds. A few authors, including Bae, Yun, and Bailey 2006, and McCauley and Park 2006, suggest there may be a regional bias for investing among Japanese savers. If so, this would contribute to a preference for the development of regional bond markets.

[107] I am grateful to Martin Schulz for making this point to me.

benefit to the cities (and countries) where they are located, providing economic activities and profits across a variety of functions, and Japanese policymakers have sought to promote Tokyo as a major international financial market since the 1980s.[108]

Financial markets are increasingly becoming a scale enterprise, with smaller exchanges around the world falling by the wayside and even the largest exchanges engaging in mergers and alliances to maintain competitive advantage.[109] Increasing returns to scale means that there are potentially strong first-mover advantages regionally; moreover, gaining a large share of the issuance of rapidly growing bond markets will bolster Tokyo in its ability to attract global business versus competitors like London, New York, and Chicago.

If a regional bond market is indeed to be created, trading will likely be based in just one or two of the major regional exchanges, presumably the ones that have the largest customer basis, the lowest costs, the most sophisticated settlement systems, the most extensive menu of hedging instruments, and the greatest ease of foreign investment and repatriation of funds.[110] Tokyo, along with Singapore and Hong Kong, is clearly one of the main contenders—particularly as long as Shanghai is cloistered in a country with strict capital controls, weak bond market infrastructure, and questionable commitment to the rule of law. The longer it takes for regional bond markets to develop, however, the more competition there will be (including from Shanghai), so proactive measures are important for Japan.[111] As in so many aspects of East Asian regionalism, time is on China's side, and it is important to Japanese interests for Tokyo to act expeditiously.

Meanwhile, the effort to raise regulatory standards and harmonize regulation that is inherent in the regionalization project has political as well as economic implications. Standard-setting is not just a public good that ABMI and ABF are providing for East Asia, although that is certainly an important aspect. Standard-setting is also a competitive game, advantaging some actors and disadvantaging others. (The legal force and specific application of standards depends on the laws and regulations of the territory where a given security is issued. This means that competition among market centers directly parallels competition over standards.) Global standards of capital openness and free competition happen to coincide with the interests of Japan, and so Japan is promoting them based on its own specific regulations

---

[108] Horne 1985; Oka 1996; Study Group for the Promotion of the Internationalization of the Yen 2005; Toya 2006; IBA 2007; Working Group on Financial and Capital Markets 2007.

[109] See, for example, Committee on Capital Markets Regulation 2006, Section II.

[110] Scott 2007. For the general argument as applied to U.S. markets, see Committee on Capital Markets Regulation 2006.

[111] IBA 2007; Working Group on Financial and Capital Markets 2007; PIFS 2006b, 2007b; Grimes 2008.

and business practices. Moreover, it is promoting standards and trying to create viable regional markets *before* China is in a position to take advantage of its potentially massive market power to situate Shanghai or Hong Kong as East Asia's premier regional financial market and to advocate less transparency and sophistication of markets and regulation than Japanese financial institutions are capable of handling. Meanwhile, locking China into global financial standards will guarantee access to potentially lucrative financial opportunities in China, which is an important aim for Japanese financial institutions. Chinese policymakers would of course like to push Shanghai as a regional market center, but at the moment they have limited means of doing so. Nonetheless, China too has been active in trying to improve its bond markets in order not to lose the race.[112]

U.S. Standards without the United States?

Turning to our third great regional power, East Asian bond market initiatives appear to fit perfectly with the stated preferences and ongoing efforts elsewhere of the United States and IMF. These initiatives also meet the interests of U.S. investors (who have access to the private sector funds created under ABF2 and other opportunities for investing in local-currency bond markets equivalent to those of regional investors) and U.S. financial institutions (which are explicitly involved in ABF2 and which may be able to gain access to underwriting or other business in local markets). So it is striking that the U.S. government is explicitly excluded from the entire exercise. After all, at first glance, one might imagine that governments seeking to build their financial markets would be interested in receiving U.S. technical support and participation in specific projects. Nonetheless, official cooperation is occurring primarily within ASEAN+3 and EMEAP. There is no meaningful program within APEC, and the demise of the Manila Framework means that there is really no other direct means for the U.S. government to push its own agenda regarding East Asian bond markets.[113] This is especially surprising given both the agenda described above and the considerable role of the United States and IMF in encouraging capital liberalization in East Asia in the early and mid-1990s. What is perhaps even more surprising is that the U.S. Treasury appears to be unconcerned about its exclusion from the intergovernmental process.[114]

[112] PIFS 2007a, 23–25. "China Move Starts Corporate Bond Surge," *FT,* August 15, 2007.

[113] As noted in chapter 4, it appears that the U.S. Treasury was instrumental in terminating the Manila Framework, which was its only viable access point to the whole conversation. Personal communication with John Taylor.

[114] I have found no official statements to the contrary, nor have I come across any U.S. or Asian market participant or official who suggests that U.S. concerns are in any way an issue.

How can we understand this phenomenon of U.S. standards without the United States from a political economy point of view? With regard to content, it is possible that, as constructivists authors argue, the ASEAN+3 governments are concerned that their agendas might diverge in future from the U.S. preference for global standards.[115] In particular, governments may be concerned about keeping the right to set limits on the inward reach of financial globalization, whether through capital controls, differential tax treatment for foreign investors, or approvals-based regulation. Although all have nominally agreed to the long-term goal of developing bond markets by approaching global standards, concerns about economic effects or foreign influence may persist.

Such preferences, if indeed they exist, should presumably influence institutional design. If individual ASEAN+3 members are unsure about their commitment (whether short-term or long-term) to openness on developed economies' terms, they are likely to prefer the current arrangements to ones that include the United States. U.S. involvement would bring pressure for firm commitments and explicit timetables. Japan, as a weaker leader, is unable to adopt more than moral suasion and positive incentives in the form of self-assessments and demonstration projects.

Thus, it could be argued that the regional identity approach is compatible to some extent with what we observe—in other words, the United States is excluded because East Asian states wish to reject the totalizing ideology of financial free markets. In fact, however, we can explain that exclusion without having to make the case for some specific ideology, but instead by focusing on power and interests. Those states that most identify their interests with regional bond market development are most in favor of it, while others prefer lower levels of participation. But advocates cannot make laggards move faster, because they lack the power to do so. In other words, this is a classic case of regional public goods provision; in this case, the absence of a clear leader to provide liquidity and enforcement (although not all ABMI participants would necessarily see enforcement in a positive light) means that they are simply not being provided and cooperation is thus limited.

The exclusion of the United States fits broader themes in East Asian regionalism as well. Rather than providing yet another venue for U.S. pressure, Japan and other East Asian governments have actively sought to expand the scope of ASEAN+3 cooperation, contributing to a strategic hedge against excessive reliance on the United States. It also constitutes a means of communicating to East Asian partners that Japan is not simply an agent of U.S. policies. For Japan, bond market development is an attractive

---

[115] Higgott 1998; Breslin and Higgott 2000; Lee 2006.

opportunity to exclude the United States from regional decision making, because China is unable to provide regional leadership. This means that Japan does not feel the imperative of U.S. help in balancing Chinese influence in this issue area. The downside of this hedge for Japan is that, in the absence of U.S. support, it may prove difficult to lock China into acceptance of global standards and Japanese leadership over the longer term, unless the economic benefits to China and other ASEAN+3 members are convincingly large.

Challenging the Dollar?

While most of the debate over bond market initiatives has been over issues of regional efficiency and volatility, these efforts are also relevant to the systemic challenge discussed in chapter 4, namely the possibility of undermining the position of the dollar within the region and globally. The main point is that expanded use of local-currency bond markets would reduce the demand for U.S. dollar-denominated assets. Moves toward improved local-currency financial instruments would reduce the dollar's role in the region as a store of value, which (along with medium of exchange and unit of invoicing) is one of the three key functions of an international currency. Less use of dollar assets as a store of value also reduces the stake of macroeconomic authorities in maintaining the value of the dollar. Over time, this should contribute to a willingness to unwind foreign exchange reserves, forcing U.S. authorities to take responsibility for the dollar rather than relying on benign neglect to transfer costs to others. If regional settlement systems could be put into place at a reasonable cost—admittedly an unlikely possibility, although discussions are ongoing in the context of ABMI—the dollar's role as medium of exchange would also be undermined.

It is significant in this regard that Japanese financial policymakers see financial regionalism as a "package deal," comprising cooperation in all three of the issue areas covered in this book (in addition to enhanced surveillance and communication), although this perspective is not yet universally held by the ASEAN+3 governments. The effect on the status of the dollar would be increased if bond market development were to proceed in tandem with other aspects of financial regionalism that tend to insulate the East Asian economies from major fluctuations in the dollar. As we have seen, intraregional currency stabilization would reduce the effect on regional economies of fluctuations in the value of the dollar; the possible development of a regional synthetic currency (unlikely though it may be in the absence of clear leadership) would be an even more powerful step. In this regard, it is worth noting that there are several proposals for developing synthetic currency bonds as a means of concentrating attention on regional currency stability.[116] The logic of emergency liquidity arrangements, as seen in the Chiang Mai Initiative (and possibly more ambitious efforts in the longer run), is also to insulate regional economies from currency crises. The development of local-currency bond markets is meant to be one more form of insulation against fluctuations in the value the dollar. When all three are put together, the result should be less concern by East Asian governments about maintaining the stability of the current dollar-based system. If local bond markets lose their cost disadvantages relative to dollar assets, that could precipitate the move out of the dollar that observers concerned about U.S. balance-of-payments sustainability and the "dollar overhang" have been fearing for over three decades.

Regionalism, Insulation, and Globalization

Finally, new sources of instability and stability are not confined to the role of the dollar in the region. One of the dilemmas of regional financial-market cooperation is that the very efforts that are meant to reduce the vulnerability of currencies and economies to swings in the value of the dollar actually invite new vulnerabilities. At least in their current forms, regional bond efforts are configured to support financial globalization rather than just regionalization, as can be seen in both the adherence to global standards and in the self-conscious courting of foreign investors and financial institutions. The reemergence of an agenda of capital liberalization less than a decade after the 1997–98 crisis is striking to say the least. (Some observers may describe it as ominous.)[117] Certainly, it calls into question constructivist approaches to financial regionalism. How the new gospel of openness is actually implemented in East Asian financial markets remains to be seen, but there can be little doubt that insulation through internationalization involves clear trade-offs between different types of vulnerability to foreign capital.[118]

It is also important to bear in mind that, despite the regionalism that is at the core of the East Asian bond market promotion efforts, the practical effect may well be to hasten globalization rather than just to further regional integration. This is a risk that Japanese policymakers, who after all are already global players, are willing to take. But it is less obvious that policymakers in other ASEAN+3 economies with less internationalized currencies and less structural power in global finance will see the trade-offs in the same way. This may result in their greater-than-intended integration

---

[116]Eichengreen 2006b; Kimura 2006; Ogawa and Kawasaki 2006.
[117]That would appear to be the implication of Higgott 1998; Blyth 2003; Best 2005.
[118]This concept is developed in Grimes 2003a and 2003b.

into the global financial system, once again making them more vulnerable to globalized finance and U.S. structural power. More likely, it will mean stop-and-go policies that vary across countries and times, further slowing the process of bond market development and the creation of truly regional markets.

Conclusion

Currency and Contest in East Asia

Financial regionalism is happening in East Asia. Its pace can be slow and its destination is decidedly unclear, but there is no question that cooperative efforts are expanding and that they will be a key component of East Asian economic regionalism and regionalization more broadly. With East Asia as the home of the world's second- and third-largest economies, not to mention the bulk of world foreign exchange reserves and vast amounts of net savings, it is essential that we better understand where regional financial cooperation is likely to go.

I have argued that financial regionalism can best be understood in the context of great power rivalry among Japan, China, and the United States. In other words, financial regionalism is not just about managing interdependence and surmounting practical obstacles to regional economic stability, important though those goals may be. Regional financial efforts have important political implications both within East Asia and globally, with Japan, China, and the United States all seeking to shape the regional financial architecture in ways that will offer them economic and strategic advantage while limiting their own vulnerability. Driving this phenomenon are two major forces—regional economic integration and the rapid rise of China as an economic and political power—that have fundamentally changed the dynamics and implications of regional cooperation.

Regional Financial Challenges and Cooperation

Regional cooperative efforts are both functionally and politically driven. In any discussion of East Asian financial regionalism, the Asian Financial

Crisis looms large as both an economic and a political event. The extent of the crisis, the perceived inappropriateness of the IMF-organized rescue packages, and the often unforthcoming approach of the United States created a major incentive to seek regional solutions. This story is most straightforward for explaining the appearance of regional liquidity provision arrangements, but it also applies to attempts to deepen local-currency financial markets and to stabilize regional currencies.

As we have also seen, however, both the economics and the politics are contested in each of these aspects of financial regionalism—it is, to borrow the subtitle of an influential book on monetary politics, a case of "ambiguous economics, ubiquitous politics."[1] The economic uncertainties have contributed to a tendency among analysts of East Asian financial regionalism to focus on problem solving and sequencing. But, practically speaking, they also open up space for politics to enter the fray more directly. In order to understand the regional dynamics, in this book I have sought to address both aspects on their own terms.

In liquidity provision, the original AMF proposal was shot down at least partly due to suspicions on the part of the United States and China that Japan was trying to create institutions that would give it de facto regional leadership. Although regional liquidity arrangements returned (with far less overt opposition) in 2000 in the form of the Chiang Mai Initiative, CMI looked very different from the AMF. Most ironically, the inability of Japanese and Chinese authorities to solve the problem of moral hazard through regional means led to their ceding much of the decision-making power to the IMF. Still, CMI constitutes a significant hedge against U.S. and IMF capriciousness; the over $80 billion committed to the swap network serves not just to augment IMF funds in the event of a crisis but also constitutes an implicit threat of creating an alternative to the IMF. Thus the Chiang Mai Initiative simultaneously serves three purposes: it significantly supplements the resources available to regional economies in the event of another currency crisis, it solves the political problem for potential creditors like Japan and China of how to make liquidity provision more "credible" and less likely to promote moral hazard, and it raises the likelihood that the IMF and U.S. government will act supportively rather than punitively in the event of a future regional crisis in East Asia.

Unlike emergency liquidity, bond market initiatives are divisible in nature, allowing member states to proceed at their own paces. In the absence of clear carrots or sticks, ABMI has been based on self-assessment and voluntary action. The amount and impact of official funds through ABMI and ABF has been unimpressive, but then again the amount of funds needed to jump-start bond markets is likely to be very large indeed and would be

---

[1] Kirshner 2003.

at considerably greater risk than money provided under CMI swap agreements. Thus, the ability of leading economies to buy compliance in ABMI is much lower than in CMI. Meanwhile, participants assign varying levels of costs and benefits to the development of their financial markets, and their individual, self-paced actions under those initiatives reflect that. No state has been willing or able to take the lead in ensuring collective action by providing sufficient public goods (such as liquidity) or by pressuring its counterparts into compliance. My analysis suggests that we should not expect that to happen any time soon; if regional bond markets are to develop, it will be the result of the unilateral actions of one or two market centers in a competitive rather than cooperative process.

Currency coordination too is contested both conceptually and practically. The 1997 experience of vulnerability created by pegged exchange rate regimes, along with differing levels of economic development and divergent macroeconomic conditions among countries, would seem to make the value of currency stability questionable unless some level of macroeconomic policy coordination were to be achieved.[2] From an economic perspective, currency stabilization around either an internal or external basket is not a particularly complicated assignment, but the actual installation of effective surveillance, enforcement mechanisms, and symmetrical intervention obligations requires a level of confidence in the future actions of regional partners that will be difficult to achieve in the absence of clear leadership from the dominant economies. Given the differences in opinion and interest between Japan and China, not to mention their very different economic imperatives, a "bi-gemony" of the type that France and Germany provided in the evolution of European currency cooperation seems unlikely to say the least. Nonetheless, demand for currency cooperation among East Asian states is likely to keep the issue on the table. This derives from a common preference to hedge against the U.S. dollar (and thus the U.S. "power to deflect") and the potential need to manage foreign exchange and currency policies in the event of a crisis driven by abrupt dollar depreciation.

Power Shifts, Leadership, and Regionalization

East Asian regional economic cooperation is developing in a unique context. Economic regionalization has proceeded rapidly, but it has not been

---

[2] In contrast, the East Asian dollar standard and Bretton Woods II arguments claim that there are significant benefits to be derived from regional currency stability, but only when nested inside a global, dollar-based system. McKinnon 2005; Dooley, Folkerts-Landau, and Garber 2003.

supported by extensive intergovernmental cooperation. Japan, the most economically advanced and (measured by exchange rate) the richest country in the region, is challenged for leadership by China, a large, poor country that is nevertheless a bigger economy in purchasing-power terms. The two are together driving regional cooperation, but their own bilateral relations are characterized by political bitterness and mistrust, even as their economic interdependence grows unabated. Japan continues to rely on its bilateral alliance with an external superpower for its long-term security, while simultaneously shifting its international economic transactions toward Asia. Conversely, China and the United States remain wary—and indeed often suspicious—of each other while experiencing rapidly increasing economic interdependence. Meanwhile, formal trade cooperation in East Asia in the form of preferential trading agreements is driven by competition among regional and extraregional states to conclude the earliest and most beneficial deals.

None of this sounds promising as the background for serious regional economic cooperation. And yet we are in the midst of the most ambitious project of regional cooperation that East Asia has ever seen. The easy part of the story is that globalization and technological changes have created the opportunity for integrated East Asian regional production networks, which in turn have induced government cooperation to support them. Politically, competition among key players has actually driven economic cooperation in many instances. This is particularly evident in the establishment of preferential trading agreements, where China and Japan have each sought first-mover advantage, while the United States has pushed not to be excluded from lucrative markets. All three (as well as other regional and extraregional states) have sought to lock in access by securing official agreements that mutually commit them to their counterparts. For Japan, in particular, regionalism is an uncertain, high-stakes game. Hedging simultaneously against China (politically and militarily) and the United States (economically), it risks both military antagonism with China and abandonment by the United States.

Meanwhile, the role of the other ASEAN+3 states cannot be ignored or assumed away. While my analysis focuses on the great powers, South Korea and the leading ASEAN states operate as veto players. For the moment, at least part of the great power competition is over their affections. For these states, the best guarantee of a reasonable level of autonomy is continued involvement of all three major powers but with none assured of hegemony. At the same time, Japanese and Chinese willingness to provide a level of crisis support that U.S. and global financial actors clearly did not in 1997–98 makes the regional economic hedge (as embodied in particular in the Chiang Mai Initiative) an attractive one for their ASEAN+3 counterparts.

Realists in a Liberal World

Even economists and technocrats who write about designing a new regional financial architecture inevitably find themselves bringing up "politics" or "political will" in an effort to explain the difficulty of cooperation. Most political analysis to date has been based on neoliberal or constructivist approaches, largely to the exclusion of power politics. Perhaps one reason for the lack of power-based analysis is that it is not immediately obvious how realist political economy theory and observations should best be applied to understanding East Asian financial regionalism. Many analysts assume that realism means exclusive focus on relative gains and that therefore realist political economy is about reducing vulnerability through pursuing autarky or creating more or less exclusive economic blocs. Clearly, this kind of analysis does not take one very far in the modern, increasingly global economy.

One of my goals in this book has been to adapt principles of realist political economy to globalized finance. The enduring concepts of focus on relative gains and attempting to exclude competitors from lucrative opportunities are tempered by the facts on the ground created by globalization, such that even small or weak economies have access to alternative opportunities for finance, trade, and technology acquisition that make exclusion impractical if not impossible. Thus, the traditional focus on autarky must be replaced with looking at market-based attempts at insulation from currency swings. Mercantilist urges remain, however, in the way in which states define their interest in stability and seek to advantage domestic financial institutions and exchanges. We also expect that powerful states will seek to create rules and frameworks that promote their interests above those of potential rivals. Realist political economy sees economic and security issues as fundamentally intertwined and tensions as likely to arise if the distribution of power is not reflected in economic rules over the long run.

Analytically, in this book the key prism for understanding the actions of great powers of financial regionalism has been the concepts of hedging, commitment, and leverage. Japan in particular needs to hedge against U.S. abandonment without concretely harming U.S. economic interests. At the same time, it is trying to force China to commit to a liberal financial order, while trying to gain leverage on the future actions of the IMF in the event of another regional financial or currency crisis. From a mercantile point of view, it is trying to position its financial firms and savers to profit from new opportunities and reduction of vulnerability while also positioning Tokyo as the major regional financial market center. Thus, Japan is trying to gain security (in the dual senses of reducing financial vulnerability and maintaining U.S. vital interests in East Asia), advantage vis-à-vis its major partners and competitors, and prosperity for its citizens.

For China, the story is different. Like Japan, it has a strong interest in preventing financial volatility in the region and in insulating itself from the negative effects of future U.S. macroeconomic policies, and it is willing to commit at least some resources to achieving those goals. Politically, a leadership role in East Asia seems assured, but the web of U.S. alliances and quasi alliances in the region will be an important constraint unless those alliances can be weakened. The U.S.-Japan relationship is particularly problematic for China over the long run, as it combines its two greatest regional rivals for power; in the long run, China's preference must be either to weaken that alliance or to isolate Japan in Asia. But in the short term, this is neither realistic nor attractive—not only is China heavily economically intertwined with both, but a Japan that is militarily autonomous before Chinese regional dominance has been clearly established is a recipe for a security dilemma.[3] It also needs to continue to play a reassurance game with South Korea and the ASEAN states in order to prevent them from investing in a balancing coalition with Japan, the United States, and possibly India or Australia as well. Meanwhile, Chinese financial and economic development still depends heavily on the United States and Japan.

For the United States, continuation of the status quo would be ideal. This means maintenance of alliances and quasi alliances with Japan, South Korea, and ASEAN states as a potential balancing coalition against China, while also maintaining positive economic relations with China. Equally important is the maintenance and further development of a liberally oriented global financial architecture centered on the dollar, "global standards," and IMF-based crisis resolution. Regional financial cooperation is tolerable as long as that cooperation is nested in the global status quo, which encourages foreigners to take on dollar-denominated debt without a risk premium, and which allows U.S. financial institutions ready access to attractive local and regional markets. Regional macroeconomic and currency cooperation may also be attractive, if it contributes to the gentle unwinding of global payments imbalances; if it detracts from that goal or threatens dollar hegemony, it is problematic from the U.S. perspective.

Some of the interests of the great powers lead to shared preferences, while others conflict. Where conflicts appear, states must try to play one actor off against another or to buy off opposition. While this version of realist political economy may not appear as theoretically neat and tidy as the old expectations of exclusive blocs, I submit that it much more accurately reflects the way in which power games are played in the real world. (Of course,

---

[3]Christensen 2003 makes the latter point effectively. Wu (2005–06) makes the argument that China has concluded that the U.S.-Japan alliance is *already* injurious to its security interests, but he seems to be in the minority for the moment.

in the long run, something like exclusive blocs could arise from these strategies. But over the next decade or two, contestation is likely without that kind of breakdown in globalization.)

Finally, an important part of the realist political economy story has to do with the "hegemony" of the dollar. The broad reach of the dollar and of U.S. financial markets and institutions has given the United States enormous privilege in setting rules, acting as a de facto leader in shaping financial globalization, and deferring or even deflecting the adjustment costs created by large-scale and continuing current account deficits. Those states that have been most burdened with the resulting adjustment costs—including Japan, key members of the EU, and (sooner or later) China—have an incentive to disengage from the dollar system or otherwise pressure the United States to bear those costs on its own. Europe has collectively been moving in that direction since 1973; financial regionalism in East Asia raises the possibility that Japan and China will also be in a position to reduce the U.S. "power to deflect."

Ironically, Chinese foreign exchange intervention has been helping to maintain the role of the dollar in the system, leading to claims of a stable Bretton Woods II system, despite mutual political suspicions. However, it is not at all clear that the specific economic incentives that have so far driven massive Chinese dollar purchases will persist over time, as Chinese officials began to make clear in the latter half of 2007. If they do not, ASEAN+3 cooperation could provide the opportunity for a major shift in the role of the dollar, or at least the way that the U.S. government deals with its value. It also would significantly increase the leverage of East Asian states over U.S. economic policy. Japan, as ever, would be in a singularly awkward position in such a case, having to balance its economic and political interests.

What a multicurrency world would look like remains unclear, but it seems likely that basic leadership functions like providing a market for distressed goods would be much harder to handle on a global basis. For the moment, the network effects of dollar dominance and the continued role of the United States as a dominant global political actor make a multicurrency, regionally based financial system unlikely. But if it does develop, East Asian currency insulation efforts (along, of course, with European developments) will be a key factor.

Institutional Design as a Lens into Great Power Rivalry

While power-based approaches to the study of political economy suggest principles on which to base analysis, their use in analyzing specific situations has been hampered by the problem of operationalization. Trying to deduce expected behavior from realist principles can easily lead to multiple, debatable predictions. Thus, even if great power rivalry is a plausible explanation of a given situation, the analysis is susceptible to charges that the specific "realist" narrative has been shaped to fit rather than to test the facts at hand.

I have sought to minimize that problem in this book by using analysis of economic incentives and institutional design to tease out the opportunities and vulnerabilities inherent in each issue area. For example, debates over the meaning and likely future of the Chiang Mai Initiative often focus on questions of regional identity or the need to overcome U.S. hostility to exclusive regional organizations, leading participants to see shifts in the IMF link as the measure for the significance of regional cooperation. But the institutional analysis in chapter 3 demonstrates that the wholesale shift to an AMF style of regional organization is not in the interests of Japan or China. Thus, the main place to look for power politics is not in the percentage of linked funds or the mechanisms of surveillance; rather, it is in the creation of credible hedges (and thus leverage) against arbitrary actions by the IMF. It is also to be seen in the potential ability of China to expose Japan to a painful trade-off between defending its own interests in reducing moral hazard and not antagonizing the United States, on the one hand, and not antagonizing its ASEAN partners, on the other.

In regional currency cooperation, the European experience of gradual development of monetary cooperation may appear to offer a feasible functionalist pathway, and indeed advocates have looked to that model. But both the economic conditions and the institutional design of ASEAN+3 currency stabilization attempts belie the comparison. The institutional design of ASEAN+3 currency initiatives is at this point still minimal. There are no provisions for collective decision making, autonomous surveillance, or even mutual obligation to intervene around a set of target rates, nor is there a regional currency that functions or even could function as a de facto nominal anchor as the deutschemark did in Europe. And what state in East Asia is in a position to fulfill the basic requirements of a currency leader, that is, create liquidity, lend into crises, and be a market for distressed goods? The very implausibility of the current discourse on East Asian currency cooperation redirects our attention to the political issues that matter: insulation from U.S. macroeconomic irresponsibility and the leverage gained by developing a credible threat of systemic disruption.

In bond market cooperation, the network effects of global finance, reflecting the power of the United States and the dollar, fundamentally constrain regional efforts at insulation, forcing states to follow a strategy of insulation through internationalization. But the actual institutional design of ABMI and ABF reflects the inability of either Japan or China to provide sufficient liquidity to stimulate local-currency markets, to pressure other states to change their policies, or to establish regional standards of behavior of their own. Meanwhile, the impracticality of setting up truly regional markets turns our focus to the basic competition among states to establish their own markets as regional financial market centers.

China's Rise and Financial Regionalism

Financial regionalism responds to functional challenges arising from the desire to support and promote regional economic interactions, but it is impossible to ignore the vastly increased role and capabilities of China in all aspects of regionalization and regionalism. While China has not been the primary innovator in terms of creating and promoting specific regional financial efforts, it has played a key role as veto player and facilitator. In terms of emergency liquidity provision, the reluctance of the Chinese government to participate or even nod approvingly toward the AMF concept effectively prevented serious discussion of a regional solution until at least 1999. Although the plan that was approved in Chiang Mai in 2000 closely resembled Japanese thinking on the subject at that time, concrete regional cooperation was a nonstarter until Chinese officials decided that it was not a vehicle for Japanese influence in East Asia. Once China was on board, negotiations proceeded rapidly.

Similarly, even preliminary discussions among officials about currency cooperation in East Asia were impossible until China officially abandoned the RMB's dollar peg in July 2005. The rapid rise of Chinese economic and political clout—and even more so, expectations that the rise will continue—naturally underlie its role as veto player. This point holds even in financial market initiatives, in which no one expects it to have anything approaching dominance or even parity with Japan for years to come.

What is interesting about China's rise is that it does not translate directly into a position of power in regional economic and political cooperation. This is because the Chinese government is also very fundamentally involved in a reassurance game vis-à-vis its neighbors in Southeast Asia and South Korea (albeit less so with Japan). In particular, the basic strategic imperative of Chinese regionally oriented policies for the time being is to reduce the attractiveness to ASEAN and South Korea of entering into an implicit containment coalition with the U.S.-Japan alliance at its core. Thus, at some level, the *fact* of "cooperation" is more important than its *content*—as can be seen, for example, in the "early harvest" provisions of the ASEAN-China trade agreement and the consistent Chinese emphasis that ASEAN is at the center of East Asian cooperation. And so, while China certainly does not appear to be entering into unfavorable agreements, it is not exactly driving a hard bargain with neighbors other than Japan.[4]

The combination of these effects of China's rise means that the next few years constitute an important opportunity for East Asia to create regional economic (including financial) institutions—China is clearly eager to be

[4]This may be changing, if news reports are true of China playing hardball with East Asian emerging economies over their complaints about product safety of imports from China. "Asians Say Trade Complaints Bring Out the Bully in China," *Washington Post*, September 5, 2007, 1.

a constructive participant but is not yet in a position to dictate terms. For its neighbors, this is an opportunity to attempt to embed Chinese foreign and economic policymaking in a cooperative, transparent architecture. For Japan, this is likely to be the last good chance to shape that architecture to its advantage, emphasizing free access to financial markets, currency stability, and the potential role of Tokyo as a regional financial market. This parallels a similar story at the global level, where U.S. policy has actively sought to increase China's stake in existing regimes, as reflected in both its support of Chinese entry into the WTO and more recent efforts to increase the quota and role of China in the IMF.

Can Japan Satisfy Its Yen for Asia?

East Asian financial regionalism is a collective enterprise, and its ultimate fate depends on the actions of the various state and market actors in the region. Japan faces the most interesting and challenging menu of options of any of the participants or potential participants (such as the United States) in the process. Japan's economic interests in financial regionalism are generally straightforward: it seeks to lower the likelihood of currency crises, to reduce its own vulnerability to shifts in the yen-dollar exchange rate, to secure access to East Asian financial markets for its firms and financial institutions, and to attract regional financial activity to the Tokyo markets. Accomplishment of these goals—by no means a simple or certain task— would contribute to its ability to continue to profit from East Asian economic growth and to avoid bearing the costs of U.S. balance-of-payments adjustments. Financial regionalism on an ASEAN+3 basis has been an important means through which Japan has sought to achieve these goals since the Asian Financial Crisis.

While the goals are fairly straightforward, the trade-offs are not so simple. Japan's overall strategic situation is entering its most unstable phase since the end of World War II as a result of the rise of China, reemergence of the "history issue" in East Asia, and increasing doubts about the sustainability of both the dollar-based global economic system and the U.S. commitment to acting as a regional balancer. In the long run Japan faces a choice between Chinese hegemony, on the one hand, and partnership (albeit not equal partnership) with the United States, on the other. Given the inherent uncertainties for Japan of how China will behave as a regional leader, ongoing political rivalry, and history-based antagonisms between the two, as well as Japan's increasing convergence with the United States in terms of international economic interests, Japanese leaders have across the board made clear their intention to stick with the United States. Thus, a key goal is to keep the United States embedded in East Asian political and economic structures. In economic issues, this means emphasizing common interests in stability and financial market access and development, while avoiding conflict.

At the same time, Japan must seek to address some important economic interests that differ from those of the United States. One clear issue is that the increasing importance of East Asia to Japan's economic fortunes calls for greater emphasis on creating institutional support for further integration, including with China. Of more concern from the point of view of keeping the Americans in, the Japanese government seeks to insulate its economy from some of its excessive vulnerability to U.S. economic policy choices.[5]

All of this makes Japan's participation in financial regionalism into something of a tightrope walk between hedging and commitment strategies. Moreover, time appears to be on China's side. Nonetheless, Japan brings significant strengths to the table, which it will need to use quickly to solidify a regional financial architecture that minimizes its commitment costs and still manages to lock China into cooperative, noncoercive behavior over time. These include financial-system strengths relative to neighbors and a potential to be a bridge between East Asia and the major international financial institutions. Japan may also be in a position to leverage its position as the essential balancing partner for both the United States and China. U.S. authorities understand that any sort of long-term strategy to balance or potentially militarily contain China will require partnership with Japan, due to its geographic position, size of economy, air and naval capabilities, and post–World War II role as lynchpin of U.S. strategy in the Asia-Pacific region. So abandonment is not a likely short-term or even medium-term prospect (even though Japan has made recent efforts to hedge even that remote possibility by courting cooperation with India and Australia). Meanwhile, despite China's charm offensive in ASEAN, Southeast Asian states understandably appear to prefer a balance of power to the possibility of domination by one power or another. As long as the U.S.-Japan alliance remains stable, close relations with Japan will remain an attractive prospect for the ASEAN states.

Complicating Matters: Agenda for Further Research

I have argued that great power rivalry is an essential prism for understanding the development of financial regionalism in East Asia and its implications. Rivalry, insecurity, and uncertainty create an environment in which

---

[5] Katz 2007b shows that Japan's dependence on U.S. economic trends has actually *increased* since 2000.

the major players seek to further their own interests through strategies of engagement, hedging, and commitment. These objective realities constrain the willingness and ability of states to pursue their regional and global economic interests.

But that does not mean that other factors are somehow irrelevant or that power structure will necessarily lead to some determinable outcome. The fact is that no coherent theoretical approach to a complicated phenomenon can fully account for relevant facts. In this case, we are addressing cooperative interstate efforts in a region that has a limited track record. These efforts include multiple official actors operating bilaterally, subregionally, regionally, and extraregionally, and they are linked to a variety of other regional, superregional, and global political and economic interactions. Meanwhile, the rubric of "financial regionalism" covers a coherent but logically separable set of issues, and moreover those issues have distributional consequences within economies. So I conclude this book both with confidence in the explanatory power of the framework I have used and with a deep appreciation of the need for scholars, policymakers, and journalists to address other factors as well. Only with the development of a broader literature will we be able to fully comprehend the ways in which international rivalries play out in the actual course of events.

Four research objectives will be particularly important in furthering our collective knowledge and understanding of East Asian economic financial regionalism. These include interactions with other forms of functional cooperation, the roles of South Korea and the Southeast Asian states in shaping financial regionalism, the domestic politics of interest formation, and the role of ideas in creating opportunities or obstacles to cooperation.

Financial regionalism is developing within the context of a much broader project of economic regionalization and official cooperation within and across regions. One important example is regional trade cooperation. Financial cooperation in East Asia has proceeded on a regional basis and with an emphasis on public goods and global standards, whereas trade cooperation has been largely bilateral (and often cross-regional) while emphasizing private gains by the participating economies.[6] But regional trade and financial architectures are also developing in complementary ways that reflect the importance of regional and global production networks and the growth of economic interdependence. Regional cooperation is neither completely coherent nor simply a set of discrete and loosely related functional efforts. States are likely to emphasize or deemphasize different aspects of and venues for economic and political interactions at various times and in response to specific events, perceived shifts in advantage, linkage strategies,

---

[6] Solís and Katada 2007.

and domestic politics. These choices are to a great extent unpredictable, but we need to have a much more holistic picture of the moving parts of the system in order to better understand those choices.

A second issue that calls for further research is the role of South Korea and of the Southeast Asian states (and potentially India and Australia) in the shaping of regional financial cooperation.[7] I have focused on the formative role of great powers, but in practice the preferences of other states are closely scrutinized by Japanese and Chinese financial authorities as they assemble proposals and plan negotiating strategies. This is especially true given the efforts of both Japan and China to reassure and win the allegiance of their regional partners. The structure of ASEAN+3 and China's stated claim that ASEAN should determine the pace and direction of regional cooperation also lock regional leaders into a process that requires respect for the interests of their partners. It would be useful to have a clearer and more nuanced understanding of their perspectives and stakes in the regional financial project in order to go beyond the first cut that this book provides.

Third, there remains considerable scope for analyzing the formation of states' interests in regional financial cooperation. I have presented state interests as being coherent and structurally determined, in order to avoid ad hoc explanations of key events and policies. But there is clearly more to the story than this. Indeed, probably the strongest potential criticism of this book is that it has not determined states' interests empirically. There is a vast literature that points to domestic political economy as determining states' economic "interests" in Japan and the United States, and the domestic political economy approach has become the default option for studies of their foreign economic policies. I believe that I am on solid ground in using a reductionist approach to financial regionalism, both because I am trying to isolate the degree to which "high politics" shapes regional economic policies and because domestic preferences regarding international financial issues tend to be much less conflictual than in trade and to involve fewer domestic actors. Moreover, based on extensive discussions over the years with U.S., Japanese, and (to a much lesser extent) other East Asian officials and financial professionals, I believe that my approach is largely empirically correct as well. Nonetheless, there remains a need to analyze the domestic politics more rigorously.

Finally, we need more constructivist studies of the effects of regional identity and elite socialization. Regional identity certainly appears in regionalist rhetoric, suggesting that there is at least some attraction within

---

[7] I thank Nobuhiro Hiwatari for alerting me to the importance of this avenue of research. Koo 2006 offers a preliminary examination of Korea's efforts to play a "balancing role" in East Asian regionalism.

the region to some sort of "East Asian" identity. And it is at least plausible that beliefs about the global financial system might constrain the types of financial policies and international regimes that key state actors perceive to be attractive or even possible. My own assessment is that these factors play at most a minor role compared to objective factors such as power and economic interests. But it is difficult to make a scholarly judgment about the validity of identity-based explanations of regionalism, given that there is no consensus among authors about what an East Asian regional identity might actually be, how widely it is held, how it has changed over time, or how it should systematically affect outcomes. A sharpening of constructivist explanations in addition to empirical investigation of public and elite attitudes and beliefs would improve the debate over East Asian regionalism, and perhaps our understanding of regionalism itself.

Looking to the Future

While I recognize the importance of a much broader research agenda than is possible for one scholar or to be addressed in one book, I return finally to my basic theme. Great power politics is clearly at play in shaping East Asian financial regionalism—not only in terms of constraints, but also in providing opportunities for cooperation and shaping the specific agenda. As long as the long-term structure of power in East Asia remains uncertain, major states will look to economic regionalism as one of many means of creating hedges for themselves and commitments for allies and adversaries, while simultaneously seeking economic prosperity in an interdependent regional and global economy. For the foreseeable future, this appears to be a formula for limited cooperation nested within the framework of the global financial architecture.

Putting together the various strands of hedges, commitments, and alignments, we can imagine a relatively stable East Asia well into the medium term. No state has an incentive to upset the status quo of supporting mutually beneficial economic integration, nor is there an obvious call to rock the political boat for the time being. It even seems likely that financial regionalism will come to support regional economic integration and development over time. But the extent of support is likely to be functional and selective rather than encompassing. In short, the most likely outcome of current efforts will be neither community nor overt conflict. If Japanese policymakers continue to seek an intermediate goal that balances security and economic interests between China and the United States, the politics are likely to work out. The economics—particularly in terms of currency stability and local-currency bond market development—will be more questionable, although the efforts are relatively low cost and generally positive, and operate in the context of market-driven interdependence. In particular, I expect that the Chiang Mai Initiative will work more or less as planned if its services are needed.

Nonetheless, there are some clouds on the horizon. One is the question of whether regional or global financial stability can be achieved if the role of the dollar is reduced. While reduced exposure to dollar swings is inherently attractive to Japan and its neighbors, a reduced role of the dollar may force them to create mechanisms for collective international liquidity provision and lender-of-last-resort functions. In the absence of effective collective leadership by Japan and China—an unlikely phenomenon for the time being— the transition from a dollar-based to a multicurrency world is likely to be a volatile one if and when it occurs. Moreover, it will have profoundly negative effects on U.S. structural power. This presents both opportunity and danger for East Asia. As the U.S. power to deflect declines, Japan (and China) will benefit from being able to pursue returns on their savings instead of propping up the dollar. But it is also likely to be destabilizing to world payments and financial systems, and potentially to the U.S.-Japan relationship as well.

The other danger is that larger political struggles will trump economic (even relative economic) interests. I have raised the possibility that China could leverage a threatened decoupling of the Chiang Mai Initiative from the IMF to weaken Japan's relationships regionally or with the United States. Alternatively, there is a possibility that a serious U.S.-China dispute surrounding trade imbalances, the value of the RMB, and the management of China's foreign exchange reserves and sovereign wealth funds could erupt. In principle, this could lead to redoubled efforts within East Asia to solidify regional financial cooperation, especially if the U.S. response were also to target the policies of other East Asian states with excessive reserves or sovereign wealth funds. More likely, it would lead to an uncoordinated response that could be injurious to East Asia, the United States, and the world. This disarray could eventually reinvigorate demand for regional financial cooperation, but at great cost and not in a manner or time frame that any advocate of regionalism would prefer.

The realist tradition is not known for its optimism. The best hope it offers in times of turbulence is a prescription for peaceful change that says that the interests and abilities of rising powers should be accommodated if serious conflict is to be avoided. As an optimist by nature but a realist by observation and training, I end this book by expressing the hope that East Asian financial regionalism will ease global adjustment to the rise of China while supporting economic benefit along the way. The conditions most likely to achieve this outcome are the maintenance of a rough balance of power between China and Japan (supported by its alliance with the United States) and a regional commitment to common standards that reduce volatility and ensure mutual gain.

References

Acharya, Amitav. 2000. *Constructing a Security Community in Southeast Asia: ASEAN and the Problem of Regional Order.* New York: Routledge.

Aggarwal, Vinod. 1998a. "Reconciling Multiple Institutions: Bargaining, Linkages, and Nesting." In *Institutional Designs for a Complex World,* ed. Vinod Aggarwal, 1–31. Ithaca: Cornell University Press.

———. 1998b. "Institutional Nesting: Lessons and Prospects." In *Institutional Designs for a Complex World,* ed. Vinod Aggarwal, 195–213. Ithaca: Cornell University Press.

———, ed. 1998. *Institutional Designs for a Complex World.* Ithaca: Cornell University Press.

Aggarwal, Vinod, and Shujiro Urata, eds. 2006. *Bilateral Trade Agreements in the Asia-Pacific: Origins, Evolution, and Implications.* New York: Routledge.

Ahearne, Alan, William Cline, Kyung Tae Lee, Yung Chul Park, Jean Pisani-Ferry, and John Williamson. 2007. "Global Imbalances: Time for Action." *Peterson Institute for International Economics Policy Brief,* no. PB07–4.

Alt, James, Randall Calvert, and Brian Humes. 1988. "Reputation and Hegemonic Stability: A Game-Theoretic Analysis." *American Political Science Review,* vol. 82, no. 2: 445–66.

Amyx, Jennifer. 2002. "Moving beyond Bilateralism? Japan and the Asian Monetary Fund." *Pacific Economic Papers,* no. 331 (September). Canberra: Australia-Japan Research Centre, Australian National University.

———. 2004a. *Japan's Financial Crisis: Institutional Rigidity and Reluctant Change.* Princeton: Princeton University Press.

———. 2004b. "A Regional Bond Market for East Asia? The Evolving Political Dynamics of Regional Financial Cooperation." *Pacific Economic Papers,* no. 342. Canberra: Australia-Japan Research Centre, Australian National University.

———. 2004c. "Japan and the Evolution of Regional Financial Arrangements in East Asia." In *Beyond Bilateralism: U.S.-Japan Relations in the New Asia-Pacific,* ed. Ellis Krauss and T. J. Pempel, 198–218. Stanford: Stanford University Press.

Anderson, Benedict. 1991. *Imagined Communities: Reflections on the Origin and Spread of Nationalism,* revised and enlarged edition. London: Verso.

Andrews, David. 2006. "Monetary Policy Coordination and Hierarchy." In *International Monetary Power,* ed. David Andrews, 91–114. Ithaca: Cornell University Press.

Andrews, David, ed. 2006. *International Monetary Power.* Ithaca: Cornell University Press.

Andrews, David, C. Randall Henning, and Louis Pauly, eds., 2002. *Governing the World's Money.* Ithaca: Cornell University Press.

Aoki, Takeshi. 2006. *Bōeki kara miru "Ajia no naka no Nihon"* ["Japan in Asia" as seen from the perspective of trade]. Tokyo: Nihon Keizai Hyōronsha.

Aramaki, Kenji. 2006. "Sequencing of Capital Account Liberalization: Japan's Experiences and Their Implications to China." *Public Policy Review* (Ministry of Finance of Japan, Policy Research Institute), vol. 2, no. 1 (January): 177–231.

Armitage, Richard, and Joseph Nye. 2007. "The U.S.-Japan Alliance: Getting Asia Right through 2020." *CSIS Report,* February.

Asian Development Bank. 2003. "Technical Assistance for the ASEAN+3 Regional Guarantee Mechanism." TAR:OTH 37352 (October).

——. 2004. *Monetary and Financial Integration in East Asia: The Way Ahead,* vol. 1, ed. Asian Development Bank. New York: Palgrave Macmillan.

——. 2005a. *Early Warning Systems for Financial Crises: Applications to East Asia.* New York: Palgrave Macmillan.

——. 2005b. "Technical Assistance: Strengthening Economic and Financial Monitoring in Selected ASEAN+3 Countries." Project no. 39579 (December).

——. 2007. "Enhancing the Capacity of Selected ASEAN+3 Countries for Assessing Financial Vulnerabilities." Project no. 40565 (March).

Asian Bond Markets Initiative. 2006. "Progress Report of the Asian Bond Markets Initiative." November. http://asianbondsonline.adb.org/documents/Progress_Report_ABMI_Nov2006.pdf, accessed September 3, 2007.

Axelrod, Robert, 1984. *The Evolution of Cooperation.* New York: Basic Books.

Axelrod, Robert, and Robert Keohane, 1986. "Achieving Cooperation under Anarchy: Strategies and Institutions." In *Cooperation under Anarchy,* ed. Kenneth Oye, 226–54. Princeton: Princeton University Press.

Bae, Kee-Hong, Young Sup Yun, and Warren Bailey. 2006. "Determinants of Bond Holdings by Foreign Investors." *BIS Papers,* no. 30: 102–28.

Baldwin, Richard. 2006. "Multilateralising Regionalism: Spaghetti Bowls as Building Blocs on the Path to Global Free Trade." *World Economy,* vol. 29, no. 11: 1451–518.

——. 2007. "Managing the Noodle Bowl: The Fragility of East Asian Regionalism." *Asian Development Bank Working Paper Series on Regional Economic Integration,* no. 7 (February).

Bank for International Settlements. 2007. *Triennial Central Bank Survey of Foreign Exchange and Derivatives Market Activity in April 2007: Preliminary Global Results.* September.

Barnett, Michael, and Martha Finnemore. 2004. *Rules for the World: International Organizations in Global Politics.* Ithaca: Cornell University Press.

Beeson, Mark. 2006. "South-East Asia and the International Financial Institutions." In *The Political Economy of South-East Asia: Markets, Power and Contestation,* ed. Garry Rodan, Kevin Hewison, and Richard Robison, 240–57. Oxford: Oxford University Press.

Bello, Walden. 1998. "East Asia: On the Eve of the Great Transformation?" *Review of International Political Economy,* vol. 5, no. 3: 424–44.

Berger, Thomas. 2003. "Power and Purpose in Pacific East Asia: A Constructivist Interpretation." In *International Relations Theory and the Asia-Pacific,* ed. G. John Ikenberry and Michael Mastanduno, 387–420. New York: Columbia University Press.

——. 2007. "The Politics of Memory in Japanese Foreign Relations." In *Japan in International Politics: The Foreign Policies of an Adaptive State,* ed. Thomas Berger, Michael Mochizuki, and Jitsuo Tsuchiyama, 179–211. Boulder: Lynne Rienner.

Bergsten, C. Fred, 1985. *Dilemmas of the Dollar: The Economics and Politics of U.S.* International Monetary Policy. New York: Council on Foreign Relations.

——. 2007. "The Dollar and the Renminbi." Statement before the Hearing on U.S. Economic Relations with China: Strategies and Options on Exchange Rates and Market Access, Subcommittee on Security and International Trade and Finance, Committee on Banking, Housing and Urban Affairs, United States Senate, May 23.

Bernard, Mitchell, and John Ravenhill. 1995. "Beyond Product Cycles and Flying Geese: Regionalization, Hierarchy, and the Industrialization of East Asia." *World Politics,* vol. 47 (January): 171–209.

Best, Jacqueline. 2005. *The Limits of Transparency: Ambiguity and the History of International Finance.* Ithaca: Cornell University Press.

Bhagwati, Jagdish. 1991. *The World Trading System at Risk.* Princeton: Princeton University Press.

Blyth, Mark. 2003. "Structures Do Not Come with an Instruction Sheet: Interests, Ideas, and Progress in Political Science." *Perspectives on Politics,* vol. 1, no. 4: 695–706.

Bowie, Alasdair, and Daniel Unger. 1997. *The Politics of Open Economies: Indonesia, Malaysia, the Philippines, and Thailand.* Cambridge: Cambridge University Press.

Bowles, Paul. 2002. "Asia's Post-Crisis Regionalism: Bringing the State Back In, Keeping the (United) States Out." *Review of International Political Economy,* vol. 9, no. 2: 244–60.

Bowles, Paul, and Baotai Wang. Forthcoming. "The Rocky Road Ahead: China, the U.S. and the Future of the Dollar." *Review of International Political Economy,* vol. 15, no. 3.

Bracken, Paul. 2007. "Financial Warfare," *Orbis,* vol. 51, no. 4: 685–96.

Breslin, Shaun, and Richard Higgott. 2000. "Studying Regions: Learning from the Old, Constructing the New." *New Political Economy,* vol. 5, no. 3: 333–52.

Calder, Kent, and Min Ye. 2004. "Regionalism and Critical Junctures: Explaining the 'Organization Gap' in Northeast Asia." *Journal of East Asian Studies,* vol. 4, no. 2 (May–August): 191–226.

Calomiris, Charles. 1998. "The IMF's Imprudent Role as Lender of Last Resort." *Cato Journal,* vol. 17, no. 3: 275–94.

Cargill, Thomas, Michael Hutchison, and Takatoshi Ito. 1997. *The Political Economy of Japanese Monetary Policy.* Cambridge: MIT Press.

Chang, Michele, 2003. "Franco-German Interests in European Monetary Integration: The Search for Autonomy and Acceptance." In *Monetary Orders: Ambiguous Economics, Ubiquitous Politics,* ed. Jonathan Kirshner, 218–35. Ithaca: Cornell University Press.

Chinn, Menzie, and Jeffrey Frankel. 2005. "Will the Euro Eventually Surpass the Dollar as Leading International Reserve Currency?" *NBER Working Paper,* no. 11510.

Chinn, Menzie, and Hiro Ito. 2006. "What Matters for Financial Development? Capital Controls, Institutions, and Interactions." *Journal of Development Economics,* vol. 81, no. 1: 163–92.

Christensen, Thomas. 2001. "Posing Problems without Catching Up: China's Rise and Challenges for U.S. Security Policy." *International Security,* vol. 25, no. 4: 5–40.

——. 2003. "China, the U.S.-Japan Alliance, and the Security Dilemma in East Asia." In *International Relations Theory and the Asia-Pacific,* ed. G. John Ikenberry and Michael Mastanduno, 25–56. New York: Columbia University Press.

Chua, Beng Huat. 2004. "Asian Values: Is an Anti-Authoritarian Reading Possible?" In *Contemporary Southeast Asia: Regional Dynamics, National Differences,* ed. Mark Beeson, 98–117. New York: Palgrave Macmillan.

Chung, Duck-Koo, and Barry Eichengreen, 2007. "Exchange Rate Arrangements for Emerging East Asia." In *Toward an East Asian Exchange Rate Regime,* ed. Duck-Koo Chung and Barry Eichengreen, 1–21. Washington, DC: Brookings Institution.

——, eds., 2007. *Toward an East Asian Exchange Rate Regime.* Washington, DC: Brookings Institution.

Clift, Jeremy. 2006. "People in Economics: The Quiet Integrationist." *Finance and Development*, vol. 43, no. 1.

Cline, William. 2005. "The Case for a New Plaza Agreement." *Policy Briefs in International Economics*. Washington, DC: Institute for International Economics, no. PB 05–4.

Cohen, Benjamin J., 1993. "The Triad and the Unholy Trinity: Lessons for the Pacific Region." In *Pacific Economic Relations in the 1990s: Cooperation or Conflict?* ed. Richard Higgott, Richard Leaver, and John Ravenhill, 133–58. Boulder: Lynne Rienner.

——. 1998a. *The Geography of Money*. Ithaca: Cornell University Press.

——. 1998b. "When Giants Clash: The OECD Financial Support Fund and the IMF." In *Institutional Designs for a Complex World: Bargaining, Linkages, and Nesting*, ed. Vinod Aggarwal, 161–94. Ithaca: Cornell University Press.

——. 2004. *The Future of Money*. Princeton: Princeton University Press.

——. 2006. "The Macrofoundations of Monetary Power." In *International Monetary Power*, ed. David Andrews, 31–50. Ithaca: Cornell University Press.

——. 2007. Toward a leaderless currency system? Presented at conference on "Whither the Key Currency? American Policy and the Global Role of the Dollar in the Twenty-first Century." Cornell University, October 12–14.

Committee on Capital Markets Regulation. 2006. *Interim Report*. November 30. http://www.capmktsreg.org/pdfs/Summary_11.30interimreport.pdf.

Cooper, Scott. 2006. "The Limits of Monetary Power: Statecraft within Currency Areas." In *International Monetary Power*, ed. David Andrews, 162–83. Ithaca: Cornell University Press.

Dalla, Ismail. 2003. *Harmonization of Bond Market Rules and Regulations in Selected APEC Economies*. Manila: Asian Development Bank.

Deng, Yong. 2006. "Reputation and the Security Dilemma: China Reacts to the China Threat Theory." In *New Directions in the Study of China's Foreign Policy*, ed. Alastair Iain Johnston and Robert Ross, 186–214. Stanford: Stanford University Press.

Destler, I. M., and C. Randall Henning. 1989. *Dollar Politics: Exchange Rate Policymaking in the United States*. Washington, DC: Institute for International Economics.

Dooley, Michael, David Folkerts-Landau, and Peter Garber. 2003. "An Essay on the Revived Bretton Woods System." *NBER Working Paper*, no. 9971.

——. 2004. "The U.S. Current Account Deficit and Economic Development: Collateral for a Total Return Swap." *NBER Working Paper*, no. 10727.

Duffield, John. 2003. "Asia-Pacific Security Institutions in Comparative Perspective." In *International Relations Theory and the Asia-Pacific*, ed. G. John Ikenberry and Michael Mastanduno, 243–70. New York: Columbia University Press.

Dupont, Alan. 1996. "Is There an 'Asian Way'?" *Survival*, vol. 38, no. 2: 13–33.

East Asia Study Group. 2002. *Final Report of the East Asia Study Group*. Presented at Phnom Penh ASEAN+3 Summit. November 4. http://www.aseansec.org/viewpdf.asp?file=/pdf/easg.pdf.

East Asia Vision Group. 2001. *East Asian Community: Region of Peace, Prosperity and Progress*. Submitted to ASEAN+3 leaders. October 31. www.mofa.go.jp/region/asia-paci/report2001.pdf.

Eichengreen, Barry, 1996. *Globalizing Capital: A History of the International Monetary System*. Princeton: Princeton University Press.

——. 1999. *Toward a New International Financial Architecture: A Practical Post-Asia Agenda*. Washington, DC: Institute for International Economics.

——. 2004. "The Unintended Consequences of the Asian Bond Fund." Address to the annual meeting of the Asian Development Bank, May, Jeju Island, South Korea. http://emlab.berkeley.edu/users/eichengr/policy/jejuisl&mar29–04.pdf#search=%22Asian%20bond%20fund%22, accessed October 4, 2006.

——. 2006a. "The Development of Asian Bond Markets." *BIS Papers*, no. 30: 1–12.

————. 2006b. "The Parallel-Currency Approach to Asian Monetary Integration." *American Economic Review*, vol. 96, no. 2: 432–36.

Eichengreen, Barry, and Ricardo Hausmann, eds. 2005. *Other People's Money: Debt Denomination and Financial Instability in Emerging Market Economies*. Chicago: University of Chicago Press.

Eichengreen, Barry, Ricardo Hausmann, and Ugo Panizza. 2003. "Currency Mismatches, Debt Intolerance and Original Sin: Why They Are Not the Same and Why It Matters." *NBER Working Paper*, no. 10036 (October).

Eichengreen, Barry, and Pipat Luengnaruemitchai. 2006. "Why Doesn't Asia Have Bigger Bond Markets?" *BIS Papers*, no. 30: 40–77.

Ernst, Dieter. 1994. "Mobilizing the Region's Capabilities? The East Asian Production Networks of Japanese Electronic Firms." In *Japanese Investment in Asia: International Production Strategies in a Rapidly Changing World*, ed. Eileen Doherty, 29–55. Berkeley: Berkeley Roundtable on the International Economy.

Eschweiler, Bernhard. 2006. "Bond Market Regulation and Supervision in Asia." *BIS Papers*, no. 30: 335–52.

Evans, Paul. 2005. "Between Regionalism and Regionalization: Policy Networks and the Nascent East Asian Institutional Identity." In *Remapping East Asia*, ed. T. J. Pempel, 195–215. Ithaca: Cornell University Press.

Executives' Meeting of East Asia-Pacific Central Banks, 2006. *Review of the Asian Bond Fund 2 Initiative*. http://www.emeap.org/ABF/ABF2ReviewReport.pdf, accessed October 8, 2007.

Experts' Group on Asian Economic and Financial Issues. 2005. *Dai 20 kai Ajia keizai/kin'yū no shomondai ni kansuru senmon bukai gijiroku* [transcript of the 20th meeting of the Experts' Group on Asian Economic and Financial Issues], May 20, Tokyo. http://www.mof.go.jp/singikai/kanzeigaitame/giziroku/baig170520gijiroku.htm, accessed July 17, 2005.

Foreign Exchange Commission. 1999. *Internationalization of the Yen for the 21st Century: Japan's Response to Changes in Global Economic and Financial Environments*, April 20.

Frankel, Jeffrey, and Miles Kahler. 1993. Introduction to *Regionalism and Rivalry: Japan and the United States in Pacific Asia*, ed. Jeffrey Frankel and Miles Kahler, 1–19. Chicago: University of Chicago Press.

Frasher-Rae, Michelle. 2008. *Malign Neglect: The Transatlantic Battle for the Soul of Money*. Unpublished book manuscript.

Friedberg, Aaron. 2005. "The Future of U.S.-China Relations: Is Conflict Inevitable?" *International Security*, vol. 30, no. 2: 7–45.

Frieden, Jeffrey, and Ronald Rogowski. 1996. "The Impact of the International Economy on National Policies: An Analytical Overview." In *Internationalization and Domestic Politics*, ed. Robert Keohane and Helen Milner, 25–47. Cambridge: Cambridge University Press.

Fukao, Kyoji, Hikari Ishido, and Keiko Ito. 2003. "Vertical Intra-Industry Trade and Foreign Direct Investment in East Asia." *RIETI Discussion Paper Series*, no. 03-E-001.

Funabashi, Yoichi. 1989. *Managing the Dollar: From the Plaza to the Louvre*. Washington, DC: Institute for International Economics.

————. 1995. *Asia Pacific Fusion: Japan's Role in APEC*. Washington, DC: Institute for International Economics.

Garrett, Geoffrey, and Peter Lange. 1996. "Internationalization, Institutions, and Political Change." In *Internationalization and Domestic Politics*, ed. Robert Keohane and Helen Milner, 48–77. Cambridge: Cambridge University Press.

Gavin, Francis. 2003. "Ideas, Power, and the Politics of U.S. International Monetary Policy during the 1960s." In *Monetary Orders: Ambiguous Economics, Ubiquitous Politics*, ed. Jonathan Kirshner, 195–217. Ithaca: Cornell University Press.

Geithner, Timothy. 2007. "Reflections on the Asian Financial Crises." Presented at conference on "The Asian Crisis Revisited: Challenges over the Next Decade," Federal Reserve Bank of San Francisco, June 20. http://www.frbsf.org/banking/asiasource/events/2007/0706/papers/geithner.pdf.

Ghosh, Swati. 2006. *The Road to Robust East Asian Financial Markets*. Washington, DC: World Bank.

Gill, Indermit, and Homi Kharas. 2006. *An East Asian Renaissance: Ideas for Economic Growth*. Washington, DC: World Bank.

Gilpin, Robert. 1987. *The Political Economy of International Relations*. Princeton: Princeton University Press.

——. 2000. *The Challenge of Globalization*. Princeton: Princeton University Press.

——. 2001. *Global Political Economy*. Princeton: Princeton University Press.

——. 2002. "The Evolution of Political Economy." In *Governing the World's Money*, ed. David Andrews, C. Randall Henning, and Louis Pauly, 19–37. Ithaca: Cornell University Press.

Girardin, Eric, 2004. "Information Exchange, Surveillance Systems, and Regional Institutions in East Asia." In *Monetary and Financial Integration in East Asia: The Way Ahead*, vol. 1, ed. Asian Development Bank, 53–96. New York: Palgrave Macmillan.

Goldstein, Avery. 2005. *Rising to the Challenge: China's Grand Strategy and International Security*. Stanford: Stanford University Press.

Goldstein, Morris. 1998. *The Asian Financial Crisis: Causes, Cures, and Systemic Implications*. Washington, DC: Institute for International Economics.

——. 2002. *Managed Floating Plus*. Washington, DC: Institute for International Economics.

Goldstein, Morris, and Nicholas Lardy. 2005. "China's Role in the Revived Bretton Woods System: A Case of Mistaken Identity." *Institute for International Economics Working Paper*, no. 05–2.

——. 2006. "China's Exchange Rate Policy Dilemma," *American Economic Review*, vol. 96, no. 2: 422–26.

Goldstein, Morris, and Philip Turner. 2004. *Controlling Currency Mismatches in Emerging Markets*. Washington, DC: Institute for International Economics.

Goldstein, Morris, and Anna Wong, 2005. "The Next Emerging-Market Financial Crisis: What Might It Look Like?" In *Financial Crises: Lessons from the Past, Preparation for the Future*, ed. Gerard Caprio, James Hanson, and Robert Litan, 121–210. Washington, DC: Brookings Institution.

Gowa, Joanne. 1994. *Allies, Adversaries, and International Trade*. Princeton: Princeton University Press.

Grabel, Ilene. 2003. "Ideology, Power, and the Rise of Independent Monetary Institutions in Emerging Economies." In *Monetary Orders: Ambiguous Economics, Ubiquitous Politics*, ed. Jonathan Kirshner, 25–52. Ithaca: Cornell University Press.

Green, Michael. 2001. *Japan's Reluctant Realism: Foreign Policy Challenges in an Era of Uncertain Power*. New York: Palgrave Macmillan.

——. 2002. "Balance of Power." In *U.S.-Japan Relations in a Changing World*, ed. Steven Vogel, 9–34. Washington, DC: Brookings Institution.

Grieco, Joseph. 1988. "Anarchy and the Limits of Cooperation: A Realist Critique of the Newest Liberal Institutionalism." *International Organization*, vol. 42, no. 3: 485–507.

Grimes, William W., 1999. "Japan and Globalization: From Opportunity to Constraint," *Asian Perspective*, vol. 23, no. 4: 167–98.

——. 2001. *Unmaking the Japanese Miracle: Macroeconomic Politics, 1985–2000*. Ithaca: Cornell University Press.

——. 2002. "Purchasing Credibility in East Asia, but at What Cost? Japan and Regional Currency Arrangements." Presented at "Japan and the Transforming International Order: Bilateral Relations, Regional Arrangements, and Global Regimes," June 20–22, Sophia University, Tokyo.

——. 2003a. "Internationalization as Insulation: Dilemmas of the Yen." In *Japan's Managed Globalization: Adapting to the 21st Century*, ed. Ulrike Schaede and William W. Grimes, 47–76. Armonk, NY: M. E. Sharpe.

——. 2003b. "Internationalization of the Yen and the New Politics of Monetary Insulation." In *Monetary Orders: Ambiguous Economics, Ubiquitous Politics*, ed. Jonathan Kirshner, 172–94. Ithaca: Cornell University Press.

——. 2005. "Japan as the 'Indispensable Nation' in Asia: A Financial Brand for the 21st Century," *Asia-Pacific Review*, vol. 12, no. 1: 40–54.

——. 2006. "East Asian Financial Regionalism in Support of the Global Financial Architecture? The Political Economy of Regional Nesting." *Journal of East Asian Studies*, vol. 6, no. 3: 353–80.

——. 2008. "Tōkyō shijō ga Ajia no chūshin dearu tame ni subeki koto" [What must be done to make Tokyo the financial-market center of Asia]. *Ekonomisuto*, January 8, 80–84.

Grossman, Gene, and Elhanan Helpman. 1995. "The Politics of Free-Trade Agreements." *American Economic Review*, vol. 85, no. 4: 667–90.

Haas, Peter. 1992. "Introduction: Epistemic Communities and International Policy Coordination." *International Organization*, vol. 46, no. 1: 1–35.

Haggard, Stephan. 2000. *The Political Economy of the Asian Financial Crisis*. Washington, DC: Institute for International Economics.

Hall, Peter, and Rosemary Taylor. 1996. "Political Science and the Three New Institutionalisms." *Political Studies*, vol. 44, no. 5: 936–57.

Hamilton-Hart, Natasha. 2002. *Asian States, Asian Bankers: Central Banking in Southeast Asia*. Ithaca: Cornell University Press.

——. 2006. "Creating a Regional Arena: Financial Sector Reconstruction, Globalization, and Region-Making." In *Beyond Japan: the Dynamics of East Asian Regionalism*, ed. Peter Katzenstein and Takashi Shiraishi, 108–29. Ithaca: Cornell University Press.

Hanson, James. 2005. "Postcrisis Challenges and Risks in East Asia and Latin America: Where Do They Go from Here?" In *Financial Crises: Lessons from the Past, Preparation for the Future*, ed. Gerard Caprio, James Hanson, and Robert Litan, 15–61. Washington, DC: Brookings Institution.

Hatch, Walter, and Kozo Yamamura. 1996. *Asia in Japan's Embrace*. Cambridge: Cambridge University Press.

Hayami, Masaru. 1995. *En ga sonkei sareru hi* [The day when the yen will be respected]. Tokyo: Tōyō Keizai Shimpōsha.

Hayashi, Shigeko. 2006. *Japan and East Asian Monetary Regionalism: Towards a Proactive Leadership Role*. New York: Routledge.

Helleiner, Eric. 1994. *States and the Reemergence of Global Finance: From Bretton Woods to the 1990s*. Ithaca: Cornell University Press.

——. 2000. "Still an Extraordinary Power, but for How Much Longer? The United States in World Finance." In *Strange Power: Shaping the Parameters of International Relations and International Political Economy*, ed. Thomas Lawton, James Rosenau, and Amy Verdun, 229–47. Aldershot, UK: Ashgate Publishing.

——. 2006. "Below the State: Micro-Level Monetary Power." In *International Monetary Power*, ed. David Andrews, 72–90. Ithaca: Cornell University Press.

Henning, C. Randall. 1994. *Currencies and Politics in the United States, Germany, and Japan*. Washington, DC: Institute for International Economics.

Henning, C. Randall. 2002. *East Asian Financial Cooperation*. Washington, DC: Institute for International Economics.

——. 2006. "The Exchange-Rate Weapon and Macroeconomic Conflict." In *International Monetary Power*, ed. David Andrews, 117–38. Ithaca: Cornell University Press.

Hettne, Björn. 2005. "Beyond the 'New' Regionalism." *New Political Economy*, vol. 10, no. 4: 543–71.

Higgott, Richard. 1998. "The Asian Economic Crisis: A Study in the Politics of Resentment." *New Political Economy*, vol. 3 no. 3: 333–56.

Hirschman, Albert, 1945 [1969]. *National Power and the Structure of Foreign Trade*. Berkeley: University of California Press.

Hisane, Masaki. 2007. "'Axis of Democracy' Flexes Its Military Muscles." *Asia Times Online*, March 31.

Hiwatari, Nobuhiro. 1996. "The Domestic Sources of U.S.-Japan Economic Relations." Presented at the annual meeting of the American Political Science Association, San Francisco.

——. 2003. "Embedded Policy Preferences and the Formation of International Arrangements after the Asian Financial Crisis." *Pacific Review*, vol. 16, no. 3: 331–59.

Horiuchi, Akiyoshi. 1998. *Kin'yū shisutemu no mirai: Furyō saiken mondai to biggu ban* [The future of the financial system: The nonperforming loan problem and Big Bang]. Tokyo: Iwanami Shinsho.

——. 1999. *Nihon keizai to kin'yū kiki* [Japan's economy and the financial crisis]. Tokyo: Iwanami Shoten.

Horne, James. 1985. *Japan's Capital Markets: Conflict and Consensus in Policymaking*. London: Allen and Unwin.

Hoshi, Takeo, and Anil Kashyap. 2001. *Corporate Financing and Governance in Japan: The Road to the Future*. Cambridge: MIT Press.

Hu, Xiaolian. 2007. "China's Approach to Reform." *Finance and Development*, vol. 44, no. 3 (September).

Hutchison, Michael, and Frank Westermann, eds. 2006. *Japan's Great Stagnation: Financial and Monetary Policy Lessons for Advanced Economies*. Cambridge: MIT Press.

Ikenberry, G. John, David Lake, and Michael Mastanduno. 1988. "Introduction: Approaches to Explaining American Foreign Economic Policy." *International Organization* (special issue: "The State and American Foreign Policy Making"), vol. 42, no. 1: 1–14.

Institute for International Monetary Affairs. 1999. "Internationalization of the Yen: Implications for Stabilization of Financial Systems and Currencies in Asia." Conference report, March. Tokyo: Institute for International Monetary Affairs.

——. 2002a. *Executive Summary of Research Papers and Suggestions of Kobe Research Project*. http://www.mof.go.jp/jouhou/kokkin/tyousa/tyou058.pdf.

——. 2002b. *Policy Evaluation of Japan's Support to Countries Affected by the Asian Currency Crisis* [translation of *Gaibu hyōka: Wagakuni no Ajia tsūka kiki shien no seisaku hyōka*]. Tokyo: Institute for International Monetary Policy. www.mof.go.jp/english/hyouka/14nendo/sougou1–2.pdf.

——. 2005. "Ajia ni okeru saiken shijō kenkyūkai" [Asia Bond Markets Study Group], March.

——. 2007. *Research Papers and Policy Recommendations on "Toward Greater Financial Stability in the Asian Region: Exploring Steps to Create Regional Monetary Units (RMUs)."* ASEAN Secretariat, March. http://www.aseansec.org/20729.pdf, accessed October 2, 2007.

International Bankers Association of Japan. 2007. *Recommendations to Promote Tokyo as a Global Financial Center*. Tokyo: International Bankers Association, March 16.

International Financial Institutions Advisory Commission. 2000. *Report*. Washington, DC: U.S. Congress.

International Monetary Fund. 2003. "Access Policy in Capital Account Crises: Modifications to the Supplemental Reserve Facility (SRF) and Follow-up Issues Related to Exceptional Access Policy." January 14. http://www.imf.org/external/np/tre/access/2003/011403.htm, accessed August 17, 2007.

——. 2006. "De Facto Classification of Exchange Rate Regimes and Monetary Policy Framework." December 22. http://www.imf.org/external/np/mfd/er/2006/eng/0706.htm, accessed August 28, 2007.

——. 2007. *IMF Staff Report on the Multilateral Consultation on Global Imbalances with China, the Euro Area, Japan, Saudi Arabia, and the United States.* June 29. http://www.imf.org/external/np/pp/2007/eng/062907.pdf, accessed August 28, 2007.

Ito, Keiko, and Kyoji Fukao. 2003. "Vertical Intra-Industry Trade and the Division of Labor in East Asia." *Hitotsubashi University Institute of Economic Research, Discussion Paper Series,* a444.

Ito, Takatoshi. 2004. "Promoting Asian Basket Currency Bonds." In *Developing Asian Bondmarkets,* ed. Takatoshi Ito and Yung Chul Park, 67–89. Canberra: Asia Pacific Press.

——. 2007. "A Case for a Coordinated Basket for Asian Countries." In *A Basket Currency for Asia,* ed. Takatoshi Ito, 124–41. New York: Routledge.

——, ed. 2007. *A Basket Currency for Asia.* New York: Routledge.

Ito, Takatoshi, and Yung Chul Park. 2004. "Exchange Rate Regimes in East Asia." In *Monetary and Financial Integration in East Asia: The Way Ahead,* vol. 1, ed. Asian Development Bank, 143–88. New York: Palgrave Macmillan.

Jervis, Robert. 2006. "Thinking Systemically about China." *International Security,* vol. 31, no. 2: 206–8.

Johnston, Alastair Iain. 2003a. "Is China a Status Quo Power?" *International Security,* vol. 27, no. 4: 5–56.

——. 2003b. "Socialization in International Institutions: The ASEAN Way and International Relations Theory." In *International Relations Theory and the Asia-Pacific,* ed. G. John Ikenberry and Michael Mastanduno, 107–62. New York: Columbia University Press.

——. 2004, "China's International Relations: The Political and Security Dimensions." In *International Relations of Northeast Asia,* ed. Samuel Kim, 65–100. Lanham, MD: Rowman and Littlefield.

Kahler, Miles. 2000. "Legalization as Strategy: The Asia-Pacific Case." *International Organization,* vol. 54, no. 3 (Summer): 549–71.

Kaiser, Karl. 2004. *Asia and Europe: The Necessity for Co-operation.* Tokyo: Council for Asia-Europe Cooperation.

Kaminsky, Graciela, and Carmen Reinhart. 1999. "The Twin Crises: The Causes of Banking and Balance-of-Payments Problems." *American Economic Review,* vol. 89, no. 3: 473–500.

Kang, David. 2003a. "Getting Asia Wrong: The Need for New Analytical Frameworks." *International Security,* vol. 27, no. 4: 57–85.

——. 2003b. "Hierarchy and Stability in Asian International Relations." In *International Relations Theory and the Asia-Pacific,* ed. G. John Ikenberry and Michael Mastanduno, 163–90. New York: Columbia University Press.

——. 2003–04. "Hierarchy, Balancing, and Empirical Puzzles in Asian International Relations." *International Security,* vol. 28, no. 3: 165–80.

Kapstein, Ethan. 1991. "Supervising International Banks: Origins and Implications of the Basle Accord." *Princeton Essays in International Finance.*

——. 1994. *Governing the Global Economy: International Finance and the State.* Cambridge: Harvard University Press.

Katada, Saori. 2001. *Banking on Stability.* Ann Arbor: University of Michigan Press.

Katada, Saori. 2002. "Japan and Asian Monetary Regionalization: Cultivating a New Regional Leadership after the Asian Financial Crisis." *Geopolitics,* vol. 7, no. 1: 85–112.

——. 2004. "Japan's Counterweight Strategy: U.S.-Japan Cooperation and Competition in International Finance." In *Beyond Bilateralism: U.S.-Japan Relations in the New Asia-Pacific,* ed. Ellis Krauss and T. J. Pempel, 176–97. Stanford: Stanford University Press.

——. Forthcoming. "From a Supporter to a Challenger? Japan's Currency Leadership in Dollar-Dominated East Asia," *Review of International Political Economy,* vol. 15, no. 3.

Katada, Saori and Mireya Solís. Forthcoming. "Under Pressure: Japan's Institutional Response to Regional Uncertainty." In *Northeast Asian Regionalism: Ripe for Integration?* ed. Vinod Aggarwal, Min Gyo Koo, Seungjoo Lee, and Chung-in Moon. Berlin: Springer.

Katz, Richard. 2007a. "Risk Business: Households Still Risk Averse." *Oriental Economist,* March: 9–10.

——. 2007b. "The Japan Fallout from U.S. Credit Woes: No 'Decoupling'." *Oriental Economist,* September: 11–12.

Katzenstein, Peter. 1997. "Introduction: Asian Regionalism in Comparative Perspective." In *Network Power: Japan and Asia,* ed. Peter Katzenstein and Takashi Shiraishi, 1–44. Ithaca: Cornell University Press.

——. 2005. *A World of Regions: Asia and Europe in the American Imperium.* Ithaca: Cornell University Press.

Katzenstein, Peter, and Takashi Shiraishi, eds. 1997. *Network Power: Japan and Asia.* Ithaca: Cornell University Press.

Kawai, Masahiro. 2005. "East Asian Economic Regionalism: Progress and Challenges." *Journal of Asian Economics,* vol. 16: 29–55.

——. 2007. "Toward a Regional Exchange Rate Regime in East Asia." *ADB Institute Discussion Paper,* no. 68.

Kawai, Masahiro, and Shigeru Akiyama. 2000. "Implication of the Currency Crisis for Exchange Rate Arrangements in Emerging East Asia." *World Bank Policy Research Working Paper,* no. 2502.

Kawai, Masahiro, and Shinji Takagi. 2005. "Strategy for a Regional Exchange Rate Arrangement in East Asia: Analysis, Review and Proposal." *Global Economic Review,* vol. 34, no. 1: 21–64.

Keidanren. 2001. *Japan-China Relations in the 21st Century: Recommendations for Building a Relationship of Trust and Expanding Economic Exchanges between Japan and China.* February 20. http://www.keidanren.or.jp/english/policy/2001/006.html, accessed August 22, 2007.

Keizai Dōyūkai. 2000. *A Private-Sector Perspective on the Internationalization of the Yen: A Study on Japanese and Asian Stability and Growth.* Tokyo: Keizai Dōyūkai.

Kenen, Peter. 2001. *The International Financial Architecture: What's New? What's Missing?* Washington, DC: Institute for International Economics.

Kenen, Peter, and Ellen Meade. 2008. *Regional Monetary Integration.* New York: Cambridge University Press.

Keohane, Robert. 1980. "The Theory of Hegemonic Stability and Changes in International Economic Regimes, 1967–1977." In *Change in the International System,* ed. Ole Holsti, Randolph Siverson, and Alexander George, 131–62. Boulder: Westview Press.

Keohane, Robert. 1984. *After Hegemony: Cooperation and Discord in the World Political Economy.* Princeton: Princeton University Press.

Keohane, Robert, and Joseph Nye. 1989. *Power and Interdependence.* 2nd ed. Glenview, IL: Scott Foresman and Company.

Kikkawa, Mototada. 1998. *Manē haisen* [Defeat in the money wars]. Tokyo: Bunshun Shinsho.

Kim, Samuel. 2000. "East Asia and Globalization: Challenges and Responses." In *East Asia and Globalization,* ed. Samuel Kim, 1–31. Lanham, MD: Rowman and Littlefield.

——. 2004. "Regionalization and Regionalism in East Asia." *Journal of East Asian Studies,* vol. 4, no. 1: 39–67.

Kimmitt, Robert. 2008. "Public Footprints in Private Markets: Sovereign Wealth Funds and the World Economy." *Foreign Affairs,* vol. 87, no. 1: 119–30.

Kimura, Shigeki. 2006. "Ajia ni okeru ikinai basuketto tsūka e no michisuji" [A route toward an Asian regional basket currency]. *Gaikō Fōramu,* no. 221 (December): 59–63.

Kindleberger, Charles. 1972. "The Benefits of International Money." *Journal of International Economics,* vol. 2, no. 4: 425–42.

——. 1973. *The World in Depression, 1929–1939.* Berkeley: University of California Press.

——. 1981. "Dominance and Leadership in the International Economy: Exploitation, Public Goods, and Free Rides." *International Studies Quarterly,* vol. 25, no. 2: 242–54.

——. 1986. "International Public Goods without International Government." *American Economic Review,* vol. 76, no. 1: 1–13.

Kirshner, Jonathan. 1995. *Currency and Coercion: The Political Economy of International Monetary Power.* Princeton: Princeton University Press.

——. 1999. "The Political Economy of Realism." In *Unipolar Politics: Realism and State Strategies after the Cold War,* ed. Ethan Kapstein and Michael Mastanduno, 69–102. New York: Columbia University Press.

——. 2000. "The Study of Money." *World Politics,* vol. 52, no. 3: 407–36.

——. 2003. "States, Markets, and Great Power Relations in the Pacific: Some Realist Expectations." In *International Theory and the Asia-Pacific,* ed. G. John Ikenberry and Michael Mastanduno, 273–98. New York: Columbia University Press.

——. 2006. "Currency and Coercion in the Twenty-First Century." In *International Monetary Power,* ed. David Andrews, 139–61. Ithaca: Cornell University Press.

——. 2007. "Money, Capital, and Coercion in the Asia-Pacific Region." In *The Uses of Institutions: The U.S., Japan, and Governance in East Asia,* ed. G. John Ikenberry and Takashi Inoguchi, 187–216. New York: Palgrave Macmillan.

——, ed. 2003. *Monetary Orders: Ambiguous Economics, Ubiquitous Politics.* Ithaca: Cornell University Press.

Kishimoto, Shūhei. 1999. "Shin Miyazawa kōsō no shimei to Ajia tsūka kikin" [The mission of the New Miyazawa Plan and the Asian Monetary Fund]. *Fainansu,* May: 31–48.

Kohsaka, Akira. 1996. "Interdependence through Capital Flows in Pacific Asia and the Role of Japan." In *Financial Deregulation and Integration in East Asia,* ed. Takatoshi Ito and Anne Krueger, 107–46. Chicago: University of Chicago Press.

Koike, Ryoji. 2004. "Japan's Foreign Direct Investment and Structural Changes in Japanese and East Asian Trade." *Monetary and Economic Studies* (Bank of Japan), October: 145–82.

Komiya, Ryutaro and Miyako Suda. 1991. *Japan's Foreign Exchange Policy 1971–1982.* Sydney: Allen and Unwin.

Komori, Yoshihisa. 2002. *Nitchū yūkō no maboroshi* [The illusion of Sino-Japanese friendship]. Tokyo: Sankei Shimbunsha.

Kondō, Takehiko. 2000. *Ajia taiheiyō kyōtsū tsūka ron* [A common currency for the Asia-Pacific]. Tokyo: Japan External Trade Organization.

——. 2003. *Ajia kyōtsū tsūka senryaku: Nihon "saisei" no tame no kokusai seiji keizaigaku* [Strategy for an Asian common currency: International political economy of promoting Japan's "revival"]. Tokyo: Sairyūsha.

Koo, Min Gyo. 2006. "South Korea's Balancing Role in the Emerging Institutional Architecture in East Asia." Unpublished paper presented at the annual meeting of the American Political Science Association, Philadelphia, August 31–September 3.

Koremenos, Barbara, Charles Lipson, and Duncan Snidal. 2001. "The Rational Design of International Institutions." *International Organization,* vol. 55, no. 4: 761–99.

Krasner, Stephen. 1985. *Structural Conflict: The Third World against Global Liberalism.* Berkeley: University of California Press.

Kurlantzick, Joshua. 2006. "East Meets East." *Washington Post,* December 10, B3.

———. 2007. *Pax Asia-Pacifica: Asia's Emerging Identity and Implications for U.S. Policy.* Los Angeles: Pacific Council on International Policy.

Kuroda, Haruhiko. 1989. "Socrates: the Dollar Dialogue." *International Economy* March/April: 92–95.

———. 2005. *Tsūka no kōbō: En, doru, yūro, jinmingen no yukue* [The rise and fall of currencies: The fate of the yen, dollar, euro, and renminbi]. Tokyo: Chūō Kōronsha.

Kuroda, Haruhiko, and Masahiro Kawai. 2003. "Strengthening Regional Financial Cooperation in East Asia." *PRI Discussion Paper Series* (Ministry of Finance of Japan), no. 03A–10.

Kwan, C. H. 1997. "Ajia no tsūka kiki, sono taishitsu to kyōkun" [The Asian Financial Crisis, its characteristics and lessons]. *Sekai,* no. 640 (October): 35–38.

———. 2001. *Yen Bloc: Toward Economic Integration in Asia.* Washington, DC: Brookings Institution.

Lampton, David. 2007. "Faces of Chinese Power." *Foreign Affairs,* vol. 86, no. 1: 115–27.

Laurence, Henry. 2001. *Money Rules: The New Politics of Finance in Britain and Japan.* Ithaca: Cornell University Press.

Lee, Jong-Wha, and Changyong Rhee. 2007. "Crisis and Recovery: What We Have Learned from the South Korean Experience?" *Asian Economic Policy Review,* vol. 2, no. 1: 146–64.

Lee, Young Wook. 2006 "Japan and the Asian Monetary Fund: An Identity–Intention Approach." *International Studies Quarterly* vol. 50, no. 2, 339–66.

Legro, Jeffrey. 2007. "What China Will Want: The Future Intentions of a Rising Power." *Perspectives on Politics,* vol. 5, no. 3: 515–34.

Leheny, David. 2006. "A Narrow Place to Cross Swords: 'Soft Power' and the Politics of Japanese Popular Culture in East Asia." In *Beyond Japan: The Dynamics of East Asian Regionalism,* ed. Peter Katzenstein and Takashi Shiraishi, 211–33. Ithaca: Cornell University Press.

Lejot, Paul, Douglas Arner, and Qiao Liu. 2006. "Contemporary Markets for Asian Debt Capital Market Instruments." In *Asia's Debt Capital Markets: Prospects and Strategies for Development,* ed. Douglas Arner, Jae-Ha Park, Paul Lejot, and Qiao Liu, 57–115. New York: Springer.

Lejot, Paul, Douglas Arner, and Frederick Pretorius. 2006. "Promoting Market Development with Structured Finance and Regional Credit Enhancement." In *Asia's Debt Capital Markets: Prospects and Strategies for Development,* ed. Douglas Arner, Jae-Ha Park, Paul Lejot, and Qiao Liu, 269–90. New York: Springer.

Letiche, John. 2000. "Lessons from the Euro Zone for the East Asian Economies." *Journal of Asian Economics,* vol. 11, no 3: 275–300.

Lincoln, Edward. 2004. *East Asian Economic Regionalism.* Washington, DC: Brookings Institution.

Lipscy, Phillip. 2006. "A Market-Based Theory of Change in International Organizations." Paper presented at the annual meeting of the American Political Science Association in Philadelphia, August 31–September 3.

Lowery, Clay. 2007. "Remarks by Acting Under Secretary for International Affairs Clay Lowery on Sovereign Wealth Funds and the International Financial System." Paper presented at "The Asian Crisis Revisited: Challenges over the Next Decade," Federal Reserve Bank of San Francisco, June 21. http://www.frbsf.org/banking/asiasource/events/2007/0706/papers/lowery.pdf.

Lukes, Steven. 1974. *Power: A Radical View.* New York: Macmillan.

Ma, Guonan, and Eli Remolona. 2005. "Opening Markets through a Regional Bond Fund: Lessons from ABF 2." *BIS Quarterly Review,* June: 81–92.

Malik, Mohan. 2005. "The East Asia Summit: More Discord than Accord." *YaleGlobal,* 20 December.

Manchin, Miriam, and Annette Pelkmans-Balaoing. 2007. "Rules of Origin and the Web of East Asian Free Trade Agreements." *World Bank Policy Research Working Paper,* no. 4273.

Mauzy, Diane K. 1997. "The Human Rights and 'Asian Values' Debate in Southeast Asia: Trying to Clarify the Key Issues." *Pacific Review,* vol. 10, no. 2: 210–36.

McCauley, Robert. 2003. "Unifying Government Bond Markets in East Asia." *BIS Quarterly Review,* December: 89–98.

McCauley, Robert N., and Yung-Chul Park. 2006. "Developing the Bond Market(s) of East Asia: Global, Regional or National?" *BIS Papers,* no. 30: 19–39.

McKendrick, David, Richard Doner, and Stephan Haggard. 2000. *From Silicon Valley to Singapore.* Stanford: Stanford University Press.

McKinnon, Ronald. 2004. "The East Asian Dollar Standard." *China Economic Review,* vol. 15, no. 3: 325–30.

——. 2005. *Exchange Rates under the East Asian Dollar Standard.* Cambridge: MIT Press.

McKinnon, Ronald, and Kenichi Ohno. 1997. *Dollar and Yen: Resolving Economic Conflict between the United States and Japan.* Cambridge: MIT Press.

McKinnon, Ronald, and Gunther Schnabl. 2003. "Synchronized Business Cycles in East Asia: Fluctuations in the Yen-Dollar Exchange Rate." *World Economy,* vol. 26: 1067–88.

——. 2004. "The East Asian Dollar Standard, Fear of Floating, and Original Sin." *Review of Development Economics,* vol. 8, no. 3: 331–60.

Mearsheimer, John, 2001. "The Future of the American Pacifier." *Foreign Affairs,* vol. 80, no. 5 (September/October): 46–61.

——. 2006. "China's Unpeaceful Rise." *Current History,* vol. 105, no. 690 (April): 160–62.

Medeiros, Evan. 2005–06. "Strategic Hedging and the Future of Asia-Pacific Stability." *Washington Quarterly,* vol. 29, no. 1: 145–67.

Medeiros, Evan, and M. Taylor Fravel. 2003. "China's New Diplomacy." *Foreign Affairs,* vol. 82, no. 6: 22–35.

Meng, Fang. 2005. "Chūgoku keizai no naka no Nihon" [Japan in the Chinese economy]. In *Nihon no higashi Ajia senryaku* [Japan's East Asia strategy], ed. Toshio Watanabe, 129–46. Tokyo: Tōyō Keizai Shinpōsha.

Mercer, Jonathan. 1996. *Reputation and International Politics.* Ithaca: Cornell University Press.

Mieno, Yasushi. 2000. *Ri o mite, gi o omou* [Pursuing gain, remembering duty]. Tokyo: Chūō Kōronsha.

Mikitani, Ryoichi, and Adam Posen, eds. 2000. *Japan's Financial Crisis and Its Parallels to U.S. Experience.* Washington, DC: Institute for International Economics.

Milne, R. S., and Diane Mauzy. 1999. *Malaysian Politics under Mahathir.* New York: Routledge.

Milner, Helen. 1997. *Interests, Institutions, and Information: Domestic Politics and International Relations.* Princeton: Princeton University Press.

Ministry of Foreign Affairs of Japan. 2006. *Japan Diplomatic Bluebook.* Tokyo: Ministry of Foreign Affairs.

Mittelman, James. 2000. *The Globalization Syndrome: Transformation and Resistance.* Princeton: Princeton University Press.

Mohanty, M. S., and Philip Turner. 2006. "Foreign Exchange Reserve Accumulation in Emerging Markets: What Are the Systemic Risks?" *BIS Quarterly Review*, September: 39–52.

Moore, Thomas. 2004. "China's International Relations: The Economic Dimension." In *International Relations of Northeast Asia*, ed. Samuel Kim, 101–34. Lanham, MD: Rowman and Littlefield.

——. 2006. "Cooperating to Compete: East Asian Regionalism in Chinese Foreign Policy." Paper presented at the annual meeting of the American Political Science Association, Philadelphia, August 31–September 3.

——. 2007. "China's Rise in Asia: Regional Cooperation and Grand Strategy." In *The Evolution of Regionalism in Asia*, ed. Heribert Dieter, 34–56. London: Routledge.

Mukōyama, Hidehiko. 2005. "Sangyō kōzō kōdoka to Nihon no kyōryoku" [Industrial structure improvement and Japanese cooperation]. In *Nihon no higashi Ajia senryaku* [Japan's East Asia Strategy], ed. Toshio Watanabe, 75–100. Tokyo: Tōyō Keizai Shinpōsha.

Munakata, Naoko. 2004. *Transforming East Asia: The Evolution of Regional Economic Integration*. Washington, DC: Brookings Institution.

Murase, Tetsuji. 2000. *Ajia antei tsūkakan: Yūro ni manabu en no yakuwari* [A stable Asian currency zone: The role of the yen, as learned from the euro]. Tokyo: Keisō Shobō.

Nanto, Dick. 1998. "The 1997–98 Asian Financial Crisis." *Congressional Research Service Report*, February 6.

Narine, Shaun. 1997. "ASEAN and the ARF: The Limits of the 'ASEAN Way'." *Asian Survey*, vol. 37, no. 10: 961–78.

——. 2003. "The Idea of an 'Asian Monetary Fund': The Problems of Financial Institutionalism in the Asia-Pacific." *Asian Perspective*, vol. 27, no. 2: 65–103.

Narongchai Akrasanee and David Stifel. 1994. "The Political Economy of the ASEAN Free Trade Area." In *Asia Pacific Regionalism: Readings in International Economic Relations*, ed. Ross Garnaut and Peter Drysdale, 327–38. Pymble, Australia: HarperCollins.

National Intelligence Council. 2004. *Mapping the Global Future: Report of the National Intelligence Council's 2020 Project*. Washington, DC: Government Printing Office.

Nelson, Patricia. 2003. "Integrated Production in East Asia: Globalization without Insulation?" In *Japan's Managed Globalization: Adapting to the Twenty-First Century*, ed. Ulrike Schaede and William Grimes, 124–56. Armonk, NY: M. E. Sharpe.

Nemoto, Yoichi. 2003. "An Unexpected Outcome of the Asian Financial Crisis: Is ASEAN+3 a Promising Vehicle for East Asian Monetary Cooperation?" *Princeton University Program on U.S.-Japan Relations Monograph Series*, no. 7.

Nihon Keizai Chōsakai. 1998. *Ajia no keizai-tsūka kiki to Nihon no yakuwari* [Asia's economic and financial crisis and Japan's role]. Tokyo: Nihon Keizai Chōsakai Gikai.

Nishi, Fumiaki, and Alexander Vergus. 2006. "Asian Bond Issues in Tokyo: History, Structure and Prospects." *BIS Papers*, no. 30: 143–70.

Noble, Gregory. 1997. "From Island Factory to Asian Centre: Democracy and Deregulation in Taiwan." *Department of International Relations Working Paper*, no. 5. Canberra: Australian National University.

North, Douglass. 1990. *Institutions, Institutional Change and Economic Performance*. New York: Cambridge University Press.

Ōba, Mie. 2004. *Ajia taiheiyō chiiki keisei e no dōtei* [The journey toward formation of an Asia-Pacific region]. Tokyo: Minerva Shobō.

Obstfeld, Maurice, and Kenneth Rogoff. 2004. "The Unsustainable U.S. Current Account Position Revisited." *NBER Working Paper*, no. 10869.

Odell, John. 2000. *Negotiating the World Economy*. Ithaca: Cornell University Press.

Ogawa, Eiji. 2002. "The U.S. Dollar in the International Monetary System after the Asian Crisis." *JBIC Institute Discussion Paper*, no. 1.

——. 2005. "AMU: Higashi Ajia no kawase seisaku kyōchō o mezashite" [AMU: Toward East Asian currency policy coordination]. Paper presented at the Research Institute of Economy, Trade, and Industry, Tokyo, Japan, October 17. Summary at http://www.rieti.go.jp/jp/events/bbl/05101701.html.

Ogawa, Eiji, and Kentarō Kawasaki. 2006. "Higashi Ajia ni okeru kyōtsū tsūka seisakukan" [A common currency policy sphere in East Asia]. *Finansharu Rebyū*, May: 58–80.

Ogawa, Eiji, and Junko Shimizu. 2007. "A Common Currency Basket in Bond Markets in East Asia." In *A Basket Currency for Asia*, ed. Takatoshi Ito, 142–76. New York: Routledge.

Oh, Gyutaeg, and Jae-Ha Park. 2006. "Creation of a Regional Credit Guarantee Mechanism in Asia." *BIS Papers*, no. 30: 224–40.

Ohta, Takeshi. 1991. *Kokusai kin'yū: Genba kara no shōgen* [International finance: Testimony from the front line]. Tokyo: Chūō Kōronsha.

Oka, Masao. 1996. *En ga kijiku tsūka ni naru hi* [When the yen becomes a key currency]. Tokyo: Kadokawa Shoten.

Olarn, Chaipravat. 2004. "Reserve Pooling in East Asia: Beyond the Chiang Mai Initiative." In *Monetary and Financial Integration in East Asia: The Way Ahead*, vol. 1, ed. Asian Development Bank, 97–142. New York: Palgrave Macmillan.

Olson, Mancur. 1965. *The Logic of Collective Action: Public Goods and the Theory of Groups.* Cambridge: Harvard University Press.

Olson, Mancur, and Richard Zeckhauser. 1966. "An Economic Theory of Alliances." *Review of Economics and Statistics*, vol. 48, no. 3: 266–79.

Ōnishi, Yoshihisa. 2005. *Ajia kyōdō tsūka: Jitsugen e no michi shirube* [A common Asian currency: The path to making it a reality]. Tokyo: Sōsōsha.

Oye, Kenneth. 1986. "Explaining Cooperation under Anarchy: Hypotheses and Strategies." In *Cooperation under Anarchy*, ed. Kenneth Oye, 1–24. Princeton: Princeton University Press.

——. 1993. *Economic Discrimination and Political Exchange*. Princeton: Princeton University Press.

Park, Jae-Ha, and Gyutaeg Oh. 2006. "Developing Asian Bond Markets Using Securitization and Credit Guarantees." In *Asia's Debt Capital Markets: Prospects and Strategies for Development*, ed. Douglas Arner, Jae-Ha Park, Paul Lejot, and Qiao Liu, 33–56. New York: Springer.

Park, Yung Chul, and Daekeun Park. 2004. "Creating Regional Bond Markets in East Asia." In *Developing Asian Bondmarkets*, ed. Takatoshi Ito and Yung Chul Park, 16–66. Canberra: Asia Pacific Press.

Pauly, Louis. 1997. *Who Elected the Bankers? Surveillance and Control in the World Economy*. Ithaca: Cornell University Press.

Pempel, T. J. 2005. "Introduction: Emerging Webs of Regional Connectedness." In *Remapping East Asia: The Construction of a Region*, ed. T. J. Pempel, 1–28. Ithaca: Cornell University Press.

——. 2006. "The Race to Connect East Asia: An Unending Steeplechase." *Asian Economic Policy Review*, vol. 1, no. 2: 239–54.

——, ed. 2005. *Remapping East Asia: The Construction of a Region*. Ithaca: Cornell University Press.

Peng, Dajin. 2000. "The Changing Nature of East Asia as an Economic Region." *Pacific Affairs*, vol. 73, no. 2: 171–91.

Press, Daryl. 2005. *Calculating Credibility: How Leaders Assess Military Threats*. Ithaca: Cornell University Press.

Program on International Financial Services. 2006a. *Building the Financial System of the 21st Century: An Agenda for China and the United States*. Cambridge: Harvard Law School, Program on International Financial Services. http://www.law.harvard.edu/programs/pifs/pdfs/2006China_finalreport.pdf, accessed September 3, 2007.

——. 2006b. *Building the Financial System of the 21st Century: An Agenda for Japan and the United States.* Cambridge: Harvard Law School, Program on International Financial Services. http://www.law.harvard.edu/programs/pifs/pdfs/2006%20Japan%20 Final%20Report.pdf, accessed September 3, 2007.

——. 2007a. *Building the Financial System of the 21st Century: An Agenda for China and the United States.* Cambridge: Harvard Law School, Program on International Financial Services. http://www.law.harvard.edu/programs/pifs/pdfs/2007chinafinalreport. pdf, accessed September 3, 2007.

——. 2007b. *Building the Financial System of the 21st Century: An Agenda for Japan and the United States.* Cambridge: Harvard Law School, Program on International Financial Services. http://www.law.harvard.edu/programs/pifs/pdfs/japan07sympreport.pdf, accessed April 11, 2008.

Radelet, Steven, and Jeffrey Sachs, 1998. "The East Asian Financial Crisis: Diagnosis, Remedies, Prospects." *Brookings Papers on Economic Activity,* no. 1: 1–74.

Ravenhill, John. 2001. *APEC and the Construction of Pacific Rim Regionalism.* Cambridge: Cambridge University Press.

Rhee, Yeongseop. 2004. "East Asian Monetary Integration: Destined to Fail?" *Social Science Japan Journal,* vol. 7, no. 1: 83–102.

Rodan, Garry, Kevin Hewison, and Richard Robison. 2006. "Theorising Markets in South-East Asia: Power and Contestation." In *The Political Economy of South-East Asia: Markets, Power and Contestation,* ed. Garry Rodan, Kevin Hewison, and Richard Robison, 1–38. Oxford: Oxford University Press.

Rolfe, Jim. 2003. "Welcome in Asia: China's Multilateral Presence." In *Asia's China Debate,* ed. Satu Limaye. Honolulu: Asia-Pacific Center for Security Studies. http:// www.apcss.org/Publications/SASChinaDebate/Asias%20China%20Debate%20 Complete.pdf, accessed October 11, 2007.

Rose, Andrew. 2006. "A Stable International Monetary System Emerges: Bretton Woods, Reversed." *Centre for Economic Policy Research Discussion Paper,* no. 5854, September.

Rozman, Gilbert. 2005. *Northeast Asia's Stunted Regionalism: Bilateral Distrust in the Shadow of Globalization.* Cambridge: Cambridge University Press.

Rubin, Robert, and Jacob Weisberg. 2003. *In an Uncertain World.* New York: Random House.

Ruggie, John, ed. 1993. *Multilateralism Matters: The Theory and Praxis of an Institutional Form.* New York: Columbia University Press.

Sakakibara Eisuke. 1998. *Kokusai kin'yū no genba: Shihonshugi no kiki o koete* [The arena of international finance: Moving beyond the crisis of capitalism]. Tokyo: PHP Shinsho.

——. 1999. Mr. Yen managing crises: International intervention averted global depression. *Daily Yomiuri,* August 6, 1.

——. 2005. *Keizai no sekai seiryokuzu* [Map of world economic power]. Tokyo: Bungei Shunjū.

Samuels, Richard. 2007. "Securing Japan: The Current Discourse." *Journal of Japanese Studies,* vol. 33, no. 1: 125–52.

Sano, Jun'ya. 2005. "Higashi Ajia renkei ni Nitchū wa ika ni kakawaruka?" [How are Japan and China linked in East Asian cooperation?]. In *Nihon no higashi Ajia senryaku* [Japan's East Asia strategy], ed. Toshio Watanabe, 147–78. Tokyo: Tōyō Keizai Shinpōsha, 2005.

Sato, Yoichiro. 2003. "Mixed Feelings: East Asia's Debate about China's Growth and Regional Integration." In *Asia's China Debate,* ed. Satu Limaye. Honolulu: Asia-Pacific Center for Security Studies.

Schamis, Hector. 2003. "The Political Economy of Currency Boards: Argentina in Historical and Comparative Perspective." In *Monetary Orders: Ambiguous Economics, Ubiquitous Politics,* ed. Jonathan Kirshner, 125–49. Ithaca: Cornell University Press.

Schelling, Thomas. 1966. *Arms and Influence.* New Haven: Yale University Press.

Scollay, Robert, and John Gilbert. 2001. *New Regional Trading Arrangements in the Asia Pacific?* Washington, DC: Institute for International Economics.

Scott, Hal. 2007. "The Development of Asian Bond Markets: The Offshore Option." *Harvard Law School Harvard Public Law Working Paper,* No. 07–06.

Shambaugh, David. 2004–05. "China Engages Asia: Reshaping the Regional Order." *International Security,* vol. 29, no. 3: 64–99.

Shimizu, Yūji. 2005. "Higashi Ajia kinyū kyōryoku no naka no Nihon" [Japan in East Asian financial cooperation]. In *Nihon no higashi Ajia senryaku* [Japan's East Asia strategy], ed. Toshio Watanabe, 43–74. Tokyo: Tōyō Keizai Shinpōsha.

Shinohara, Hajime. 1999. "Asian Currency Settlement System." *Institute for International Monetary Affairs Newsletter,* no. 1, January 19.

———. 2007. "Currency Policy to Enhance Regional Cooperation (Part 4)," *Institute for International Monetary Affairs Newsletter,* no. 2, February 1.

Shiraishi, Takashi. 2006. "The Third Wave: Southeast Asia and Middle-Class Formation in the Making of a Region." In *Beyond Japan: The Dynamics of East Asian Regionalism,* ed. Peter Katzenstein and Takashi Shiraishi, 237–71. Ithaca: Cornell University Press.

Shultz, George, William Simon, and Walter B. Wriston. 1998. Who needs the IMF? *Wall Street Journal,* 3 February: A22.

Singer, David Andrew. 2007. *Regulating Capital: Setting Standards for the International Financial System.* Ithaca: Cornell University Press.

Snidal, Duncan. 1985. "The Limits of Hegemonic Stability Theory." *International Organization,* vol. 39, no. 4: 579–61.

Sohn, Injoo. 2005. "Asian Financial Cooperation: The Problem of Legitimacy in Global Financial Governance." *Global Governance,* vol. 11, no. 4: 487–504.

———. 2007. "East Asia's Counterweight Strategy: Asian Financial Cooperation and Evolving International Monetary Order." *UNCTAD G-24 Discussion Paper Series,* no. 44, March.

Solís, Mireya, and Saori Katada. 2007. "Understanding East Asian Cross-Regionalism: An Analytical Framework." *Pacific Affairs,* vol. 80, no. 2: 229–57.

Solomon, Robert. 1977. *The International Monetary System, 1945–1976.* New York: Harper and Row.

———. 1999. *Money on the Move: The Revolution in International Finance since 1980.* Princeton: Princeton University Press.

Steil, Benn, and Robert Litan. 2005. *Financial Statecraft: The Role of Financial Markets in American Foreign Policy.* New Haven: Yale University Press.

Stein, Arthur. 1990. *Why Nations Cooperate: Circumstance and Choice in International Relations.* Ithaca: Cornell University Press.

Stiglitz, Joseph. 2002. *Globalization and Its Discontents.* New York: W. W. Norton.

Stone, Randall. 2002. *Lending Credibility: The International Monetary Fund and the Post-Communist Transition.* Princeton: Princeton University Press.

Strange, Susan. 1986. *Casino Capitalism.* Oxford: Blackwell Publishers.

———. 1994. *States and Markets,* 2nd ed. London: Pinter Publishers.

———. 1996. *The Retreat of the State: The Diffusion of Power in the World Economy.* Cambridge: Cambridge University Press.

Stubbs, Richard. 2002. "ASEAN+3: Emerging East Asian Regionalism?" *Asian Survey,* vol. 42, no. 3: 440–55.

———. 2004. "ASEAN: Building Regional Cooperation." In *Contemporary Southeast Asia: Regional Dynamics, National Differences,* ed. Mark Beeson, 216–33. New York: Palgrave Macmillan.

———. 2005. *Rethinking Asia's Economic Miracle: The Political Economy of War, Prosperity and Crisis.* New York: Palgrave Macmillan.

Study Group for the Promotion of the Internationalization of the Yen. 2000. *Interim Summarization.* Ministry of Finance of Japan, June 30.

———. 2005. *En no kokusaika no suishin: "En no kokusaika suishin kenkyūkai" zachō torimatome* [Promoting internationalization of the yen: Chairman's summary of the Study Group for the Promotion of the Internationalization of the Yen]. Tokyo, January 23.

Summers, Lawrence. 2004. "The United States and the Global Adjustment Process." Speech at the Institute for International Economics, March 23. http://www.iie.com/publications/papers/paper.cfm?researchid=200.

Sutter, Robert. 2006. "China's Rise: Implications for U. S. Leadership in Asia." *Policy Studies* (East-West Center), no. 21.

Suzuki, Sanae. 2004. *Chairmanship in ASEAN+3: A Shared Rule of Behavior.* Tokyo: Institute of Developing Economies Discussion Paper, no. 9 (October).

Tadokoro, Masayuki. 2001. *"Amerika" o koeta doru* [The dollar beyond "America"]. Tokyo: Chūō Kōronsha.

Takeuchi, Atsushi. 2005. "Study of Impediments to Cross-Border Bond Investment and Issuance in Asian Countries." ABMI Working Group on Foreign Exchange Transactions and Settlement Issues, December. http://asianbondsonline.adb.org/documents/ABMI_WG_FETS_Impediments_to_CrossBorder_Bond_Invesment_Issuance.pdf, accessed September 3, 2007

———. 2006. "Identifying Impediments to Cross-Border Bond Investment and Issuance in Asian Countries." *BIS Papers,* no. 30: 246–60.

Tamura, Hideo. 2004. *Jinmingen, doru, en* [Renminbi, dollar, yen]. Tokyo: Iwanami Shinsho.

Taniguchi, Tomohiko. 1993. "Japan's Banks and the Bubble Economy of the Late 1980s." *Princeton University Center of International Studies U.S.-Japan Relations Monograph Series,* no. 4.

———. 2005. *Tsūka moyu* [Currencies on fire]. Tokyo: Nihon Keizai Shimbunsha.

Terada, Takashi. 2003. "Constructing an 'East Asian' Concept and Growing Regional Identity: From EAEC to ASEAN+3." *Pacific Review,* vol. 16, no. 2: 251–77.

———. 2004. "Creating an East Asian Regionalism: The Institutionalization of ASEAN+3 and China-Japan Directional Leadership. *Japanese Economy,* vol. 32, no. 2: 64–85.

Thomson Financial, 2007. *Debt Capital Markets Review,* Second Quarter. http://www.thomson.com/pdf/financial/league_table/de/2Q2007/2Q07_Debt_Capital_Markets, accessed August 31, 2007.

Thorbecke, Willem, and Masaru Yoshitomi. 2006. "Trade-FDI-Technology Linkages in East Asia." Prepared for the NEAT Working Group on "Trade-FDI-Technology Linkages in East Asia," July 21. http://www.ceac.jp/e/pdf/neat_04wg07.pdf, accessed March 26, 2007.

Toya, Tetsuro. 2006. *The Political Economy of the Japanese Financial Big Bang: Institutional Change in Finance and Public Policymaking.* Oxford: Oxford University Press.

Tran, Hung, and Jorge Roldos. 2004. "The Role of Securitisation and Credit Guarantees." In *Developing Asian Bondmarkets,* ed. Takatoshi Ito and Yung Chul Park, 129–44. Canberra: Asia Pacific Press.

United Nations Committee on Trade and Development (UNCTAD). 2006. *World Investment Report 2006—FDI from Developing and Transition Economies: Implications for Development.* New York: United Nations.

U.S. House of Representatives Select Committee on U.S. National Security and Military/Commercial Concerns with the Peoples' Republic of China. 1999. *Final Report.*

Utsumi, Makoto. 1999. "Yūro ga Nihon keizai to en ni ataeru eikyō" [The effect of the euro on the Japanese economy and the yen]. In *Yūro to Nihon keizai* [The euro and the Japanese economy], ed. Utsumi Makoto, 3–12. Tokyo: Tōyō Keizai, Shinpōsha.

Vogel, Steven. 1996. *Freer Markets, More Rules: Regulatory Reform in Advanced Industrial Countries.* Ithaca: Cornell University Press.

Volcker, Paul, and Toyoo Gyohten. 1992. *Changing Fortunes: The World's Money and the Threat to American Leadership.* New York: Times Books.

Wade, Robert. 1998. "From 'Miracle' to 'Cronyism': Explaining the Great Asian Slump." *Cambridge Journal of Economics,* vol. 22: 693–706.

Wade, Robert, and Frank Veneroso. 1998. "The Asian Crisis: The High Debt Model versus the Wall Street–Treasury–IMF Complex." *New Left Review,* no. 228, March–April.

Walt, Stephen. 1990. *The Origins of Alliances.* Ithaca: Cornell University Press.

Wan, Ming. 2001. *Japan between Asia and the West.* Armonk, NY: M. E. Sharpe.

Wang, Hongying. 2003. "China's Exchange Rate Policy in the Aftermath of the Asian Financial Crisis." In *Monetary Orders: Ambiguous Economics, Ubiquitous Politics,* ed. Jonathan Kirshner, 153–71. Ithaca: Cornell University Press.

Watanabe, Toshio. 2004. "Ajiaka suru Ajia" [Asianizing Asia]. In *Higashi Ajia keizai renkei no jidai* [The era of East Asian economic cooperation], ed. Toshio Watanabe, 3–16. Tokyo: Tōyō Keizai Shinpōsha.

——. 2005. "Higashi Ajia kyōdōtai wa seiritsu suru ka?" [Will an East Asian union be created?]. In *Nihon no higashi Ajia senryaku* [Japan's East Asia strategy], ed. Toshio Watanabe, 207–19. Tokyo: Tōyō Keizai Shinpōsha, 2005.

Weatherbee, Donald. 2005. *Southeast Asia: The Struggle for Autonomy.* Lanham, MD: Rowman and Littlefield.

Webb, Michael, 1995. *The Political Economy of Policy Coordination: International Adjustment since 1945.* Ithaca: Cornell University Press.

Wendt, Alexander. 1992. "Anarchy Is What States Make of It: The Social Construction of Power Politics." *International Organization,* vol. 46, no. 2: 391–425.

——. 2001. "Driving with the Rearview Mirror: On the Rational Science of Institutional Design." *International Organization,* vol. 55, no. 4: 1019–49.

Woods, Ngaire. 2006. *The Globalizers: The IMF, the World Bank, and Their Borrowers.* Ithaca: Cornell University Press.

Working Group on Financial and Capital Markets. 2007. *Toward the Establishment of Truly Competitive Financial and Capital Markets: The First Report of the Working Group on Financial and Capital Markets Expert Committee on Reforms Addressing Globalization Council on Economic and Fiscal Policy.* Tokyo: Cabinet Council on Economic and Financial Policy, April 20.

Wu, Xinbo. 2005–06. "The End of the Silver Lining: A Chinese View of the U.S.-Japanese Alliance." *Washington Quarterly,* vol. 29, no. 1: 119–30.

Xiao, Geng. 2004. "People's Republic of China's Round-Tripping FDI: Scale, Causes and Implications." *ADB Institute Discussion Paper,* no. 7 (June). Tokyo: Asian Development Bank Institute.

Yeo, Lay Hwee. 2003. *Asia and Europe: The Development and Different Dimensions of ASEM.* New York: Routledge.

Yoshino, Naoyuki, K. Ishikawa, and Tamon Asonuma. 2004. "Asia keizai no genjō to Ajia saiken shijō" [Economic situation of Asia and Asian bond market]. In *Ajia tsūka kiki to makurokeizai seisaku* [Asian Financial Crisis and Macroeconomic Policy], ed. Naoyuki Yoshino, chap. 1. Keio University Press.

Yoshino, Naoyuki, Sahoko Kaji, and Ayako Suzuki. 2004. "The Basket-Peg, Dollar-Peg, and Floating: A Comparative Analysis." *Journal of the Japanese and International Economies,* vol. 18: 183–217.

Yoshino, Naoyuki, Sahoko Kaji, and Tamon Asonuma. 2005a. "Dynamic Effect of Change in Exchange Rate System: From the Fixed Exchange Rate Regime to the Basket Exchange Rate System." Paper presented at Keio University, July 11.

——. 2005b. "The Optimal Weight and Composition of a Basket Currency in Asia: The Implications of Asymmetry." *SCMS Journal of Indian Management,* vol. 2, no. 4: 74–87.

Yoshino, Naoyuki, Sahoko Kaji, and Tamon Asonuma. 2005c. "Optimal Exchange Rate System in East Asia and the Regional Bond Market." In *Emerging East Asian Regionalism: Trend and Response,* ed. Zhang Yunling, 233–58. Beijing: World Affairs Press.

Yoshitomi, Masaru, and Kenichi Ohno. 1999. "Capital-Account Crisis and Credit Contraction." *ADB Institute Working Paper,* no. 2. Tokyo: Asian Development Bank Institute.

Young, Oran. 1989. *International Cooperation: Building Regimes for Natural Resources and the Environment.* Ithaca: Cornell University Press.

Yu, Hyun-Seok. 2003. "Explaining the Emergence of New East Asian Regionalism: Beyond Power and Interest-Based Approaches." *Asian Perspective,* vol. 27, no. 1: 261–88.

Zhang, Yunling. 2005. "Emerging New East Asian Regionalism." *Asia-Pacific Review,* vol. 12, no. 1: 55–63.

Zheng, Bijian. 2005. "China's 'Peaceful Rise' to Great-Power Status." *Foreign Affairs,* vol. 84, no. 5: 18–24.

Index

Page numbers with an f, t, or n indicate figures, tables, or notes, respectively.